ROUTLEDGE LIBRARY EDITIONS:
AGRIBUSINESS AND LAND USE

Volume 17

NOWHERE TO GO
BUT DOWN?

T0271406

NOWHERE TO GO
BUT DOWN?

Peasant Farming and
the International
Development Game

ANDREW S. MacDONALD

Routledge
Taylor & Francis Group

LONDON AND NEW YORK

First published in 1989 by Unwin Hyman Ltd

This edition first published in 2024
by Routledge
4 Park Square, Milton Park, Abingdon, Oxon OX14 4RN

and by Routledge
605 Third Avenue, New York, NY 10158

Routledge is an imprint of the Taylor & Francis Group, an informa business

British Library Cataloguing in Publication Data
A catalogue record for this book is available from the British Library

ISBN: 978-1-032-48321-4 (Set)
ISBN: 978-1-032-47049-8 (Volume 17) (hbk)
ISBN: 978-1-032-47057-3 (Volume 17) (pbk)
ISBN: 978-1-003-38438-0 (Volume 17) (ebk)

DOI: 10.4324/9781003384380

Publisher's Note
The publisher has gone to great lengths to ensure the quality of this reprint but points out that some imperfections in the original copies may be apparent.

Disclaimer
The publisher has made every effort to trace copyright holders and would welcome correspondence from those they have been unable to trace.

Nowhere to Go but Down?

*Peasant Farming and the
International Development Game*

Andrew S. MacDonald

London
UNWIN HYMAN
BOSTON   SYDNEY   WELLINGTON

Published by the Academic Division of
Unwin Hyman Ltd
15/17 Broadwick Street, London W1V 1FP, UK

Unwin Hyman Inc.,
8 Winchester Place, Winchester, Mass. 01890, USA

Allen & Unwin (Australia) Ltd,
8 Napier Street, North Sydney, NSW 2060, Australia

Allen & Unwin (New Zealand) Ltd in association with the
Port Nicholson Press Ltd,
60 Cambridge Terrace, Wellington, New Zealand

First published in 1989

British Library Cataloguing in Publication Data

MacDonald, Andrew S.
    Nowhere to go but down: peasant farming and the
    international development game.
1. Developing countries. Agricultural
industries. Economic development
I. Title
338.1′09172′4
ISBN 0 04 4453051

Printed in Great Britain by Billings & Sons Ltd, Worcester

Contents

viii

Tables and figures

This book is dedicated to my wife, Olive, who understands, and to the peasant farmer, who understands more than is realized.

It is also dedicated to Fiona, whose C F condition was the cause of my wanderings around the world.

1 Introduction

At the risk of being considered pedantic, but to ensure that I and the reader are on the same wavelength, it is necessary to start by stating some basic assumptions which are fundamental to my understanding of the role and place of agriculture in the human society:

- Mankind, and animals, cannot survive without plants, even with today's technology levels.
- The production of sufficient food for the daily and yearly survival of the family and the community has been and is still a primary and overriding concern.
- The evolution of a stable agricultural system producing agricultural surpluses was a necessary precursor before mankind could develop other skills and improve the standard of living.
- When people do not have to devote all their available time to the production of food they are free to use surplus energy (physical or mental) in any way the community finds acceptable. They can make a Boeing 747, a swimming pool, or a rifle.

These statements remain true in spite of modern technology and 'space age' thinking, for mankind has not yet managed to master energy to the extent that he can synthesize foods independently of plants on a scale sufficient to meet a community's needs. During the Second World War people used to joke about the children from London who, evacuated to farms in the country, were astonished to see milk coming out of cows (they had always thought it came out of bottles). Nowadays, we meet seemingly well-educated men and women who are equally blinkered and who think that food is nothing more than a commodity to be purchased with money from a supermarket: the lamb chops in a cling-film packet are seldom even associated with an animal. Most certainly few of the population in a wealthy 'First World' country have any idea how or where

Fuel for cooking is always in demand in developing countries. This photograph shows two children (one pushing the cart) who earn a living bringing firewood to the town. Their future is not very inviting.

the chops were produced. Even more alarmingly, many of the whizzkids of affluent societies look upon money used in the supermarket as a real commodity, something of value in itself. Their education has been so highly specialized that they have never had the opportunity to understand what money represents: skills, and the services built on skills. Money is no more than the common denominator for the common wealth. Few bankers understand that if one gives them a suitcase full of money and transports them to a desert island they will starve. However, for the great majority of the peoples of this world, that is, those dependent on subsistence farming for survival, money has little meaning, though they are very aware of the eternal struggle to provide the daily bread.

If we are to consider the plight of the Third World countries, particularly those stagnating at or around the poverty line, then it is necessary to have a fundamental understanding of why some people are 'poor' and others are 'rich'. Sadly few advisers from the wealthy

West understand their own source of wealth, or how that wealth was built up over the centuries. Whilst acknowledging the good intentions of the initiators and compilers of the Brandt Report one has to observe that they were too remote from the subsistence farmers ever to understand their way of life, needs and aspirations, or to come up with proposals that would help the communities in which they live. How can people whose world is the world of the Mercedes, the American Express credit card, Jumbo first class travel, the House of Commons dining room or the supermarket, comprehend the motivation of a family whose world is one and a half hectares of paddy land?[1] The peasant farmer's thoughts, customs and traditions were evolved in the hard school of survival and are entirely alien to a person coasting along in the protective cocoon of a developed society. Indeed, Westerners are guilty of the cardinal sin of being patronizing in thinking that they know the peasant farmers' circumstances and what is best for them.

For a number of years now I have undertaken consultancy assignments in Third World countries, all having the objective of helping these countries to improve their agricultures, make better use of their natural resources, maximize production from the soil, upgrade their husbandry standards, and better the lot of the poorest of the poor. At the beginning I was full of enthusiasm for the task, but with time I have begun to question the value of my contributions to the well-being of the subsistence farmers. It could be that my efforts have been misdirected, and that for some Third World countries the activities of people like myself have been more negative than positive, holding them back rather than helping them forward. I look at countries like Tanzania and Sierra Leone and wonder where the progress has taken them. Might one even go so far as to say that they are progressing backwards? Why does a country like the Sudan, after so many development studies and grandiose schemes, now find itself short of food? And how does famine happen in a world that can spend $125 million on a Jumbo jet to take the people of the wealthy world to holiday on the beaches of the developing world?

One way to cause introspective gloom amongst a group of consultants, is to ask for examples of successful agricultural projects in developing countries which are the result of past feasibility studies. There are some, but one has to search for good examples. Once again the problem is that thorny question of how to define success. For some consultants a good report is an end in itself, if it is well written, reasonably bulky and quoted in other studies; the villager's or agricultural industry's interests are almost secondary. At the risk of being presumptuous it is intended that this book should serve the needs and interests of the subsistence farmers, the remote village communities, and the larger rural societies of the countries which the planners are attempting to help in their development. Unfortunately, as in all development situations whether in developed or undeveloped countries, there are conflicting sectoral interests and the word development does not necessarily mean improvement. Even within a developing country the interests of the farmers in the rural areas, where the greater part of the population lives, may be subordinated to those of the urban population, quite apart from any conflict of interests between ministries.

It is alarming that massive food shortages in developing countries are becoming increasingly commonplace. Whether these 'famines' are attributable to a failure of the subsistence farming system or to bad macro-planning on the part of governments is a matter of controversy, mainly based on opinions. The authorities tend to put the blame on nature combined with the conservatism of the subsistence farmers, their lack of cooperative spirit and unwillingness to adopt new techniques. To the city dweller the subsistence farmers are perverse, unintelligent and lacking in enterprise. Personally I neither accept these views nor regard them as valid explanations for the increasing failure of the subsistence farming system in the developing world. As shown in Chapter 3, the subsistence cultivator is an industrious and sensible person; shortcomings should be sought among the central governments of both the Third World and developed countries, and not among the people in the field.

It is hoped that this book will, to some extent, clarify the strengths and limitations of the subsistence farming system, will make more clear the complexities and tremendous difficulties encountered in achieving agricultural developments in developing countries, and by so doing provide an insight into the inevitability of future famines if present policies are persisted in.

There is some confusion in the use of the term 'Third World' in the context of underdevelopment. Thus countries such as Singapore and Trinidad, which might be thought of as developing countries, are relatively wealthy, having gross national products per capita of over $6000 (1985), putting them into the upper middle class. This book is more concerned with the thirty countries of the world whose GNP per capita is less that $400 per year – countries whose populations total about half of the world's population. To put these figures into perspective, the GNP per capita of countries such as Switzerland, USA, Norway and Canada exceeds $13,500 per year. People in such wealthy situations cannot conceive how anyone can survive for a year on an income of $400; for example, in London that amount would hardly be sufficient for a husband and wife to stay and eat for one night at a top hotel.

The term 'subsistence farming' also needs defining. In the context of this book, subsistence agriculture is interpreted as a farming system in which the family unit (within a community of such farmers) depends for its annual sustenance and survival on its own family efforts. It is a stable agricultural system, providing there is sufficient land available for the needs of each family, though production is limited to the work-energy value of the family using, *with their own hands*, simple agricultural tools, usually a spade hoe and a cutlass. Most of the family's work-energy is used up meeting its own annual food needs, with only a fraction being available for the production of cash crops, which might be surplus food crops or, in favourable environments, specific cash crops such as seed cotton. Almost invariably, subsistence farming families have small cash incomes.

Of course there are variations and modifications to the above generalizations, but essentially every family can survive independently within both the community and the nation. However, in the modern world few farming families are entirely independent for their daily needs and nearly all have access to some basic necessities, such as matches, salt, cooking oils, cooking pots, simple agricultural tools and cloth. The family's slender cash resources are quickly used up on these few purchases.

Although subsistence farming families survive by their own efforts, in practice the families are socially and culturally part of the community. In West Africa the shifting cultivation system is followed by individual families working within large blocks of land, say 100–200 acres (40–80 hectares), which have been cleared of forest or secondary bush communally (usually by slash and burn methods), the whole group moving on to new land every two or three years. In parts of Asia, where there is land pressure and agriculture is more intensive, the holdings are owned by individual families, but they can call upon the extended family for assistance when there are peak work inputs, such as at times of land preparation and harvesting. However, the individual family unit, whether in the shifting cultivation system or in an extended family situation, still has to be independent for its sustenance. A major modification is when the family can supplement hand power with animal power, though one has to recognize that the animal also requires food, which may be difficult to provide where there is extreme land pressure.

Agriculture is not a specific subject and within the discipline can be found almost every known expertise. To plough the land requires a knowledge of soils, metallurgy and farm power; to plant seeds takes us into the realms of plant breeding, plant protection, entomology and pathology; harvesting leads us into aspects of storage, marketing, markets and economics. A good agriculturalist is expected to have a wide knowledge of many disciplines, none of them necessarily his or her own specialism. A complication is that many people assume that agronomists and agriculturalists are one and the same breed. Thus an agronomist (my own speciality) may be called upon to advise on banana husbandry, land capability, improved grassland management, water requirements, cold tolerance, or what ever inspired topic is thought up for investigation. The agronomist is often expected to cover all the cropping aspects of an agricultural study (and livestock as well, if he is foolish enough to admit to even the sketchiest interest in animals), yet the only aspects of agriculture that agronomists can truly call their own are plant populations, time of planting and rotations.

Agriculture, then, is a multidisciplinary subject, requiring understanding, if not mastery, of many diverse specialisms. A person who thinks of himself as an agriculturalist may not necessarily appreciate or comprehend the multitude of interacting factors that have to be assessed when advising on agricultural developments involving large areas and sizeable communities. An agronomist may be very competent within his own specialism, e.g. tea agronomy or rangeland improvement, yet out of his depth when it comes to development planning. Likewise, it may be unwise for, say, an economist or an engineer, with their tunnel vision, to be the prime force in decision making for agricultural projects, even more so if the development is outside their home environments (irrigation schemes in developing countries managed by Western irrigation engineers, for example).

In the context of Third World countries, usually tropical, agricultural development involves a wide variety of disciplines and expertise: for example, agroclimatology, topography, infra-red photography, soil science (pedalogic and edaphic), surface and ground water hydrology, sociology, irrigation agronomy, farm power, land tenure, crop drying, world markets, prices and so on. A veritable jig-saw of pieces must be fitted together to reveal a picture of the present before we can even think about best options for development. One of the major worries I have when assembling the background data for a new project study is that one may have missed one or more of the pieces of the jig-saw, making the agronomic proposals of doubtful validity. For one project that I was involved in, in Sri Lanka, maize was an option in the proposed rotation, until my attention was drawn to the parrot problem (they take great delight in pulling corn cobs to pieces). Shooting them would no doubt be the answer of the profit-minded Westerner, but this may not be acceptable in a Buddhist society.

An agricultural planner in a developing country must also be able to relate himself to the beneficiary, who, in the context of this book, is the peasant farmer (even if the formal client is a ministry of agriculture or an international agency). Yet in recent years the opportunity for Western experts to become truly familiar with the daily and yearly farming routines and ways of life of extended families in subsistence societies has become more and more limited. There are brief encounters, quick socio-economic surveys, but almost no in-depth contacts. What is even more alarming is that in some of the developing countries the local experts, who have been trained internally or at some overseas university, do not necessarily have an intimate knowledge of local rural life either. Education took them to towns, to boarding schools, to colleges, to overseas post-graduate courses, and back to senior posts in offices or ministries.

Thus in recent years the people responsible for initiating, planning, and eventually implementing development have come from a background remote from that of the rural society which is to be aided. This, of course, may not be important for specific crop or technology development, such as introducing clonal propagation for tea plantations, or new high yielding varieties of rice, but it is important when the development involves the community in fundamental changes to their traditional way of life, for example in integrated rural development projects.

It is interesting to record (regardless of one's opinion on our imperial past) that agricultural officers serving in the colonial services did not have this remoteness, for the simple reason that standing orders required them to spend ten nights per month out of their stations in the field. Rest houses were usually, but not always, available, and quite frequently the agricultural officer was put up in village houses. He worked with the farmers in the fields during the day, talked with them at night and, if he was lucky, was taught how to play Mweso or Wari, an African board game. My first Director of Agriculture (in Sierra Leone) informed me, during an early briefing, that I would be moved around from station to station to gain experience and, if I applied myself, might become a useful agricultural officer in seven years' time. It is possible to put an unkind interpretation on his remarks, but I prefer to believe that his seven-year yardstick was, in his experience, the amount of time needed for a young officer to master the complexities of tropical agriculture, before he could be expected to make meaningful contributions in the field of agricultural development.

The broad purpose of this book is to examine the role and place of agriculture in the Third World countries, and the constraints on the development of subsistence farming. There is also an attempt to rationalize the subsistence farming system and to highlight the shortcomings of national and international policies related to development of subsistence farming societies in the poorer half of the world. It is not intended that this should be a formal textbook on subsistence agriculture and its development: rather it is the intention to present a synthesis of past experience in the field together with my more recent incursions into the strange world of the consultant agronomist, a world in which I find myself still trying to define success; it is a critique of the mismatch between the farmer's needs and what the consultants offer, from a practitioner's viewpoint. In recent years numerous textbooks, manuals, guidelines and project evaluation procedures have been published which cover, to the point of confusion, the broad and detailed aspects of agricultural development in the tropics. A list of some of those publications that I have found useful in my work on tropical agronomy is given in the references at the end of the book.

Many people are interested in the background of subsistence farming, and in the difficulties that can be encountered in bringing about development, but fewer may wish to read about the more technical aspects of development planning. As a consequence this book is divided into two parts, the first being concerned with the subsistence farming system, the second with development planning, and the final chapter with conclusions and recommendations. For those only concerned with the basic issues of the development of subsistence farming in the Third World, Part II can be omitted without losing any of the fundamental background.

Notes

1 The average small holding size in Bangladesh is 1.42 hectares (3 $\frac{1}{2}$ acres) [9].

Part I

Subsistence Agriculture and its
Development

2   Setting the scene

Geography

We tend to think of subsistence farming as a system to be found in the very undeveloped, 'primitive' backwaters of the world, but this is incorrect. Firstly, subsistence agriculture is not a primitive farming system, but a system that has evolved over many centuries, requiring considerable skill on the part of the farmers who practise it on their holdings. In Bangladesh farmers may have to follow several different rotations on their small holdings, with a possibility of three crops per year, on land that may be covered with twenty feet of water during the rainy season and be dry during the 'winter' period. Mastering the seasons, storing seeds, and integrating the

Table 1   *Rural population of the world – 1985 data*

Economies	GNP per capita (US$)	Rural %	Population Total (millions)	Rural
1 Low income	less than 400	78	2,439	1,902
2 Middle income	400 – 1,600	52	1,242	646
3 Upper middle income	1,600 – 7,000	35	567	198
4 High income (oil exporters)	7,000 – 20,000	27	18	5
5 Industrial (market)	4,000 – 17,000	25	737	184
6 Eastern European (non market)	not available	35	362	127
Total			5,365	3,062

Source: World Development Report (41)

crops with each other in order to provide sustenance for the family throughout the year, is no easy task, requiring a knowledge of crop

A woman headloading waste household organic matter to the fields.
In the wet season this road will be impassable.

husbandry that would tax many Western factory farmers. Secondly,
the subsistence farming system is not to be found only in the
backwaters, but is the basis of life for nearly half of the population
of the world. Examination of Table 1, derived from the World
Development Report of 1985, shows that 2500 million people are
rural in the two poorer economic groups.

Most, though not all, low income countries, comprising
72,128,000 sq km, or 47 per cent of the land area of the world, are
located in the tropical parts of Africa and the Far East. Within these
land areas are to be found a wide range of environments from
deserts to tropical rain forests, each with its own subsistence
farming system. Fertility of the soils is frequently low but, having
said that, some of the oldest cultivated lands of the world are
located in these areas, such as the Nile Delta and ancient irrigation
projects in Sri Lanka. I have stood on top of a small temple carved
out of living rock at Anuradhapura, and looked down upon a small
irrigated block of land that is known to have been cultivated for

more than 2000 years, which makes one ponder over generalizations about the poor fertility of the tropical soils.

The World Development Report for 1987 [41] includes the following thirty-seven countries within the 'low income' group with a GNP per capita of less than $400 per year:

1 Ethiopia	14 Niger	26 Sierra Leone
2 Bangladesh	15 Benin	27 Senegal
3 Burkina Faso	16 Central African	28 Ghana
4 Mali	Republic	29 Pakistan
5 Bhutan	17 India	30 Sri Lanka
6 Mozambique	18 Rwanda	31 Zambia
7 Nepal	19 Somalia	32 Afghanistan
8 Malawi	20 Kenya	33 Chad
9 Zaire	21 Tanzania	34 Kampuchea, Dem.
10 Burma	22 Sudan	35 Lao PDR
11 Burundi	23 China	36 Uganda
12 Togo	24 Haiti	37 Viet Nam
13 Madagascar	25 Guinea	

Climate

It is not intended to examine climate in the meteorological sense, that is, using time series of data for temperature, sunshine hours, rainfall, humidities, wind speeds, etc., but rather to discuss the interaction of climate and agriculture. It hardly needs saying that climate is an important determinant of a country's agriculture. This was particularly so in the past, though now modern technology allows man to modify the climate to permit the production of crops in almost any part of the world. Thus irrigation, using groundwater, has turned parts of Saudi Arabia into wheat and lucerne belts, but for the great majority of the world's farmers high-priced inputs are not available. They have to depend on rain-fed agriculture or, as in Bangladesh, on seasonal floods originating in the Himalayas. For such farmers, almost entirely subsistence-orientated, the farming system followed is related to the climate in the first instance. There are interactions with other factors, such as topography, soil characteristics, and the presence or absence of diseases and pests which threaten not only plants, but also human beings (river blindness being a classic example of a sickness keeping people out of otherwise fertile lands). Climate, however, is the prime limiting factor. A good example of the importance of climate in determining a country's agriculture is seen in Mauritius. Mauritius, originally uninhabited, covered with forest, and the home of the Dodo and other now extinct birds, is some 720 square miles in size. Known to the Arabs in early times, but not considered worthy of settlement, it remained untouched until the beginning of the sixteenth century when it became a refuge for Portuguese flotillas, though there was still no permanent settlement. In 1598 eight Dutch ships, caught in a violent storm, became separated and five of them discovered 'Cirne'. They were delighted with the whole ambience of the island and the matelots found a large bird, the Dodo, whose flesh 'n'etait pas tres mauvaise'. They called the island Maurice, in honour of the Stathouder de la Hollande, Maurice de Nassau. During the seventeenth century the Dutch made the Dodo extinct and stripped the island of its timber resources, in particular, ebony. In 1715 the French took possession of the island and in 1735 Bernard Francois Mahe, Comte de Labourdonnais, arrived to commence the 'veritable fondation de l'ile maurice'. He encouraged agriculture, established the Jardin Royal de Montplasir and initiated the sugar cane industry.

If one visits Mauritius now, the Dodos have all gone, as have all but a handful of ebony trees, and the indigenous vegetation (over a thousand species), is now restricted to a few hectares located between Mare aux Vacoas and the Black River Gorges. The island is well vegetated, but what one sees are mainly imported exotics, dominated by the sugar cane plant and the sugar plantations. When the first settlers arrived they would not have found the island particularly bountiful as far as food supplies were concerned. The indigenous plants, which had had a separate evolution of their own, were not edible at all, their main characteristic being leaves that had strong attachments to the stems as a defence against the high wind speeds during the cyclone seasons. It was said that one could write one's name on a leaf, using pinpricks, and come back several years later to find the leaf still attached to the shrub.

The cyclones are important and necessary as they bring the rain for the sugar crop, and there will be several cyclones as a normal feature of each year. If there were no cyclones then there would be drought conditions. Most of them are harmless blankets of cloud, a few will cause concern, and once every ten years or so there will be one that is devastating, with lives being lost. As a generalization, up to 80 miles per hour (128 km/hr), the damage is linear, but above 80 mph (128 km/hr), the damage starts becoming geometric. Cyclone

Carol in 1962 was known to have reached 125 miles per hour (200 km/hr), because it was at that speed that the anemometer snapped. One of the bad aspects of the cyclonic winds is that they are not constant in direction and are turbulent and gusty. I have seen coffee trees corkscrewed out of the ground, and mature palms bend over parallel to the ground before snapping upright, yet at no time did I experience wind speeds exceeding 100 mph (160 km/hr). Wind speeds over 125 mph (200 km/hr), must be rather unnerving. The cyclones are, as already stated, an annual feature of the island and it is interesting to observe that whilst the exotic plants have their leaves shredded during a bad cyclone, the indigenous plants' leaves remain firmly fixed. After a cyclone the roads are littered with shredded leaf fragments.

It is on account of the prevalence of the cyclones that sugar cane has become the major crop on the island, it being one of the few crops that will tolerate high wind speeds. Even if badly damaged (that is, snapped off, rather than just being shredded) in a severe cyclone, it will recover and produce a good crop in the following year. Indeed, there may be some compensatory growth, resulting in an above normal yield in the following year. The other crop that is suitable, surprisingly for a cyclone area, is tea, simply because in the plantations it is grown as a flat 'table', which reduces the wind resistance. Mauritius is, thus, a splendid example of the influence of climate on agriculture, with some 93 per cent of the land devoted to agriculture under sugar cane. It is worth mentioning that Mauritius has virtually no cattle industry, in spite of being covered by a 'grass' species this is due not to climatic factors but to a pest factor, the Stomoxys fly menace. This is a biting fly so fierce that it will worry livestock to death if they are kept in the open, and as a consequence the few cattle are kept in darkened byres fumigated with wood smoke. This is a pity as the sugar cane industry has by-products which make useful animal feeds.

Though climate is an obviously important factor in determining the crop species and cultivars that can be grown in one area (and these areas can be quite small, no more than a few acres in extent in environments such as the flood plains of Bangladesh), breeding work has produced varieties of crops that can grow under extreme conditions. For example, the Katumani maizes were bred to produce a yield under very low rainfall regimes; wheat varieties were bred which were suitable for the 'winter' period in Bangladesh, which are so successful that wheat has become a major

crop during the dry 'winter' season; and potatoes are now being
grown widely in the tropics. Climate is an important constraint on
agriculture, but modern technology has greatly widened the
ecological range under which specific crops can grow successfully.

History

It is one of my opinions that Western contemporary educationalists
give inadequate attention to the history of mankind. I do not mean
by this that there should be increased emphasis on masses of dull
dates. The important thing is to impart an understanding of how
mankind has arrived at the present state of development. If a
population does not have that understanding it is easy to take the
present for granted and to discount the hard work put into
development by earlier generations. Without that understanding, a
society's present social well-being may be undervalued, and even,
by neglect, lost or allowed to wither. Because of this opinion, I have
included some words, in general, on the historical background to
development in the world.

Conventional mythology, usually perpetuated by entrenched
religions, blandly explained the creation of the universe as an act of
God or Gods: 'In the beginning there was God....' Creation, or
genesis, according to one prominent religion, took place over a
period of six days, whilst the mythology of Persia describes six
creative periods of a thousand years. However, the sciences of
geology and evolution eventually cast doubts on simplistic myths,
and the most recent of mankind's creation theories are those that
revolve around a 'big bang'. Though complete understanding of the
true nature of the universe must remain rudimentary to blinkered
mankind, the species has determined an evolutionary timetable for
the world in which he lives. A plausible interpretation of the origin
of life and its evolution has also been devised.

Mankind assumes that life originated in water two to three
thousand million years ago. About 1000 million years later life split
into animal and plant forms, with a further split into vertebrate and
invertebrate animals some 300–400 million years after that. These
developments took place in water until about 250–300 million years
ago when, with the evolution of the amphibians, molluscs, ferns,
etc., life forms appeared on dry land. Over the next 200 million
years slow evolution is assumed, by man, to have led to the creation
of the higher plants and animals. Mankind, the most advanced life
form to date, appeared one to two million years ago and now

numbers some 5000 million persons, occupying the whole land surface (apart from the extreme environments such as the polar caps, deserts and the highest altitudes). *Homo sapiens* is the present peak of an evolutionary process, which through the millenniums has produced over one and a half million forms of life.

Physically the earth's crust had cycles of tectonic activity, involving movement of great plates (continents), first together and then apart. The present positions of the planet's continents had their origins in the splitting of Pangaea (an ancient land mass thought to have split into Gondwanaland and Laurasia at the end of the Palaeozoic era), commencing 200–300 million years ago at the beginning of the age of the giant reptiles. Flowering plants appeared some 100 million years later after the continents had commenced their drift. Life on this planet is dependent on the process of photosynthesis, whereby the sun's energy is used to combine carbon dioxide and water into carbohydrates or organic matter. The process only occurs in members of the plant kingdom, which in turn are directly or indirectly the source of energy for members of the animal kingdom. At the present level of technology mankind cannot survive in the absence of plants.

It is interesting to note that when the continents split, it was in Africa that the least number of edible plants evolved – edible in the sense that they could be consumed directly by man. Of course, other animals could consume a wider range of plants and probably this is why pastoralism became a feature of African agriculture in prehistoric times. We tend to assume that the food plants commonly cultivated in Africa have always been there, but this is not so. Though there are a few indigenous wild rice species, the main species grown nowadays came from Asia, as did the banana, some two to three thousand years ago. Other common food plants, such as cassava, sweet potatoes, maize, groundnuts, the common bean (*Phaseolus vulgaris*), tomatoes, capsicums, passion fruits, guavas, pawpaws, cashews, avocados, and some of the yams, all had to wait for the discovery of the Americas before they were introduced into Africa. Before the arrival of the New World food crop species (which is historically a recent event), survival must have been difficult in Africa south of the Sahara, there being relatively few indigenous food plants. Even those that were available, such as some species of sorghums, millets, cowpeas, oil palms and *bambarra* groundnuts, were not necessarily spread evenly throughout the vast continent.

Earliest man was a hunter, a gatherer of herbs. Human beings were to be found in scattered groups, and, like the lion, their numbers were in balance with the ecology of the area in which they lived. Under favourable conditions there would be not more than one person per square kilometre, compared to, for example, 650 per square kilometre in Bangladesh at the present time. Over the next few thousand years man the hunter developed simple agricultural techniques, probably associated in the first instance with fishing communities in South East Asia. Development of settled agriculture meant that mankind's life style no longer consisted wholly of seeking food. Although still primitive, mankind had evolved to a level where he had leisure, which allowed the species time to ponder and develop other faculties and skills. For example, the controlled use of fire, the smelting of metals for tools, the devising of housing and the further development of languages as a means of communication.[1] Eventually man's enquiring and ingenious mind came up with the written word[2] and created numerals, essential keys to the future expansion of mankind's corporate knowledge needed in his quest for progress.

It must be stressed that in the civilizing of mankind the development of agricultural skills – in growing crops and raising of livestock, also in storing agricultural surpluses – was a necessary precursor. Nature, however, was and is a fickle master, not to be treated lightly or disrespectfully. The sun, rain and earth were raised to the status of gods, rites of propitiation were performed and members of the community who challenged the traditions were ostracized, driven out of the community or sacrificed. Farming systems that were stable and ensured the survival of the community, and which had taken centuries to be mastered, were not to be trifled with. Agricultural practices that were proven by the simple fact that the community survived from generation to generation were revered by all and protected by the elders. Change was abhorrent, the society was ultra-cautious, conservative to an extreme, and this was everywhere not just in the tropics. In Britain the Norfolk four-course rotation, the backbone of the country's agricultural wealth, was standard practice from the middle of the eighteenth century up to the beginning of the twentieth.

We must not assume, though, that the traditional farming methods of the past were foolproof. Famine and pestilence raised their heads from time to time: seven famine years are recorded in the old writings, impressed into men's minds for all time. The grain baskets of North Africa are now only of archaeological interest. Ephesus, a city of 300,000 people when St Paul visited it, is now in ruins, set in amongst eroded hills. The hinterland to the west of Trincomalee, in Sri Lanka, once highly populated, with enormous tanks and equally giant *dagobas* (Buddhist shrines), is now covered with rather indifferent forest, and what happened is a matter of speculation. No wonder man was cautious.

Famine was always a real threat to communities up to, and even after the Second World War. Communications, before 1939, were not so well developed, administrators were preoccupied with the problems of keeping populations fed, and Directors of Agriculture had to report monthly on the food situation. Famines were treated as a problem that had to be anticipated and solved locally. In some areas customary laws required farmers to have a three-year supply of small grains, such as finger millet, in store as reserves. Cassava had a special status amongst administrators because it could be stored, living, in the ground. Most root crops can only be left in the ground for a few weeks once the tubers or roots have matured, but cassava will continue growing for one or two years, and, although the roots become rather fibrous and its palatability may decline, it can still be eaten in periods of food shortage. In Tothill's book, *Agriculture in Uganda* [86], published in 1940, reference is made to the importance of cassava as a famine reserve, it being a root crop that stored well in the ground and had the further advantage that it was not attacked by the migratory locust. The Baganda farmers in the fertile crescent to the north of Lake Victoria were required to maintain quarter acre plots of cassava on their small holdings as a famine reserve, though by the late 1950s the order was not enforced.

In Uganda in 1967, five years after Independence, the first policy objective of the Department of Agriculture was still 'to ensure adequate supplies of the foodstuffs which can be efficiently produced under local conditions' [88].

A good example of the recognition of the importance of food and the pragmatic approach of Departments of Agriculture is seen in the agricultural policy priorities for Sierra Leone, listed in the *Annual Report* for 1955 [77], as follows:

A The provision of adequate food for the people.
B The cultivation of cash crops and the exploitation of wild trees for export purposes.
C Soil conservation.

D The improvement in the preparation, quality and marketing of produce.

E Agricultural education, and

F Research.

Having met the first priority of food security the Departments of Agriculture then turned their attention to cash crops. Almost invariably they were primary products which were exported to the developed countries for processing, and included such crops as cotton, palm kernels, unrefined sugar, rubber, tea, coffee, cocoa, spices, pyrethrum, sisal and jute. In terms of world trade, it seemed a balanced and stable situation, but it was to be upset by the Second World War.

It is pertinent to note that although the provision of food for the people was the top priority of the colonial administrations, the major research stations established in the tropics were almost all concerned with cash crops: WACRI, the West African Cocoa Research Institute, the Tea Research Institute at Kericho in Kenya, the Rubber Research Institute in Malaysia. It is only in recent years that major research institutes, such as the International Institute for Tropical Agriculture at Ibadan, Nigeria, were established for research into annual food crop production.

Immediately after the Second World War there was a general, world-wide shortage of food – food was rationed in the United Kingdom up until the beginning of the 1950s. This was the incentive for the Groundnut Scheme in Tanganyika, and similar ventures such as poultry in the Gambia. Neither of them could be called successful, and it was said, unkindly, that the Gambia exported more groundnuts than Tanganyika: nevertheless, these were early examples of the agricultural development game in the developing countries.

Though food shortages after the Second World War focused attention on agricultural production in the world, it was not this temporary situation that was to be the major influence on the future of agriculture in the backward parts of the world.[3] In fact, after the Second World War the political, social and economic world scene was to wholly change, and in many of the developing countries it was to the natural resources sector of the economy that the new administrations looked for development funds, which for most countries meant that the small scale subsistence farmers were the ones to carry the burden of national aspirations and change.

The Second World War was portrayed as a battle of principles between democratic, communist and fascist regimes, but in fact it was a battle for power and influence. The result was a win for the democracies and their communist allies, but it also toppled the select band of industrial powers from their position of dominance. Not for much longer were they to have the monopoly of production. No longer were the underdeveloped nations to be mere suppliers of raw materials and markets for the products of the industrial powers. As well as the coming shift in industrial power, the Second World War heralded a new age in communications. Cheap radios flooded the post-war world and in a relatively short period of time most houses throughout the world had a radio, or access to one. At the time of the world musical festival organized to raise aid for the famine-struck countries of the Sahel it was estimated that there were 600 million TV sets in the world. The result was increased general awareness of what was going on in the rest of the world. The development of air transport took a little longer to achieve, but was still incredibly rapid. Travel was no longer the privilege of the few, but increasingly open to the masses. Countries that were previously almost unknown became tourist centres overnight, supporting a vast international tourist industry.

Concurrent with the increased movement of the masses about the world, there were major medical advances making the movement of the masses less hazardous. For example, effective drugs to control malaria, antibiotics for gastro-enteric diseases, and the control and subsequent disappearance of smallpox all facilitated overseas travel. Without these advances mass travel world-wide would not have been possible. Alarmingly, a new disease, AIDS, has appeared on the scene; its impact on the world socio-economic scene, if no cure is found quickly, remains to be seen.

At the same time, the old Keynesian structure of world economics received a jolt when a new manufacturing power appeared on the scene. Japan was to be followed in due course by such unlikely places as Taiwan, Korea, Singapore, India, China and others. There followed in the 1950s, 1960s and 1970s a world-wide explosion of manufacturing capacity. The world had found materialism. Cars were produced everywhere; a belch of manufactured goods flooded the world markets; packaging became an industry; advertising cost millions and waste disposal was a serious problem. But storm clouds were appearing on the horizon for the Keynesian economic world. The classical boom and bust cycle was no longer a valid theory; governments were losing their safety valve or market regulator function – the techniques were tried but they no longer worked. Governments spent money (increasingly available through fiscal drag in taxation), created inflation, and became the victims of their own high interest rates. Indeed the rates were so high as to be usury rather than interest, exceeding 30 per cent in many years. Governments became bankrupt and needed international aid to bail them out of their follies. The old socio-economic order was, and still is, collapsing, and no new order has emerged. Indeed, many reactionary interests refuse to see the changes and await patiently the return of the good old days.

Among all this confusion we had the creation of newly independent states from former colonies, protectorates or dominions who previously had been tied markets of the imperial homelands. Although now free to pursue policies of their own making, the new governments soon realized that they had limited funds and resources for their development enthusiasms (if they had had any worthwhile resources they would have been exploited already by the colonial masters). They naturally turned to their one common natural resource, the land,[4] and the farmer was called upon, in the national interest, to grow more exportable cash crops. Diversification was the 'in' word. Departments of Agriculture, in dozens of newly independent countries, desperately sought out new crops to grow: vanilla, black pepper, fibres, coffee, cocoa, tropical fruits to export by air, orchids, cashews, macadamia nuts, jojoba beans, sugar cane, sugar cane for methanol, canning tomatoes, mangoes, citrus – every month a new crop would be the wonder crop that was to transform the economy. All this was actively encouraged by the hordes of advisers that poured into the new states as doors were opened to ever more and more embassies. Colonies that had never known anyone other than British or French administrators suddenly found that the world was made up of Americans, Russians, Germans, Norwegians, Japanese, Chinese and others, all keen to set up an embassy, to give advice and, sometimes, aid. For most countries, the aid was more than infrastructures and stretched bureaucracies could cope with, but in general it was positive and helpful.

Unfortunately this happy situation for the developing countries was not to last, particularly in Africa, but also in other continents. Internal politics and strife resulted in military takeovers, which

Table 2 *Imports of crude oil into Bangladesh, 1972–1982*

Year	Quantity (thousands of metric tons)	Value (millions) US$	Value (millions) taka	Unit value (US$ per metric ton)
1972–73	718.9	15.61	121.43	21.71
1973–74	350.9	20.55	165.27	58.66
1974–75	832.3	78.50	814.46	94.32
1975–76	936.0	90.13	1,352.00	96.29
1976–77	1,092.0	103.84	1,604.73	95.09
1977–78	1,064.0	104.11	1,592.88	97.09
1978–79	1,039.9	123.70	1,855.43	118.94
1979–80	1,277.7	244.46	3,666.90	191.33
1980–81	1,304.7	325.41	5,016.90	249.41
1981–82	1,177.9	314.29	6,820.09	267.00

Source: Bangladesh Petroleum Corporation [9]

Table 3 *Per capita energy consumption of selected countries (kilograms of oil equivalent)*

Country	Years 1965	Years 1985	Country	Years 1965	Years 1985
Nepal	6	17	China	178	515
Ethiopa	10	17	Malaysia	312	826
Bangladesh	–	43	Brazil	287	781
Afghanistan	30	73	Iran	537	1,026
Sierra Leone	104	82	Japan	1,474	3,116
Kenya	114	103	Poland	2,027	3,438
Sri Lanka	107	139	United Kingdom	3,481	3,603
India	100	201	Saudi Arabia	1,759	3,653
Pakistan	136	218	Germany F.R.	3,197	4,451
Indonesia	91	219	USSR	2,603	4,885
Philippines	160	255	United States	6,586	7,278
Thailand	80	343	Norway	4,650	8,920

Source: World Development Report 1987 [41]

were not conducive to continued development, whether agricultural or otherwise. However, a more important world phenomenon was to have a major impact on agricultural development, and that was the incredibly sharp and sudden rise in the price of oil, as exemplified in Table 2.

Suddenly fertilizers became much more expensive to import, and likewise the operating costs of tractors rocketed up, making the inputs for high-yielding varieties of wheat and rice a serious burden for subsistence farmers and governments, who had to find the foreign exchange to pay for these inputs, quite apart from all the other non-agricultural imports.

It should be noted that although the price rises for imported energy were disastrous for the developing countries with their limited foreign exchange funds, these countries were using relatively small quantities of the world's energy resources, as seen in Table 3.

With the rise in oil prices governments of developing countries found that their precious foreign exchange, usually obtained by the export of low-priced primary commodities, was purchasing less and less, and that surpluses for new development were no longer being generated. What was even worse was that the prices of imported commodities other than oil were also going up whilst world market prices for their primary commodities were not rising at the same pace. Sugar was a good example of world overproduction after newly independent countries had decided to grow the crop and then had to compete with each other for the markets. The Third World governments were squeezed for development funds and found themselves getting poorer whilst the developed and industrialized countries seemed to be able to take the oil price hikes in their stride and get richer in the process.

The governments of the developing countries decided that they had to emulate the developed countries and industrialize, in which endeavours they were actively supported by the multinationals, and as a consequence cotton processing in Lancashire declined markedly. Peasant farmers were encouraged to grow more cotton for home processing (though when tractors and oil became so expensive the day of the buffalo and the ox looked like returning).

Amongst all these political, social and economic changes in the way the world was ordered, the scenario was set for the Development Game.

Demography, land availability and farm size
At the beginning of the Agricultural Revolution, say 8000 BC, there were probably between 5 and 10 million people on earth. By the beginning of the Industrial Revolution in 1750 the total had reached around 750 million persons, rising to 1.2 billion in 1850, 2.5 billion in 1950, and about 5 billion in 1987, with 6 billion estimated by the year 2000. These increases are incredible and not sustainable, if for

no other reason than that they will impose impossible strains on the agricultural industry of the world.

The inexorable rise in the world's population has become of increasing concern to all countries in the developing world. Strangely enough this rise in population has often been encouraged by the politicians of the developing countries – more people meant national strength, so they advocated. This was a philosophy that fitted in with the subsistence farmers' own ideas, it being commonly believed that having many children meant a secure old age. Combined with political encouragement, improved preventative medicine meant that the expectation of life increased, more babies survived, they lived longer, and populations became unstable as the average age of the population went down. For many countries 45 per cent of the population is now under the age of fifteen – in Bangladesh the average age of the population is seventeen. Family planning is the popular cry, but even if we could get the presently unwed to limit their future family size to two children the populations will still nearly double in the next twenty years. Unfortunately those areas with the worst food shortage seem to have the highest birth rates. Regional data on average annual population growth rates is given in Table 4. What is not often realized is the speed at which populations can double, as shown in Table 5.

Table 4 *Average annual population growth rates (%), 1960–1982*

Area	1960–70	1970–79	1980	1981	1982
All developing regions	2.3	2.2	1.9	2.0	2.2
Africa south of the Sahara	2.4	2.8	2.8	3.2	3.2
E. Asia and Pacific	2.2	1.7	1.4	1.5	1.7
Latin America and Caribbean	2.8	2.5	2.4	2.3	2.3
N. Africa and Middle East	2.7	3.0	3.3	3.0	3.0
South Asia	2.4	2.4	2.4	2.2	2.3
Southern Europe	1.6	1.6	1.6	1.5	1.6
Industrialized countries	1.1	0.8	0.6	0.7	0.6

Source: World Bank Annual Report 1984 [40]

With a population growth rate of 3 per cent per year every twenty-five years or so one has to double the amount of food produced, the number of houses, the number of teachers, the number of buses, in fact everything, just in order to stand still. Think of this as a food

Table 5   *Population growth rates and the doubling effect*

Annual population growth rate as a percentage	Number of years to double the population
1.0	70
1.5	47
2.0	35
2.5	28
3.0	24
3.5	20
4.0	18

production problem for the agricultural sector in a developing country. At present Kenya has a growth rate of about 4 per cent and is probably doubling its population every eighteen years, India's population is increasing at over a million a month, more than three times the population of Norway each year, and China is attempting to get its birthrate down to one child per family.

Undoubtedly population increases in the world have become one of the most serious constraints on the development of Third World countries. The scale of the problem is well illustrated in Table 6, which gives some data on the change in population in Sri Lanka over a hundred-year period.

Table 6   *Population of Sri Lanka, 1871–1980*

Year	Population (thousands)	Annual growth (%)	Density/sq mile
1871	2,400	—	95
1921	4,498	0.9	178
1953	8,098	2.8	320
1971	12,690	2.2	501
1975	13,496	1.7	533
1976	13,717	1.6	541
1977	13,942	1.7	550
1978	14,184	1.9	560
1979	14,490	2.0	572
1980	14,738	1.8	582

Source: Central Bank of Ceylon, Review of the Economy 1980 [13]

The serious food security problems which faced the world after the Second World War, when population numbers were increasing rapidly, were masked for a time by the Green Revolution. This was a brilliant piece of breeding work by researchers working in Mexico and the Philippines, who bred short stiff-strawed varieties of wheat and rice that could stand up to high nitrogen fertilizer applications and which had high yield potentials. The result was almost unbelievable increases in grain production. Whilst oil prices were low the package of inputs required by the high yielding varieties were affordable by all, even by countries who had only negligible amounts of foreign exchange. Though governments were not always consistent in their priorities,[5] it is true to say that the use of fertilizers and farm machinery increased quite markedly in the developing countries in the 1960s and 1970s. In Bangladesh, for example, the use of commercial fertilizers rose from 275,000 tons in 1969/70 to 830,000 tons in 1981/82 – a significant increase, though still small compared to the 48 million tons used in the USA in 1982. In my opinion population control is the most urgently needed 'development' in the Third World. Without population control the future is bleak for the rural masses of the developing world, that is, for the hundreds of millions of subsistence farmers and their families. The reasons why this is so are discussed more fully in Chapters 4 and 5.

One of the results of the rising world population is that land pressure problems are becoming more evident. Farm sizes are decreasing, fragmentation is common (in Bangladesh a farmer has on average five to six parcels of land), and landless families are commonplace. As the pressure mounts, so people are forced into increasingly adverse environments, e.g. the char lands (emerging sandbanks), in the Bay of Bengal or the infertile podsols of Sumatera. In some reports the term 'functionally landless', meaning rural families with less than half an acre (0.2 ha), is being used. More and more, the hills are being denuded and the forest cover removed: for example, the hills immediately above Freetown in Sierra Leone are now red scars, whereas thirty-five years ago they were renowned throughout West Africa for their rich green cover of jungle.

In 1798 Malthus brought out his 'Essay on the Principle of Population'. He theorized that there was a natural tendency for population to increase faster than the means of subsistence, and that the ultimate check to population is the want of room and food. This essay led to what became known as Malthusianism, though Malthus would not necessarily have supported all the subsequent theories that sprang from his essay. Indeed, Malthus approved only of the principle of moral restraint: 'do not marry until you have a fair prospect of supporting a family'. For most of the world, then, and at least half of the world now, this meant having access to sufficient land on which to grow the food necessary for the family's yearly survival.

When population pressure is low there are no real problems, there being more land available than the population needs, or can work with its own hands. In countries such as Sierra Leone land tenure was not an important issue in the past: land was plentiful, its ownership being vested in the tribal authorities, village chiefs, etc. In recent times, however, rising populations resulted in land pressure, and land ownership became an issue around the 'infant' urbanizations. I recall the District Commissioner at Magburaka in Tonkolili District, Sierra Leone, commenting in the 1950s that he was having to deal, increasingly, with land ownership litigation, usually regarding boundary disputes.

Yet, within the subsistence farming system, land availability is not in itself a constraint on development; it is, however, a constraint on survival when there is insufficient land to meet the family's annual sustenance needs. When there is plenty of land it is the energy value of the farm family that limits development and an improving standard of living.

Where land is plentiful, like air or water, it is not greatly valued in itself, and its use is traditional. The sons and daughters of the parents have the right of use over village/tribal lands to provide for the needs of their families, often with no precise allocation of areas or boundaries. In the case of the shifting cultivators of Sierra Leone, with its unfavourable soils and environment, the lands were worked in blocks (which were cleared and fired by the whole community together), within which individual families cultivated, during the next two to three years, sufficient land to provide them with their food requirements. After this two-year period, as the fertility and yields declined, the community would move to a new block and the former block would be abandoned and left to lie fallow, allowing the secondary bush to regenerate. Of course, as the population increased so the blocks being cleared would become proportionately larger, but there would be no discernible changes in the system, except that over the decades the rest/fallow period would shorten and the cycle of clearing would, for example, decline from twenty-five to twelve years. In the remoter parts of Tonkolili District, when I was there in the 1950s the cycle was said to be about twenty-five years, but around Magburaka, a population centre, it had declined to three years. Eventually the rest/fallow period becomes insufficient for the restoration of soil fertility and yields decline, causing in turn an increase in the area worked per family in order to maintain the level of food production. This results in a quickening of the cycle and an accentuation of the decline in fertility. The end result is disaster, unless there are inputs such as fertilizers, which the subsistence family cannot afford.

In the early stages the land pressure effect is seen around the towns, but it spreads out with increasing population pressure. The end point comes when families are forced into increasingly smaller areas of land and into unfavourable agricultural environments, such as steeply sloping lands, watersheds, poor soils, rocky areas, and so on. The forests are destroyed, the ecology adversely changed and the environment becomes unsuitable for agriculture, much as has happened in parts of Ethiopia.

In more favoured lands, such as the rice lands of Asia, a similar cycle would have operated, but in this case the response to land pressure was to increase productivity vertically by land levelling, bunding, irrigation, multiple cropping, etc. However, even in such favourable areas, population rises result in farm sizes eventually becoming so small that even with improved technology a holding can no longer support the family. This results in what is now termed 'functional landlessness'. Yields per unit area could be further increased, but at considerable cost. Sadly, the subsistence farmers at the 'functionally landless' level no longer can generate enough cash to purchase the needed inputs, nor do they have the group organizational skills to deal with the situation they find themselves in.

It is not possible to quantify the minimum small holding size necessary for family survival. Depending on the general environment and whether the soils are fertile and reasonably level, and on the rainfall characteristics, the farming system could be intensive or extensive, but the objective remains the same: to grow enough food to sustain a family unit throughout the year, year in and year out.

In Uganda it is estimated that 1.3 acres (0.53 ha), are cultivated per person per year (see page 45), whilst in the pastoral areas of East Africa it might be related to the cattle carrying capacity of the land, possibly in the range of 10–20 acres (4–8 ha) per beast. In Karamoja, a mainly pastoral area in the north-east of Uganda, in 1965 there were estimated to be 604,000 cattle, 220,000 sheep and 255,000 goats. Using the 1958 census estimate of 156,000 people for

the district, this means that there were 3.8 cattle, 1.5 sheep and 1.6
goats per head of population or, if the family size was five, then the
figures per family would be 17 cattle, 7.5 sheep and 8 goats.

Another way of quantifying the holding size needed to support an
individual is on the basis of calorific needs. If an average person
needs 2500 calories per day and, for example, one pound (0.45 kg)
of rice has a calorific value of 1620, then an individual needing
912,500 calories per year would require 563 lbs (255 kg) of rice
(equal to 853 lbs or 387 kg of paddy). A family of five would need
4250 lbs (1927 kg) of paddy per year, if we assume that was all they
ate. In the period 1971 to 1979 the average yield per acre per year
(two crops possible) in System A in Sri Lanka (near Trincomalee)
was around 4900 lbs (2222 kg). In Bangladesh the average yield of
all rice varieties grown is less than a ton per acre and in Africa yields
of maize (the staple food for many tribes) of 600–1000 lbs (272–454
kg), per acre are frequently quoted. Yields of 400–600 lbs (181–272
kg) per acre are often quoted for minor cereals (see page 45). The
whole question of farm size and diet is complicated by the fact that
the subsistence farmers grow more that one crop on their holdings.
This is not quite so true in the rice growing areas of the world, but in
Sierra Leone a farmer may grow more than twenty different crops
on his holding during a year [44].

Notes

1 Up to 4000 languages are thought to have had an existence in the world.
North America, for example, had over 500, though there is some
controversy as to what constitutes a distinct language as opposed to a
dialect.
2 Phoenician, which arose out of the 6000-year-old Egyptian hieroglyphic
picture painting.
3 Through the years the newly independent states went from backward, to
underdeveloped, to developing, to less developed (LDCs), with Third
World and North-South as options.
4 As recently as 1974 top priority was given in the Sierra Leone 1974-9
National Development Plan to the development of agriculture, it 'being
consistent with both our national needs and the policies of Government.
Price incentive was to act as a powerful stimulus for agricultural
expansion' [79].
5 Third World countries are now spending nearly $9000 million per year on
imported armaments [81]

3 Subsistence agriculture

Background to survival

Before examining the subsistence farming system, the farmers, and their way of life, it is pertinent to address some of the broader issues of survival in the world in more recent times.

In the 'good old days' change was something to be treated with great caution. Development did take place but slowly and only after being well and truly tested. This was certainly true of the colonial regime before 1939. Stability was all important; the need for change was recognized, just, but controlled. This, then, was the service I joined in 1950: a cautious, slumbering giant, which in a few years was to wither away. Consideration of why this happened is outside the scope of this book – suffice it to say that the service and its central direction, consciously or unconsciously, was incapable of meeting changed political and economic circumstances after the Second World War.

As a newly appointed agricultural officer in Sierra Leone in 1950, I had insufficient experience to recognize areas where development was possible or, more importantly, to know whether developments were technically, socially or economically feasible. I was too busy trying to understand and master the new environment in which I found myself employed. Consequently, I had little appreciation of the immense difficulties that could be encountered in initiating even quite modest schemes (conflicts between senior staff, tractors sinking into rivers, fuel being stolen, targets not being met, and so on). This lack of appreciation was soon to disappear as I and most of the agricultural staff of the Department of Agriculture were thrown in at the deep end of a new venture, the Mechanized Rice Scheme, by the Director of Agriculture, George Lines. We were fortunate in that the Scheme's early development phasing had been well conceived by the Director. The initial mechanized trials had taken

Rice is not a crop, it is a way of life.

place at Bonthe under the direction of a Principal Agricultural
Officer. As experience led to confidence in the new techniques so
the areas cultivated expanded and, at the same time, the seniority of
the officers-in-charge was progessively lowered. The steady progress in hectarage cultivated as the various technical problems were
overcome is shown in Table 7.

As a Circle (District) Agricultural Officer involved over the years
in the Mechanized Rice Scheme in Bombali, Pujehun and Bonthe, I
regarded such developments as a rational response to the needs of
the country: to produce more rice in times of a world shortage
compounded, in the Sierra Leone case, by a distortion of local rice
production due to the realization by the local farmers that there
were alluvial diamonds in the finger swamps, finding which seemed
a more attractive proposition to them than hand cultivating the
swamps for rice.

The Sierra Leone Mechanized Rice Scheme was innovative, and
was put into effect by officers, from the top to the bottom, who had
had no previous experience of such developments. They shared this

Table 7 *Mechanical Cultivation in Sierra Leone, 1949–1955*

District	*Hectares Ploughed*						
	1949	*1950*	*1951*	*1952*	*1953*	*1954*	*1955*
Bonthe	2	28	114	188	477	922	1,648
Scarcies	–	–	32	78	2	–	5
Port Loko	–	–	–	183	278	306	405
Pujehun	–	–	13	163	252	410	465
Moyamba	–	–	–	128	160	–	10
Bombali	–	–	–	96	246	648	556
Tonkolili	–	–	–	–	127	344	901
Musaia	–	–	–	12	66	51	57
Newton	–	–	–	–	–	2	26
Total	2	28	159	848	1,608	2,683	4,073

Source: Department of Agriculture, Annual Report 1955 [77]

inexperience with almost everyone working then in the undeveloped parts of the tropical world. Methods of transporting tractors about a country with virtually no roads, problems of assembling ploughs that had been dispatched from the UK as part numbers in packing cases with no assembly instructions, training drivers to use track laying tractors (which one had never, oneself, driven before), learning the art of preparing seedbeds on a variety of soils, and so on, were all unfamiliar problems to be mastered. Few of the officers had time to query the project rationale. It is only in later years, with hindsight, that one realizes that, compared to many contemporary projects, the original project concepts had been sound, particularly the phasing. The project started off in a small way (two hectares) under the direction of the Department's most senior field officer, the strategy presumably being that the early exploratory trials, on which any further developments would be based, warranted direction by the most experienced field man. As the necessary field techniques were developed and proven so the expansionist phase could be delegated to younger and less experienced (but enthusiastic) officers. One wonders whether many of the massive schemes that are proposed, and sometimes implemented, today might not be more successful if they started small and were allowed to grow on their own success. It is easy to criticize the colonial governments for their seeming slowness in developing the areas which fell under their jurisdiction, for not doing more to speed up social and economic development. In fact, there had been

positive achievements which people nowadays do not even recognize as having happened. People take for granted everyday
community and household facilities if they have, within their own
lifetime's experience, always been there. Little thought is given to
how these developments took place, or to the effort needed by
previous generations to put them into effect: indeed many people
are guilty of assuming that many commonplace facilities have
always been there (roads, water supplies, sewage, schools, dentists,
enclosed fields, power supplies, etc). What is disturbing is that even
well-educated and responsible persons, in both the developed and
less developed countries, assume that the ordered environment of
the developed nations is easy to duplicate, with little understanding
of the immensity of the task of introducing change from scratch.

Some indication of the task may be conveyed by the statistics
relating to the cost of workplaces in the UK. The number of
employees in the manufacturing industry in the UK in December
1984 was 5.4 million using gross capital stock, at 1980 replacement
costs, of 195.3 billion pounds sterling. This is equivalent to £36,166
per workplace. The equivalent figure in the construction industry is
£12,400 per worker. Although these figures have to be used with
caution, they do give an indication, represented here in monetary
terms, of the scale and value of the inputs involved in the
development of the Western economies, and these figures do not
include all infrastructure costs, such as schools, housing, electricity,
etc. (1984 Blue Book, UK).

Some broad descriptive statistics which put the above quoted UK
data into perspective are that the New Halfa Irrigation Project, in
the Sudan, covering an overall area of 500,000 feddan (one feddan
equals 0.42 of a hectare, or just over an acre) with a net irrigable
area of just under 400,000 feddans and providing a livelihood for
22,000 tenants, had in 1978 only one qualified agricultural engineer.
Only one engineer for an area just slightly larger than the County of
Berkshire in the UK!

The caution displayed by senior colonial officials after the Second
World War, was, of course, largely a result of their experiences in
the colonies during the inter-war years, a period of traumatic slump
in the industrial nations accompanied by retrenchment and general
shortage of both capital and recurrent funds. Yet, though they were
instinctively cautious, they had been instrumental in earlier years in
laying down wide-ranging and sound foundations for future
development. This was no mean achievment. A classic example of

what was achieved in a relatively short period of time is the story of Uganda.

The source of the Nile was discovered, from a European viewpoint, by Speke and Grant in 1862. At the request of King Mtesa, English Protestant missionaries settled there in 1877, and French Catholics in 1879. In 1892 conflict broke out between sections of the people calling themselves respectively Protestant and Catholic, and as a consequence in 1896 Uganda became a British Protectorate under a Resident Commissioner. The railway from Mombasa was begun in 1895, and reached Lake Victoria by 1901: it opened up the British East African Protectorates for development, reduced import and export costs, meant the end of the porter system, and allowed the penetration of the territories by the Asian traders.

The Buganda Kingdom had a history going back several hundred years, with a formalized government structure comprising a Kabaka (King), Katikiro (Chief Minister), Lukiko (Parliament), Saza Chiefs (County Executives), Gombolola Chiefs (sub-County Chiefs) down to village chiefs. Yet the country, before 1900, was undeveloped. Roads consisted of bush tracks, there were no education facilities, medicine would have been traditional and unpredictable, and agriculture and the economy almost entirely at subsistence level. Even by 1948 health care in Uganda was not good. The 1953–1955 Royal Commission Report [25] quotes the percentage of the population over the age of 45 as 11.6 in 1948, and says that this is a population that is hard pressed by poverty and disease to maintain its numbers. There was evidence pointing to the conclusion that nearly half of all children died before reaching the age of fifteen.

One of the first preoccupations of the Special Commissioner, Sir Harry Johnston, was to generate a source of funds needed to cover the basic costs of administration. He favoured plantation development under European management. Prior to 1911 development was largely experimental but between then and 1914 there were considerable plantings of para rubber, coffee and cocoa. However, there were few settlers and subsequent Ugandan development was based mainly on peasant enterprises, particularly cotton and coffee.

It is of interest to note that in the annual report of the Agricultural Department for the year ended 31 March 1911 [87] the European

staff consisted of a chief agricultural officer, a government entomologist, a veterinary officer, two assistant superintendents of
cotton cultivation, a cotton inspector, and a farm overseer.

The annual report gives the value of agricultural exports for
1910–11 as just under £300,000 (Table 8), which equates to £1.5
million in 1962 values.

Table 8 *Agricultural Exports from Uganda, 1910–1911*

Product	Quantity		Value (£)
	cwt	tons	
Coffee	270	14	383
Chillies	17,462	887	20,492
Groundnuts	7,056	358	3,180
Sim-sim	10,589	538	4,477
Rubber wild.	898	45	13,412
Rubber plan.	5	0.25	147
Cotton ginned	32,694	1,635	120,664
Cotton unginned	50,281	2,514	44,748
Cotton seed	32,078	1,604	3,208
Bees-wax	35	1.75	162
Hides	7,551	378	20,544
Goat skins			24,920
Sheep skins			1,771
Ghee (clarified butter)	3,029	151	6,109

Source: Annual Report, Uganda Agricultural Department 1911 [87]

In 1962, one hundred years after Speke and Grant found the
source of the Nile, and sixty-six years after the country became a
Protectorate, Uganda became a self-governing state. It had a
healthy agriculture providing yearly export earnings worth over
£50 million or 84 per cent of all domestic exports. The country
had schools, teacher training colleges, agricultural colleges, a
university, a major hospital and faculty of medicine, dispensaries in
most districts, a well-established legal system and judiciary, a police
force and, regrettably, an army, a good communications network,
game parks and a tourist industry, television services and a third
share in an international airline. It cannot be gainsaid that these
achievements were impressive and had laid a sound base for further
development, in the relatively short period of sixty-six years. Not a
very long period of time, when one considers that the Second World
War, which seems so recent, started 48 years ago!

Today the plethora of publications from information departments and publicity organizations (government departments and

even research institutes often have their own information services) means that any progress, no matter how relevant, is well publicized. It would be easy to think that it is only in recent years that any worthwhile research or development has been carried out, but this is not the case. Research and development with far-reaching effects were quietly achieved by a handful of dedicated workers in the not too distant past, but their historical significance is not recognized. Having said that, one has to qualify the comments by acknowledging that even more could have been achieved if there had been more qualified officers in the field.

The Colonial Service Recruitment Memorandum No. 4 of April 1939 [16], providing information on the Colonial Agricultural Service, the Colonial Veterinary Service, the Colonial Forest Service, Other Appointments of a Biological Nature, and the Colonial Chemical Service, informs us that 'the territories comprised in the Colonial Empire cover an area of nearly two million square miles [5.18 million sq km], nearly twice the size of British India; and contain a population of over 60 millions, almost twice that of the self-governing Dominions'. At that time the total number of qualified agricultural officers in the Colonial Agricultural Service was in the region of 450. Charles Lynn, in his 1949 study of agricultural extension and advisory work [50], informs us that the total strength of the National Agricultural Advisory Service in England and Wales was 1450 officers, whilst in the United States of America the personnel in the Extension Service numbered around 11,000.

The rather blinkered attitude to the need for specialized staff in the colonies is shown in the report of a conference of directors and senior officers of overseas departments of agriculture and agricultural institutions held at Wye College, Kent, in September 1958 [18]. The place of horticulturists in departments of agriculture was one of the items discussed, and the following is an extract from the report.

In the discussion which followed it appeared that in some territories horticulture was regarded as an integral part of the duties of the Agricultural Officer whereas in others it was the concern of Specialist Officers; there was no standard pattern of organisation. Apart from special crops such as flowers and possibly pineapples the general trend seemed to be for horticultural work to be conducted by the Agricultural Officer. In this connection the need for including instruction in horticulture in the training of an agricultural officer was emphasised in view of the horticultural nature of many tropical crops and although the provision of a second stream of officers in the shape of Horticulturists was deprecated the Chairman pointed out that some graduates in horticulture were recruited as Agricultural Officers every year, often at the request of territories, particularly where tree crops were of major importance. (p.165)

In 1967 I received a Rockefeller travel grant allowing me to visit the West Indies, Mexico and the USA. During this trip I visited the USDA's main research station at Beltsville, just outside Washington, and to my astonishment I found that the Plant Sciences Division, alone, had some 3500 qualified research workers. The statistics quoted above do suggest that any lack of progress in the whole field of tropical agriculture in the former colonies may have been due to a lack of graduate support. But this may not be a correct inference or a valid criticism of the situation in the tropics at that time. We know that the agricultural industry in the United States of America is immensely strong and that productivity is very high. It is said loosely that one worker produces enough agricultural products for 35 people, of whom 5 are overseas. The high level of efficiency which has been achieved in the USA in producing crops is illustrated in Table 9.

Table 9 *Labour hours per unit of production for selected crops in the USA, 1979-83*

Crop	Hours per acre	Yield (bushels)	Hours per 100 bushels
Corn for grain	3.3	102.5	3
Sorghum for grain	3.7	56.8	6
Wheat	2.6	35.3	7
Potatoes	34.7	269.1 (cwt)	3 (per ton)
Sugarbeets	22.0	20.5 (ton)	1.1 (per ton)
Cotton	6.0	515.0 (pound)	6 (per bale)
Soyabeans	3.4	29.4	12

Source: USDA Agricultural Statistics 1984 [92]

Just why American agriculture is so strong is open to debate. Undoubtedly, the passing of the Morrill Land Grant College Act in 1862[1] must have been an important contributory factor, though Toffler suggests that agriculture was dragged along on the coat-tails of industry. In *The Third Wave* [84] Toffler writes:

The Civil War was not fought exclusively, as it seemed to many, over the moral issue of slavery or such narrow economic issues as tariffs. It was fought over a much larger question: would the new continent be ruled by farmers or industrializers, by the forces of the First Wave or the Second? Would the future American society be basically agricultural or industrial? When the Northern armies won, the die was cast. The industrialization of the United States was assured. From that time on, in economics, in politics and cultural life, agriculture was in retreat, industry ascendant. The First Wave ebbed as the Second came thundering in. (p.39)

If we accept Toffler's interpretation of the Civil War, it follows that it was industrialization and the consequent urbanization that was the stimulus to agricultural development in the United States, rather than the reverse. This does not negate the fact that Land Grant Colleges and a supporting Agricultural Extension Service were important factors in the agricultural development of that country, but it was still industrialization that provided the opportunity for research and extension services to initiate developments in the agricultural industry as a whole.

Some authorities argue that a strong agricultural sector provides a market for manufactured goods, or the services made available from the urban sector, and as a consequence emphasis should be laid on the development of the agricultural sector. Whilst I appreciate that argument I cannot accept it as being valid in societies which are predominantly rural. Contrarily, I accept that New Zealand can have an economy based on agriculture, but it must be noted that this works only if there are overseas markets for the agricultural surpluses. In other words, New Zealand's healthy agriculture developed in response to industrialization and markets for food in the United Kingdom. Take away these markets and New Zealand's economy is not so healthy.

Though I, at one time, favoured the strategy that investing in agriculture should be the top priority, I no longer hold that view. Indeed, I have moved to the other extreme of thinking that the best way that the small holder, the rural community or subsistence communities can be assisted is for investment to be directed, in the main, into non-agricultural enterprises. In this way markets are created in the towns for the locally marketable surpluses that the small holder produces. At the same time an expanding industrial society takes people away from the land and provides the opportunity for the rural community remaining on the land to improve their productivity, per man or per acre, to meet the needs of the new urban communities. If there is no urbanization then there are no markets and agriculture stagnates or only expands at a rate matching any population increase. Of course there may be a case for investment in agriculture on the basis of import substitution, or for crops which can be exported, such as tea, orchids, tropical vegetables, etc., providing markets can be found. Otherwise, investment in agriculture should be restricted to that necessary to meet immediate national needs.

That industrialization was the cause of change in agriculture, and not the other way round, was also the pattern in British agriculture. Before the First World War there were in Britain some one million work horses; by the 1930s the number was down to 700,000. In 1945 there were still twelve carthorses for every tractor but by the early 1970s there were less than 25,000 and the Ministry of Agriculture stopped recording their numbers. It would be easy to say that the demise of the farm horse was an example of the progressive ways of the British farmer: however, it is probably truer to say that as the wages in industry rose the farmer found that he could not afford to plough the fields using ploughmen, whose wages were also rising. Agricultural wages were always behind those of industry and so the farmer was also faced with a drift of labour away from the land to the towns. Another example of change is in the use of combines in the UK. When I went to university in the late 1940s I was taught that combines could not be used in the UK because the moisture content of the grain at the time of harvest was too high. Grain crops had to be cut with a binder, stooked to dry, stacked and eventually threshed. This was a very pleasant way of life, but as the cost of labour increased so the system became uneconomic and the agricultural industry was forced to use more intensive methods. Grain driers became a standard farm facility and every farmer bought or hired a combine harvester. It is unlikely that these changes would have taken place if there had not been the stimulus generated by increased industrialization. In this connection it is interesting to observe that in Spain, where industrialization was deliberately held back by Franco, the use of draught animals is still commonplace. If the country's entry into the EEC proves successful then we can expect to see the mule disappear as a feature of the Spanish countryside in the not too distant future.

The agricultural industry cannot be regarded in the same way as other industries or services. It is important in planning the development of agriculture to appreciate that there are these differences, otherwise the fundamental concepts on which any planning is based will be of doubtful validity. Many newly independent countries looked, and still look, upon the agricultural sector as an important natural resource which had been under-exploited. Unfortunately the agricultural industry is not like the consumer goods industry or other service industries, such as car, radio, computer manufacture, or tourism, which can rely on the consumer having an insatiable and ever increasing appetite for more and more material goods. Its function is to feed the people, no more and no less. Of course, there are in the world countries and areas which are exceptions to this generalization, thanks to shipping lanes and air transport, but for the world as a whole the statement is correct. Agriculture's function is to feed the people of the world, each day and every day. Storage provides some flexibility in this task, but at any one time there may be less than three months' reserves of food in the world.

Whenever possible I endeavour to obtain data on the consumption of food by the people of a country I am studying as it provides me with a rather fundamental piece of social background information. I believe that diet has an important influence on all of the characteristics of a community. People who have a good diet grow well, think well and generally organize their lives to live well. But National Food Balance Sheets also give me an opportunity to check roughly on the overall accuracy of the national crop acreages and the yield per acre estimates. One has to be careful in making such studies as the data may not be independent (statisticians may use two variables in order to derive the third), which may not be immediately obvious in the published statistics. However, if there has been a village level household consumption survey, then the findings can be compared with the National Balance Sheets, and also with the local Agricultural Department's acreage and yield estimates. Usually the various statistics match up, but occasionally there are inconsistencies that are worth following up in more depth.

In 1963 I reviewed some aspects of land utilization in Uganda, in the course of which I examined the question of food production. Using the Department of Agriculture's estimates of food crop acreages and FAO's Food Composition Tables, 1953, it was possible, using the available estimates for production per acre of the various food crops, to assess the extent to which the daily calorific requirement was met by the cultivators. This had been done by various authorities as shown in Table 10.

Table 10 *Various estimates of calories available in Uganda per head per day*

Area	Calories available per head per day
Whole of Uganda 1951 (Wilson 1954)	4,037
Whole of Uganda 1957 (Gale 1960)	3,699
1958 (Burgess 1962)	
Buganda	2,752
Eastern Province	5,912
Northern Province	4,090
Western Province	3,648
Whole of Uganda	4,134
1959 (Burgess 1962)	
Buganda	3,077
Eastern Province	6,583
Northern Province	4,032
Western Province	3,591
Whole of Uganda	4,399
Theoretical requirement	2,545

Source: A. S. MacDonald, 1963 [51]

Taking Uganda as a whole, it appeared that the cultivators were producing 60 per cent more food than was actually required to meet the needs of the population, while in Eastern Province more than twice the required food was produced. In terms of land utilization, conclusions such as these were of major concern and worthy of further study to determine their validity. In order to gain some indication of the validity of the data in Table 10 I attempted to calculate the gross calorific value of the food crops grown in Uganda for 1959 using my own estimates of crop yields. These calculations are shown in Table 11.

Using the figures in Table 11 the calories per day per person available from food crops alone are 5254, compared to 4399 estimated by Burgess for the same year (a figure which included the animal contribution as well). The revelation that the cultivator in Uganda (a rain-fed agricultural area) was seemingly producing twice as much food as he actually required, even although half of it was in the form of a perishable commodity, was a surprising conclusion. It stimulated me to study the available statistics on crop acreages, yields per acre, acreage trends and regional land use patterns in much greater detail, resulting in the paper from which the Tables reprinted here were derived. The following is an extract

Table 11 *Food crop acreages, yields per acre and total calorific value for Uganda, 1959*

Crop	Acreage (000s)	Yield/acre	Calories/lb FAO values*	Total calorific value (millions)
Beans mixed	576.5	200 lbs	1,565	180,444
Beans soya	5.0	200 lbs	1,520	1,520
Cassava	676.1	5 tons	494	3,740,726
Grams	9.0	200 lbs	1,565	2,817
Groundnuts in shell	426.8	800 lbs	1,760	600,934
Maize	359.9	800 lbs	1,615	464,991
Sorghum	705.2	600 lbs	1,555	657,952
Finger millet	1,270.5	600 lbs	1,505	1,147,261
Bulrush millet	5.9	400 lbs	1,580	3,729
Onions	2.0	2 tons	168	1,505
Pigeon peas	244.9	400 ibs	1,565	153,307
Peas field	41.4	200 lbs	1,565	9,828
Plantains	1,464.3	3 tons	320	3,148,830
Sweet potatoes	711.7	3 tons	440	2,104,354
Potatoes solanum	9.6	3 tons	317	20,450
Rice	7.4	600 lbs	1,620	7,193
Sim sim	235.0	200 lbs	2,605	122,435
Total	(Population in 1959 = 6,449,558)			12,368,276

Source: A. S. MacDonald [51]

*Calculated on the 'as purchased' basis, allowing for the quantities usually discarded as refuse.

from the summary of the paper:

Analysis of the available agricultural statistics in Uganda suggests that under a subsistence farming pattern, associated with man as the power unit, land utilization is in the region of 1.3 acres (0.52 ha) per person and that as an average for Uganda this statistic has stayed remarkably constant for a number of years. How far this statistic is influenced by social factors and conservatism of the cultivator is not known. Over-production of food also appears to be a necessary adjunct of a system where every family is responsible for its own sustenance. The degree to which over-production of food occurs is necessarily an estimation, but statistically appears considerable, without even considering losses in storage or the wastage of perishable food crops, which calorifically are of major importance in the diet. The need for marketing studies and reorganization associated with better storage methods is apparent if the full potential of the land and 'power unit' is to be realized. Yield per acre

figures are revealed as being deplorably low, particularly in Eastern
Province and the need for research into the husbandry of crops associated
with increased extension services and agricultural education is evident.
... In common with the rest of the world Uganda's human population is
rising rapidly. During the period 1948 to 1959 the population increased
by 1.5 million persons (to 6,449,558 persons), a growth rate of 2.5 per
cent per year, with the probability that the population of Uganda will be
13 million by 1990. It has been shown, if the present husbandry
standards are maintained for the next 30 years, that by 1990 the
provision of adequate food for the people is likely to be a major
problem, from the viewpoint of available cultivable land. In other words
if we assume that 60 per cent of Uganda, or 28 million acres, is
cultivable, by 1990 24 million acres will be required if there is no change
in the present farming pattern. Whilst there is no cause for immediate
concern, thought must be given to the future if a rising standard of living
is to be obtained and maintained for the people of Uganda. [51, p. 154]

In the event, Uganda's political problems turned out to be
overriding and tragic, and I do not suppose anyone is now able to
assess the food situation in the absence of a stable government. It
seems so sad that such gentle people, and here I am referring to the
Baganda farmers amongst whom I worked, should have been
exposed to so much disruptive violence since independence. The
wise man said peace, but the way of the world is war.

Returning to the question of Food Balance Sheets, it can be seen
that an examination of the available national statistics on diet for
almost any country can lead one to revealing and sometimes strange
conclusions about the people and their way of life. Table 12 has
been included in order to illustrate the difference in food consumption patterns between a developed and a less developed country.

Whilst the prime purpose of the farmer is to provide his family
and the community at large with 2500 calories per head per day, plus
50–100 grams of protein (these figures varying according to
environment, occupation, age, national body weights etc.), the
agricultural industry can have other functions, for example, the
production of primary products for processing (fibres, drugs) or
luxury products (orchids, spices, cocoa and alcohol). However the
markets for these products is relatively inelastic and sometimes in
competition with man-made products. It is interesting to speculate
on the effect of Italy's proposed ban on the use of non-bio-
degradeable plastic bags after 1990 – this could do more for the sisal
and jute industries than any aid projects.

Table 12 *Comparison of food consumption in the USA (1981) and Bangladesh (1981–1982) (lbs per capita per year)*

Item	USA	Bangladesh			
Meat	155.6				8.17
Poultry	62.8				
Fish	14.8				16.38
Eggs	33.8				18 in number
Dairy products incl. butter	303.3				15.54
Other fats, oils	56.4				0.34
Fresh fruit	84.0	Bananas	16.46	All other	
Processed fruit	55.2	Mango	4.42	veg	34.85
Melons	24.9	Pineapple	3.75		
Fresh veg	146.5	Jakfruits	4.99	Potatoes	26.4
Canned veg	45.6	Brinjal	4.46	Sweet pot.	16.65
Frozen veg	11.6	Pumpkin	1.45		
Potatoes and		Cauliflower	1.25	Pulses	4.7
sweet pots	84.3	Cabbage	1.33		
Beans, peas,		Onions	3.07		
nuts, soya	18.1	Garlic	1.00	Rice	306.8
Flour and cereal		Gourd	1.07	Wheat	51.9
products	150.9	Tomato	1.57	Minor grains	1.3
		Chillies	1.04		
Sugars and				Sugar	4.86
sweeteners	134.8			Molasses	1.89
				Gur	11.17
Coffee, tea, cocoa	11.4			Tea	0.15
Calories	3410 average available/dy/cap			Rural 1,707 Urban 1,866	
Protein	100 gms/day/cap			Rural 41.4 Urban 49.9	

Sources: USDA Agricultural Statistics 1984 [92], and Statistical Pocketbook of Bangladesh 1982 [9]

The foregoing paragraphs lead one to certain conclusions, regarding agriculture's contribution to mankind's standard of living, which are not generally appreciated. Agriculture's primary role is to meet a community's dietary needs every day, each year, no more and no less. The actual amount of food required can be related to calories and protein intake, but whether the diet consists of nearly all rice, or a mixture of lobster thermidors and choice wines, depends on the wealth of the individual and the society in which he or she lives. Gluttony is, unfortunately, a distorting factor, but in general individuals will consume only enough food to meet their dietary needs, whether as rice or lobster. We can, thus, draw a baseline for the community's food requirements based on the average calorific and protein needs of the population, weighted for the various age groups, etc. Below this baseline we have undernutrition, which is one of the world's most serious problems given rising population numbers, whilst above we have, quite simply, waste, which is another problem entirely with its geographical and political implications. Malnutrition is a different problem. Thus kwashiorkor, a protein deficiency particularly affecting children, is not so much related to under-nutrition, as to the education of the mother. Young mothers with children suffering from kwashiorkor who were brought into a Kwashiorkor Treatment Unit at Kasangati, near Kampala in Uganda (their children being treated and the mother given simple training on the dietary needs of infants), never returned to the clinic for further help. In the same way, overweight due to over-eating is malnutrition.

Once the community's dietary needs are met, agriculture has performed its primary function. If it does not fulfil this function then the community, in the past and even now if the Sahel is an example, is decimated to some degree or other. If the function is fulfilled then the scene is set for the community to improve its standard of living above the baseline. Good housing, security, education facilities, health services, the arts, leisure pursuits, are all achievable with good management and organization.

Whilst many governments of developing countries look upon the rural areas as a 'safety valve', a place where the expanding population can be accommodated, the statistics seem to indicate that it is those countries with the highest urban population percentages that have the highest per capita gross national product (Table 13).

The argument has now come full circle, back to the original proposition that the best way of helping the agricultural sector in developing countries is most likely by investing in the urban centres. As they develop they will drag the agricultural sector along with them. Presumably there will be some exploitation of the rural sector by the more organized and politically aware urban sector, which will

Table 13 *Urbanization and per capita GNP of selected countries*

Country	GNP per capita ($ 1983)	Urban population (% 1983)	Percentage of labour force in agriculture (1981)
Bangladesh	130	17	74
Nepal	160	7	93
Burma	180	29	67
India	260	24	71
China	300	21	74
Sri Lanka	330	26	54
Indonesia	550	24	58
Ivory Coast	710	44	79
Turkey	1,240	45	54
Malaysia	1,860	31	50
Yugoslavia	2,570	45	29
Trinidad	6,850	22	10
United Kingdom	9,200	91	2
Japan	10,120	76	12
Germany F.R.	11,430	86	4
USA	14,110	74	2
Switzerland	16,290	59	5

Source: World Development Report 1985 [41]

have to be carefully controlled by the central governments, but the alternative may be disastrous. If there is no urbanization, and populations continue to rise at their present rates, then once the rural population rises above that level that the land can naturally support, there must be disaster, unless the distressed area in question is given outside help from food surplus nations. It was of interest to note that whilst there was famine in the rural areas of Ethiopia and Sudan, reports indicated that there were no food shortages in the towns and cities.

It would be nice to think that the place and role of the farmer (and here I am referring to the subsistence small holder and not the factory farmer) is respected by the town dweller, but, regrettably, it is not – and not likely to be. One would think that governments would recognize the fundamental importance of the farming community, but they are politicians and being realistic only recognize power blocs. The town dweller is a concentrated and organizable force, a force that politicians will always treat with respect.

The rural population is by its very nature made up of independent individuals who are dispersed, with no organized leadership, and as a consequence has little influence on national policies that are decided centrally by the urban sector. This is a fact of life which will only change if there are shortages of food in the urban areas. Yet it is another fact of life that the city dweller with money in his pocket is rarely short of food.

The subsistence farming system

There are basically two subsistence farming systems, the first being orientated towards crops and the second towards livestock, but both systems have the primary objective of providing the subsistence pastoralist or cultivator, and their families, with sufficient food (and related end products), year in and year out. They are systems that have evolved and been proven sound over centuries and are still being practised in their essential form in the greater part of the tropical developing world. There are, of course, modifications to adapt the system to different environments and changing circumstances, but the primary objectives remain the same: independent daily and yearly sustenance.

Though many people in the developed world look down upon subsistence families and regard them as poor cousins, this is not a correct interpretation of their circumstances. The emergence of the subsistence farming system provided mankind with a very successful means of providing the family units with food and, as mentioned earlier, was the stepping stone for mankind's future progress. Once a family could adequately and reliably feed itself the way was open for it to develop other skills. With development of other skills wealth was created and mankind's standard of living improved, for the innovators and also for the associated rural and urban populations. Thus the subsistence farming system was a sound survival system and a springboard for other developments, but it was a closed system and does not contain within itself the seeds for its own development. That development could only come about as a spin-off from the other developments for which it had been the stepping stone, for example the mastery of steam, the invention of machines and the understanding of chemistry. Industrialization resulted in the demise of the subsistence farming system (see Table 9 and the related text), and the evolution of farming systems' whereby a handful of men could, using machines, provide enough food for a hundred people. However, this does not mean that the subsistence farming system is no longer a valid system – indeed, the greater part of the world's population still depends on it – though it does mean that for those peoples whose way of life is subsistence farming there is little material wealth. Sadly, the system is being overloaded by population pressures, the peoples are being driven into increasingly adverse agricultural environments, and the centuries-old traditional farming systems are no longer stable. Above all, however, it is the unthinking demands of central governments that have resulted in the excessive pressures which are causing the system to collapse.

Take for example the case of Tanzania. Since Independence in 1962 the population has doubled from around ten million to about twenty-two million, and the subsistence cultivators have manfully attempted to meet the needs of African Socialism and Self- reliance. Undoubtedly they, the cultivators, have been remarkably successful in their endeavours to meet the needs of the ideologies, but they have been hamstrung and discouraged by a breakdown of the national infrastructure, particularly those aspects relating to the production, marketing and primary processing of their traditional export crops. The scarce development funds had been spent on new developments, quite naturally, but without preserving the existing strengths – and now there are many unserviceable lorries, no spares, shortages of fuel, unmaintained roads, failures of processing plants, etc. Interestingly, the subsistence farmers have adapted to the situation and responded by creating a 'parallel economy'. This is not unique and conferences of finance authorities regularly have 'parallel economy' as an item on the agenda nowadays.

Within any environment where plants can grow, the human species has devised farming systems for food production that are stable, permitting the long term survival of the family and the associated settled communities. Some systems were primitive, such as pastoralism in East Africa (followed by the Masai, the Karamajong and the Suk, etc.), which 'uses' cattle as a means of survival in an otherwise unfavourable climatic environment. The regions involved have low and unreliable rainfalls, both within and between years, are unsuitable for reliable annual crop production, but are suitable for livestock utilizing the sparse grass/browse at low stocking rates – one animal to 5–30 ha or more – permitting man to survive (in small numbers), on lands which otherwise are unfavourable agricultural environments.

Other systems in favourable environments were more intensive, such as the shifting cultivation systems of annual crop production in West Africa, though even here the system was only stable whilst the population pressure was low. For example, in Tonkolili in Sierra Leone in 1951 I walked through extensive forested areas where there were twenty-five year rest periods between each three-year cultivation period, whilst not many miles away at Magburaka in a much more densely populated area the cycle was down to three years' cultivation and three years' rest. Undoubtedly the three years rest period is not sufficient to ensure long term stability, but the decline in productivity is hard to monitor. It only becomes obvious in extreme cases as has happened recently in Ethiopia and the Sahel in general. It is of interest to note that a recent study of by G. Farmer and T.M.L. Wigley [34] has indicated that the present adverse climate of the Sahel is not one of the historic cyclic occurrences but is a definite downward and unfavourable trend. They write, 'We believe that for West Africa, Sudan and Ethiopia, a continuation of the low rainfall levels of the 1970s and 1980s is more likely than a return to the wetter conditions of earlier decades. Future planning should assume that conditions similar to today will prevail.' Deforestation in the southern, wetter parts of West Africa has also been suggested as a possible causal factor. Sierra Leone is in the Soudano-Guinea zone to the south of the Sahel and Soudan zones.

It may be that this disastrous climatic situation is a natural occurrence, but, personally, I think it is attributable to the deforestation of these regions due to the relentless pressures of increasing populations. Shifting cultivation or subsistence agriculture is only stable whilst population pressures are low, and once population starts increasing beyond a certain level then the shifting cultivation method of farming is no longer a viable vehicle for family subsistence. Sadly, the authorities in the developing countries do not recognize this and in some cases have actively encouraged the population to have more children in the mistaken belief that numbers mean strength, by so doing increasing the pressures on the farming system and ensuring its even more rapid collapse.

The main constraint on the development of subsistence agriculture is that it is reliant on man as the source of farm power, and as a consequence productivity is limited to the farm power value of a family. Many people say, 'Why not give them tractors?' But this is not so easy as it sounds. A tractor in itself is of no value to the subsistence farmer unless it can pay for itself and make a profit, and that is difficult in a community where all the families are independent for their own sustenance and there are limited markets for surplus foods. A tractor has no advantage unless it can be used to increase production of commodities for which there are markets. If the population is predominantly rural and subsistence agriculture orientated (for the low income economies of the world nearly 80 per cent of the population is rural), then there is no market for their surplus production, or only a small market, as their neighbours are equally independent. It is interesting to observe that in Sri Lanka farmers with single axle tractors make most money hiring their machines for transport purposes. Farmers who manage to obtain one of these machines (usually trader farmers), are not too keen to hire out their machines for the more demanding task of cultivating land for their neighbours.

Well-meaning people in the Western world are concerned at the apparent breakdown of the subsistence farming system in some pressure spots and generously contribute money which they hope will rectify the situation. Sadly, all the money can do is alleviate matters. Why is this so? The reason is simple: the subsistence farming system (in whichever area we are concerned with) is no longer capable of meeting the needs of the ever increasing population. Moreover, the soils have become degraded by the pressures that have been put upon them, pressures that the stable system was never evolved to meet. In this way the ecological balance has been destroyed, the forests have gone, not only on the flat valley lands, which is acceptable, but also on the critical watersheds and river banks. There are no or few trees left in the famine areas of Ethiopia, but there were fifty years ago, and the springs have dried up. Erosion has become serious, the soils are degraded and give decreasing returns to meet increasing demands: an untenable situation indeed. Even outside the Sahel area the trees are going, as can be seen by eye in the Mwanza Region of Tanzania as the increasing population looks for more firewood and land to cultivate.

It is pointless telling a hungry family that they should not cut down the forest on the tops of the hills because it is bad for the environment, when they have nowhere else to go. But are the international agencies, the aid donors and the governments of the Third World countries seriously addressing themselves to these problems? The answer is no, as they have little understanding of the

subsistence farming system and the families that operate it; they do
not appreciate its strengths and its limitations, or the constraints
inherent in the system. Without that understanding there is little
that can be done to prevent famines. They can be alleviated for a
while, but unfortunately the population numbers keep on increasing to produce another famine in due course. Kenya is doubling its
population every eighteen years!

The subsistence farmers

People
It is difficult to generalize about the subsistence cultivator in a few
words, but now and then one comes across a brilliant simplification
which clears away the fog of confusion. In 'Production Procurement
and Agricultural Price Policy in Bangladesh' [71], Alimur Rahman,
writing about foodgrains, commences her section on the marketing
system with the sentence: 'In the early stage of development,
production in agriculture is geared to household consumption.'

Embodied in this one sentence, with all its implications, lies the
explanation of most of the problems encountered in any attempt to
improve the subsistence family's standard of living and their way of
life. Unless this sentence is understood there can be no understanding of the fundamental factors constraining development of
societies that are predominantly rural and essentially subsistence
orientated.

In a developed society individuals have very little freedom; they
are part of a highly organized community, and their education and
social background is arranged to fit them into that society. The
individual is permitted, indeed encouraged, to develop specialized
skills which are recognized as being of use to the community, and in
return as a contributor to that community the individual is allowed
to partake of the community's common wealth. The early but
cumbersome system of barter has been replaced by a money
economy which, in the developed world, is now so sophisticated
that a person can purchase goods throughout the world in almost
any currency just by presenting a credit card. In spite of this
sophistication most of the specialists have only the haziest of ideas
of how the other half lives, and what is even more important is that
the specialist doesn't appreciate that he or she can only survive in a
society of specialists. Give a banker a suitcase full of money and put
him on a desert island and he will starve.

The subsistence farmer and his family would survive if put on the same desert island. They would be in a familiar situation and as long as they had a spade hoe (the start of dependence on others), some seeds and pots and pans, would carry on as usual. Of course they would have few material possessions, but that is their lot now so they would notice nothing unusual.

The point of these laboured paragraphs is that the subsistence farmer and his family operate independently. Furthermore, they live in a community of farming families, all surviving independently of each other, to a greater or lesser extent. Obviously this is not completely true as there are very few families who are completely independent for their subsistence, and have no access to goods such as cooking oil, clothes, etc. However, many families are still basically subsistence orientated, for their purchasing power is limited to the few cash crops that can be produced after meeting the subsistence needs of the family, in a situation where the farm power is man power.

Accepting that the farmer is independent (and this gives him the strength of independence), and that he lives in a community of equally independent farmers, then he is faced with the disadvantage that there are only limited markets for the crops that he grows: markets, that is, within the community in which he lives. There may be markets for surpluses in remote towns, but he will have to get the produce there and in competition with his neighbours the price may not be attractive.

I gained experience of rural subsistence communities and their development constraints when I was an agricultural officer in Uganda in the late 1950s. Buganda Kingdom, where I was stationed, is a favoured country, lying within the fertile crescent to the north of Lake Victoria and having a good bimodal rainfall. For most peoples of the world their staple foodstuff is a storable grain, rice or wheat, but the Baganda are exceptions in that their staple foodstuff is a perishable commodity, the banana, or *matoke* as it is known locally. Steamed plantains or *matoke* are included in the diet once or twice a day, and in Buganda comprise the greater part of the daily calories intake, consumption being estimated at between 8 and 9 lbs per day (3.6–4.0 kg per day). Within Uganda there are estimated to be over a million acres (404,695 ha) of bananas, of which half are within the Buganda Kingdom. Despite this large acreage and several centuries of experience in growing the crop, yields per acre for the banana gardens were low, averaging only 3.5

tons per acre (8.75 tons per ha). During my agricultural extension safaris I had no difficulty in advising the farmers on improved techniques which would double or even treble their banana yields, but though seemingly respected my advice fell on deaf ears. This lack of response disturbed me for some time, until I realized that the problem was one of markets. The farmers were still fundamentally subsistence orientated (even if they had some cash crops such as robusta coffee), and their production methods produced more bananas than they could consume in the household. In fact large quantities of surplus bananas were made into beer or *waragi*. If they increased their production, what was the purpose? They could not sell it as their neighbours also had sufficient bananas for their family needs. My good advice was respected but of no value to the farmers in the circumstances of the community at that time.

A similar situation existed in the drier areas to the north of Uganda in the finger millet region. Because the farmers were in a rain-fed agricultural region, and knew by experience that rainfall can be unreliable within and between years, with consequent yearly fluctuations in yields per hectare, they deliberately over-produced food and stored it in their mud and wattle type granaries as an insurance against the bad years. This overproduction was quite considerable as they could not work on the production of an average year (which would mean that in any, say, ten-year period they would have been short of food for five years), but tended to pitch the target of production at a level which would provide them with just enough food in the most adverse year. In the good years the surpluses were made into beer. Here again we have the classic subsistence situation where all the farmers either have too much and no market for the surplus, or they are all short of food. This is more or less the situation that the peoples of Ethiopia and Darfur find themselves in at the moment, made worse by local political struggles.

The banana and finger millet example quoted above relates, however, to areas where land is relatively plentiful, such as is the case in the greater part of Africa (in contrast to the intense land pressure problems of the Far East). It would be easy to infer that the Ugandan farmers were inefficient, even lazy, but this would be a wrong conclusion. An equally wrong conclusion would be to assume from the peasant farmers' way of life that they are unintelligent and second-class citizens. This is by no means the case. They are in fact highly skilled men and women who have, in their particular circumstances, evolved a stable survival system using a minimum of resources. If we put a trained agriculturalist on the same desert island as the previously mentioned banker, but with a spade hoe, some seeds and pots and pans, it is unlikely that he would be able to improve greatly on the peasant farmers' techniques.

That subsistence farmers are as capable as anyone else in their ability to respond to and innovate in changed circumstances has been demonstrated by the farmers of Buganda, both in the last century and in the inter-war years. As Divisional Agricultural Officer, my area of responsibility included the Buvuma Islands in the northern part of Lake Victoria,[2] but as the islands were virtually uninhabited with a population of around 700 fishermen, I had not given them much priority when arranging my field safaris. Herbert Semambo, a Senior Assistant Agricultural Officer in charge of Kyagwe and Buvuma *sazas* (counties), suggested that I should visit the islands and, as there were reputed to be some cave paintings there, I agreed to go. I was not entirely happy at being in ignorance of what these islands looked like. I knew by hearsay that at the turn of the century they had been inhabited by a tribe known as the Bavuma, who spoke a language known as Luvuma. Also, I had heard that there had been some 30,000 of them living on the islands in the nineteenth century, an incredibly high figure which meant that the islands were supporting nearly 1000 people per square mile (386/sq km) of cultivable land. Unfortunately the people along the whole northern shore line of Lake Victoria were afflicted by sleeping sickness over the period 1901–8 and consequently the British authorities evacuated the population from the islands in the early part of the century.

The means of getting to the island was by launch and I could see, before landing on the deserted sandy beach where we pitched the tents, that the main island was uncultivated and, in general, covered by tall forest. There were, however, tracks through the forest and I explored some of them with Semambo. Within a few yards of the beach, in amongst the dense tree cover, we came across an earth face ten to twelve feet high, thickly covered with lower storey vegetation, which I assumed to be a raised beach (Lake Victoria having moved up and down over the centuries). We clambered up the rough track and within a few more yards we came across another similar face, and then more and more. I realized that 'my raised beach' theory was now suspect, and on scraping away the vegetation from one of the faces found that it was rock lined, and that we were in fact looking at hand made terraces. Over the next two days I walked over the greater part of the main island and found to my astonishment that the island had been completely terraced, even on the tops of the hills plots no more than a few square yards in size had been enclosed. A few months later I had the good fortune to be introduced to a Muvuma lady over one hundred years old who had been born on the island and who remembered living there as a young girl. She confirmed that the island had been completely terraced and stressed that no vegetation had been wasted. Cattle had been housed in pits within the houses and she could recall cutting grass on the hills and bringing bundles down to the animals. Furthermore when the pits were full of cattle manure it had been taken out and applied on the fields. Thornton and Rounce [74] reported in 1936 on a similar pre-colonial farming system on Ukara Island in the south of Lake Victoria. Interestingly, they recorded that as well as using farmyard manure on their fields the farmers on Ukara grew *Crotalaria striata* and *Tephrosia* for use as green manures, and I assume that the Bavuma also used a leguminous green manure, though the old lady was a little vague on this point.

The fact that these peoples on islands in Lake Victoria had evolved a quite sophisticated and stable farming system, involving the use of farmyard manure, green manures and terracing before Speke and Grant discovered the source of the Nile in 1862 (not many miles from the main Buvuma Island), demonstrates clearly that these farmers could be innovative and respond to need when the community circumstances changed – in this case the need to support nearly two people per acre (5 people per ha).

The second example of the subsistence farmer's ability to respond to new market situations and enterprises that give him an adequate return for effort is the development of the robusta coffee industry in Buganda. The Department of Agriculture had, quite justifiably, concentrated its research and extension effort on the production of cotton, and its importance as a crop was demonstrated by the presence in the country, at Namulonge, of a several thousand acre farm which was the main research station of the Empire Cotton Growing Corporation. But the Baganda realized that the returns from growing robusta coffee were more attractive than the rather tedious business of cultivating and harvesting cotton, and quietly over the years changed their cropping pattern (see Table 14). In 1936 the Baganda were growing over half an acre (0.20 ha) of cotton per person, compared to 0.03 of an acre (0.012 ha) of coffee. By 1964 the acreage of cotton per head had fallen to 0.14 (0.57 ha), and the area under coffee had risen to 0.27 acres (0.1 ha) per head. At the end of the 1950s the government suddenly realized that the robusta coffee crop was worth more than the cotton crop and appointed the first full-time coffee research officer.

It is often said that the subsistence farmers are lazy, conservative, inefficient, and unskilled. Conservative they may be, but that is only a pragmatic acceptance of the harsh unpredictability of nature, and if you have evolved a stable survival system over the centuries then you stay with it. Furthermore, the farmers' appreciation of their environment and their mastery of the farming cycle, and the sequence of operations taking them from one season to the next, show them to be highly skilled workers. If they do not respond to agricultural advice then the extension worker must query the validity of that advice because the farmers have shown themselves, by examples in many parts of the world, to be only too prepared to accept advice if it is valid in their circumstances, will give them an adequate and acceptable return for effort, and does not involve them in unacceptable risk.

Regarding the charge of being lazy, anyone who makes this accusation merely indicates a lack of understanding of the immensity of the task of providing food, and some cash, year in and year out for the family unit from small areas of land with one's hands as the main source of farm power.

A common criticism of the Ugandan farmers was that they planted their cotton crop too late with a consequent reduction in yields. Research work over a number of years and for a number of crops had clearly shown that there was a linear decline in yield as the time of planting was delayed. Research workers not only criticized the farmers, they also inferred that the agricultural officer's extension techniques were ineffective and did not make the best use of the research findings. Although the research workers would never acknowledge it, their criticism was uninformed and unjustified. Their research findings were correct, but they overlooked the fact that the experimental plots were almost invariably cultivated using tractors or unlimited hired labour. The farmers used *jembes* or spade hoes and anyone who has attempted to drive a spade hoe into the East African soils at the end of a long dry period immediately realizes why the farmers plant late. It is almost impossible to get the spade hoe blade into the soil without jarring

Table 14 *Cotton and coffee acreages in Buganda, 1921–1964*

Year	Population (000s)	Cotton acreage total (000s)	per head	Coffee acreage total (000s)	per head
1921	775	35	.05		
1922	785	32	.04		
1923	793	124	.16		
1924	803	185	.23		
1925	813	198	.24		
1926	822	156	.19	2	
1927	832	200	.24	2	
1928	842	200	.24	4	
1929	852	199	.23	8	.01
1930	863	195	.23	13	.02
1931	873	292	.33	14	.02
1932	894	318	.36	15	.02
1933	915	351	.38	17	.02
1934	937	425	.45	18	.02
1935	959	605	.63	20	.02
1936	982	695	.71	25	.03
1937	1,005	878	.87	27	.03
1938	1,029	727	.71	29	.03
1939	1,053	416	.40	31	.03
1940	1,079	439	.41	53	.05
1941	1,104	482	.44	48	.04
1942	1,130	307	.35	51	.05
1943	1,157	407	.44	53	.05
1944	1,185	333	.28	60	.05
1945	1,213	428	.35	127	.10
1946	1,242	409	.33	140	.11
1947	1,272	298	.23	142	.11
1948	1,302	477	.37	146	.11
1949	1,343	526	.39	148	.11
1950	1,386	508	.37	156	.11
1951	1,430	416	.29	178	.12
1952	1,475	342	.23	203	.14
1953	1,521	398	.26	228	.15
1954	1,569	432	.28	253	.16
1955	1,619	374	.23	280	.17
1956	1,670	346	.21	315	.19
1957	1,723	348	.20	385	.22
1958	1,777	384	.22	417	.23
1959	1,834	325	.18	441	.24
1960	1,892	250	.13	476	.25

Table 14 *continued*

Year	Population (000s)	Cotton acreage total (000s)	Cotton acreage per head	Coffee acreage total (000s)	Coffee acreage per head
1961	1,952	459	.24	515	.26
1962	2,014	278	.14	538	.27
1963	2,077	261	.13	562	.27
1964	2,143	293	.14	573	.27

Source: Unpublished material [52]

one's arms and hands, the soil being baked hard. Consequently the farmer, not being so foolish as people think, waits for the onset of the rains to soften the soil, by which time the land preparation is already too late for maximum yields by research station standards.

Similar criticisms have been heard about paddy farmers in Sri Lanka who have irrigation facilities and grow two crops per year. The complaint is that the farmers take too long cultivating the land between crops with a consequent delay in planting dates, which makes irrigation scheduling difficult. Whilst there is some substance to this criticism, what is not recognized is that the farmers have a considerable work load if they are to prepare their fields in time. In order to cultivate an acre of paddy land (assuming three passes in order to (a) uproot the stubble of the previous crop, (b) incorporate the decayed vegetation, and (c) final puddling of the field), the farmer using a spade hoe and digging to, say, 7.5 inches (19 cm), has to move, lift or invert some 2100 tons of soil. If he has only 21 days in which to do the operations then he has to manipulate, one way or another, 100 tons of soil per day. For a man whose staple diet may be 15.5 ounces (439 gm), of rice per day, that is quite a task. (The yearly consumption of foodgrains, excluding minor grains, in Bangladesh was 352 lbs (160 kg) in 1982–3.) When planning an irrigation scheme the question of holding size can be quite contentious, but if there is a shortage of animal or mechanical farm power and the small holder (who most probably has been moved into the project area from another district, i.e. without the extended family) is supported only by his wife, then the issue is quite simple. Anything over two acres, and he will probably encounter land preparation problems, depending on the cropping timetable.

Another classic example of the underrating of the amount of energy the subsistence small holder has to expend in producing his crops is that of the paddy farmer in Bangladesh. Though the main paddy growing season is during the summer rains, a Boro crop of rice is taken on low lying lands during the dry season using centuries-old irrigation techniques. In recent years the Boro paddy crop has assumed increasing importance with the introduction of low-lift pumps and shallow tube wells, there now being over 3 million acres (1.2 million ha) grown per year. Traditionally, however, the Boro crop was irrigated using doons, or swinging baskets, which would be used to lift the water up 2–6 feet (0.6–1.83 m) from a perennial water source on to nearby fields. These traditional methods of lifting water are still commonly in use on small plots of low lying land close to available water. In 1981–82, 881,000 acres (356,536 ha), were irrigated by doons (shaped like a canoe cut in half), and 212,000 acres (85,795 ha) by swinging baskets [9].

If we consider the case of the swinging basket, which is operated by two men each manipulating two long ropes attached to a woven triangular flat basket with two raised sides, the effort required to lift the amounts of water needed for the irrigation of the crop is more than most people would like to summon every day. Assuming that the Boro paddy crop will need 48 inches (122 cm) of water from planting to maturity, a period of, say, 105 days, this is equal to an application of 4848 tons of water per acre (12,000 tons/ha). In other words the two-man team has to lift about 50 tons of water per day when irrigating a one acre (0.4 ha) plot. Quite apart from their other work loads, this is a considerable task by any standards.

Farmers are also criticized from time to time on the grounds that they will not adopt proven packages of techniques. In this case we have to consider 'risk' and the farmers' cash incomes. In the Allai Tank area of Sri Lanka, farmers may have a cash income of only 1000 rupees per year, a figure which I refused to accept at first, but which I was unable to prove to be any higher. Weed control measures can cost Rps 700 per acre (0.4 ha), if the recommended rates are applied, but the farmers are hesitant in following the recommended rates as they take up almost all their available cash. They are justifiably unprogressive. What may seem to be a relatively small expenditure to a Westerner may be a year's cash income to the peasant farmers.

Another aspect of the subsistence way of life is the attitude of the rural family and the whole community to the staple food crop. A shortcoming in my own attitude to the place of crops in these societies was highlighted by my counterpart agronomist one day, when we were driving from Kandy to the Rice Research Station at Batalagoda and I had made some comment about rice being a cash crop. Thambiayah, who was a senior officer in the Department of Agriculture in Sri Lanka, gave me an enquiring look and said, 'Rice is not a cash crop, it is part of the people's way of life. Their whole history, their everyday actions all revolve around the crop.'

It is sometimes difficult for a Westerner brought up in an impersonal environment, where family ties are weak and people may not know their next door neighbours, to understand the intense feelings farmers have for their plots of land where generations of the same family and their neighbours have lived for centuries. They also have similar feelings for their crops and the husbandry methods that have been handed down from generation to generation.

To sum up, never underestimate the subsistence farmers. They may lack formal education, but they are not unintelligent, and they are very knowledgeable on the subject of survival. As Willem Boshoff, a colleague of mine at Makerere University College, used to say, 'They are the salt of the earth.'

Subsistence farmers and agricultural development
Though I have the greatest respect for the subsistence farmers and their farming system it does not necessarily follow that I have any illusions about the development potential of that system. The potential for development is virtually nil. That does not mean that the system cannot be 'polished', but productivity can be only marginally improved, and then only if there are adequate incentives (markets and prices) to induce the subsistence cultivator to make the effort.

The major constraint on increasing the subsistence cultivator's output and cash income is the value of man power. More than a manyear of labour (which includes the hand labour input of the husband, the wife and the children), is needed to keep the subsistence family fed, compared to the USA where the farming industry is now organized to the level where only 3.3 man hours of labour are required to cultivate an acre of corn. Of course the output per subsistence cultivator and per acre can be greatly increased by plant breeding (the Green Revolution), but once that advance has been taken up we come back to the limitation of the value of handpower. There is no way in which a subsistence cultivator can cultivate, plant, weed, and harvest an acre (0.4 ha) with a spade hoe in 3.3 hours. Of course, there are a few enterprising small holders, usually near towns, who have improved their cash income position by growing specialist crops, such as temperate vegetables for hotels, or cut flowers, satisfying the small urban market and thereby obtaining much greater rewards. If the neighbours emulate the progressive smallholder, however, the market becomes saturated and prices fall to an unattractive level.

In my experience it is quite easy for an able agricultural officer to help an individual progressive subsistence farmer, but it is not easy to do this on a community scale, because of the market limitations. Even if there are unlimited markets (say, for seed cotton), the subsistence cultivator's production is still limited to that equal to the spare energy *after* sufficient land has been cultivated to grow the food crops to meet the family needs for the year. In Uganda there was in the 1950s an average of 1.3 acres (0.53 ha) cultivated per year per head of population, of which one acre (0.4 ha) was for food and 0.3 of an acre (0.12 ha) for cash crops. For a five-person family this meant that 6.5 acres (2.6 ha) were cultivated by hand per year, which is no mean feat.

Departments of Agriculture have pondered for decades over the problem of how to develop the subsistence farming sector and never produced any real breakthrough. There were the so-called research station advances, but few advances that were accepted by the subsistence cultivators, mainly because the research findings were not relevant to their subsistence circumstances. There were, however, some specific advances in the field of applied research which were generally acceptable, particularly in the fields of plant breeding and plant protection. The breeding of disease-resistant varieties (cassava varieties resistant to virus disease), or varieties that were less susceptible to insect attack (jassid-resistant cotton cultivars), or varieties of maize that have a shorter (or longer) life cycle were advances of immediate and general acceptableness. Some of the water and soil conservation work was also beneficial, but, sadly, modern day central governments do not always recognize its importance, or are loath to enforce legislation on the 'voters'.

To many people the foregoing will sound rather negative, but the position is that the subsistence farming system is virtually unalterable as a system, only open to modest improvements. As said earlier, subsistence farming is a survival system, with, nowadays, some cash cropping superimposed, the cash crops being mainly export crops such as cotton, robusta coffee, groundnuts, jute, cocoa and spices. The system has limited flexibility because of the overriding constraints of farm power and markets, but this does not mean that the system cannot be changed, only that changes have to be proven and there has to be an incentive for accepting the changes. Thus rising population can 'force' the farmers to change from an extensive to an intensive system, increasing output per hectare by adopting better husbandry measures, but only to that point where the family needs are met. If they overproduce there will be no market for the surplus food because the neighbours will be following the same system.

The conclusion must be that subsistence farming was and is an excellent system for meeting the subsistence needs of a family, providing the population pressure is not so great as to make the system unstable, but it has limited potential for development.

Subsistence farmers and non-agricultural development
Traditionally the subsistence cultivators provided for their own family needs and any surpluses, usually small, were sold for cash in the urban markets. The urban markets in developing countries, though, are often smaller than one would expect. One of the reasons for this is that the relatively wealthy urban families often retain their share of the family lands and obtain their food supplies from these holdings. The desire is strong to keep the traditional subsistence independence, even if as absentee landlords. In this case their contribution to the rural economy is confined to employment of farm labour.

Many authorities regard the rural population as a vast untapped market for the goods manufactured by the urban sector. However, this is an illogicality, as the rural population cannot purchase manufactured goods unless it has money in its 'pocket', and it cannot have any money unless it has a market for its surplus production. Even if it has a market, the surplus production, which is always small, being dependent on hand labour, is not very great and worth only a few pounds sterling for each family. In Uganda when I was there an average cultivator might only produce 100 lbs (45 kg) of seed cotton, worth maybe 50 East African shillings, which would hardly pay for a meal for my wife and me in a restaurant in Kampala. But, in terms of development, even small per capita cash incomes multiplied by several million persons produce an appreciable grand total for central government to manipulate. Yet the amounts involved are, for many developing countries, less than the turnover of a modest firm operating in the developed countries. The Gross National Product per capita for Ethiopia in 1985 was $110, compared to $16,370 for Switzerland for the same year [41].

The colonial authorities were well aware of the need to establish a cash economy, if for no other reason than to provide a base for taxation, hence the enthusiasm of colonial administrations for crops such as cotton, groundnuts, rubber, cocoa, coffee, etc. Farmers were provided with seed or seedlings, marketing channels were established, road networks built and consumer goods outlets encouraged to provide the subsistence family units with incentives to grow the cash crops. Though the popular interpretation of these developments is that they were exploitation, these export cash crops were the essential basis for future non-agricultural development. From these developments sprang the primary schools, roads, dispensaries, etc. Once the urban centres were initiated then power plants appeared, primary processing units were erected, and from these beginnings urbanization proceeded, slowly but steadily – services were set up, water reservoirs built, and so on.

Unhappily for some developing countries, the new authorities did not recognize the importance of the primary commodities and the processing plants, e.g. ginneries, and embarked on adventurous industrialization programmes (often encouraged by 'helpful' Western representatives) which were beyond their infrastructures. Unfortunately the traditional industries were neglected in favour of the more spectacular new industries and over the next twenty years or so the original 'economic' infrastructure depreciated. In this way the traditional economic foundations for a country's development were dissipated, a classic case being Tanzania where ginneries are now in such a dilapidated state that they can barely process half the pre-Independence seed cotton crop (then 400,000 bales and now 200,000). Under these circumstances, where there are few incentive goods left in the village shops and where a country's service infrastructure (roads, transport, etc.), has broken down, the subsistence farmers finds themselves back to 'square one' and their only course is to establish a parallel economy.

Notes

1 The Morrill Land Grant Act allocated federal land to states for the purpose of establishing colleges (agriculture and military science being required disciplines though others were not excluded), each state to be

granted land on the basis of 30,000 acres for each senator (2) and each representative in Congress (the number depending on the 1860 census – Pennsylvania had 25).

2 Not everybody realizes just how high and how large Lake Victoria is – it is at nearly 4000 feet (1220 m), and 27,000 square miles (69,930 sq km) in extent, about the same size as the Republic of Ireland.

4 Development complexities and constraints

The environment

As a generalization one can say it is possible to grow almost any crop anywhere in the world. The Americans, for example, have grown lettuce on the North Pole, and vegetable production in the deserts of the Gulf States, using hydroponics, is well established. All that one requires are unlimited inputs and equally unlimited financial backing, plus the appropriate technology. Thus the environment in itself is not the main constraint on crop and animal production in the developing countries of the world. Of course, some environments are more suitable than others for agriculture, but even the worst environments can be amended by the use of, for example, irrigation, fertilizers, supplementary heating, or plant protection measures. The limiting factor is money. This is a factor that is overlooked nowadays by the affluent Western democracies, whose economies are so strong that they can afford to pour almost unlimited resources into their agricultures, to the point where the level of production is an embarrassment and a cause of political dissension. Regrettably the affluence is taken for granted by the average Westerner, in much the same way that a child assumes that water always comes out of taps. The amount of effort needed to create the system which allows the water to come out of the tap is not comprehended, nor is the source of the affuence understood.

Having made the above generalization, one now has to qualify the statement and relate it to the circumstances of Third World countries. The farmers in developing countries are dependent on the bounty that nature provides, on farms whose size is necessarily small, being related to the farm power value of man power. The system is fundamentally subsistence orientated, like that of the crofters of Scotland, utilizing incoming sunlight and the natural fertility of the soil. However, if the environment for agriculture is

Home from the field. Father and son on a buffalo in Boudre Peninsula, Philippines – an area originally tropical rain forest but now bare hills!

marginal the farmers have very limited funds available to them, or the community in which they live, for the purpose of amending it. If the soils are poor, they have no funds for the purchase of fertilizers to improve the fertility; if rainfall is low they have no funds for the purchase of water pumps and sprinkler irrigation equipment. Because the society in which they live, and its economy, is underdeveloped there is no way in which surplus funds can be generated for investment in the agricultural system. People in the West seem to have no appreciation or comprehension of the immensity of the economic resources that are available to them in comparison to those of the Third World. These resources have been built up by previous generations, accumulating over centuries – knowledge, libraries, education for all, technical know-how, road systems, communciations, trade routes, banking systems, etc.

One of the poorer agricultural environments of the world is that of Sierra Leone (many people do not realize that it is actually a 'green' desert, fooled by the lush and seemingly unexploited vegetative cover), but this country has great difficulty in purchasing the needed inputs to improve the intrinsically poor fertility of the country's soils. Present use of imported fertilizer is around 4000 tons per year (compared to the 48 million tons used per year by the USA [88]), but this quantity is not sufficient to make more than a tiny impression on the needs of the country. What is even more depressing is that because the amount of fertilizer that the country can afford to buy is so small (due to severe shortage of foreign exchange), they have to pay the high freight rates charged on quantities that do not make up a complete shipload. As a consequence the cost of urea landed in Freetown is about three times the price paid by the wealthy states who can purchase the commodity in bulk. Rather sadly, the International Agencies, influenced by some inappropriate Western economist's dogma, are pressurizing the Sierra Leone Government to discontinue subsidies on fertilizers provided to the country's subsistence farmers, which will make it even more difficult for the poor farmers to afford the fertilizer. Liberal donations of fertilizer to the poorer countries of the world might be a better gift than the dumping of unwanted food surpluses of the EEC, which bring so much chaos to the agricultural pricing policies of the developing countries. In recent years, during a maize shortage in the north of Tanzania, the country found it cheaper to import maize through Dar es Salaam than transport it from the south, where there was a surplus!

Many people will disagree with the suggestion that the environment is not one of the main limiting factors to production in the Third World, but whilst I acknowledge that it is important, it is a factor that can be easily modified with good technology. Look at the example of the Delta farming in Egypt. The transition from arid desert to green farm lands is dramatic to an extreme. One can stand on a spot and look over green farmlands, then turn through 180 degrees and survey unending desert. Where there is water there are crops and where there is no water there is sand. Then take the example of Israel. Whether one is for or against Zionism one has to acknowledge that Israeli agriculturalists have mastered what is a hostile environment for farming, to a point where many of the vegetables and fruits purchased in the greengrocers in the UK are from that country. Plant breeding has also played a part in reducing the importance of environment, the classic example being the maize plant which can now be grown from the equator up to Sweden, or wheat, which is now a major winter crop for Bangladesh. Varieties of crops with short growing periods have been bred, permitting crops to be grown in areas with short rainfall seasons, or allowing three crops per year where there are irrigation facilities.

Health factors were at one time an important environmental constraint on the development of agriculture in parts of the tropics. Though they are still a major factor, and will be discussed later, modern medicine has the technology to control most human ailments. The fact that Sierra Leone, for example, has a life expectancy of thirty-nine years is more a reflection on the scale of medical services (one doctor per 19,300 people), than on the existence of diseases for which there was no cure. This was, of course, not always so, and in recent times there were large areas of Africa which were not cultivated due to the presence of river blindness (onchocerciasis), while bilharzia remains a problem in Egypt. The debilitating effects of gastro-enteric diseases in rural areas with high population densities and no sewage facilities are still underestimated.

Although I have stated that the environment is not a major factor limiting agricultural production, given access to modern technology, there are large parts of the world for which viable and stable crop husbandry methods are still being researched. These are the high rainfall, acidic soil, tropical rainforest regions, to be found in the Amazon Basin, Sumatera and parts of West Africa, typically in Sierra Leone. Historically the lands are worked under a shifting cultivation system, employing the 'slash and burn' technique in the clearing of the land for cultivation. Usually the land is only cultivated for two years, before being abandoned due to increasing soil acidities, and then allowed to return to a bush/forest fallow. The technology for converting the shifting cultivation system to continuous annual cropping is still being determined, and requires inputs that are not readily available to subsistence farmers. So far only

Nicholaides and his co-workers [62] in South America have come up with economically viable permanent annual cropping systems for these very acid lands. Similar studies on annual cropping are being carried out at Padang in Sumatera, an island with poor acidic soils which are best suited to permanent tree crops (rubber and oil palms) on the uplands and rice on the *sawah,* or wetland rice lands.

An interesting sidelight on environmental issues is that we have a number of organizations in the industrialized countries whose objective is to protect the world's environment, particularly in the developing world. Great concern is expressed about the destruction of the world's forests and the killing of wildlife. Personally I thoroughly agree with these objectives, but I do think there is an element of unreality if these organizations expect the poorer nations of the world to be the ones that make the sacrifices. After all, who consumes all the hard woods that are being felled, who are the rich people providing the market, and then criticizing the poor for pandering to their greed? If the rich sincerely want to protect the world's environment then they must make the greater contribution.

I have seen, in Africa, cultivated hillside slopes which were so steep that the spade hoe went into the ground at the level of the farmer's head as he dug the ground – land so steep that the farmer could fall out of his holding, and I am not joking. It is easy to criticize such farmers for the wanton destruction of the hillside's protective forest cover, but such criticism is not justified. Population pressure forces the families into increasingly marginal environments, and the farmers, with their families to support, and meagre resources (often not much more than a mud hut, a cutlass and a spade hoe), can hardly be blamed for scrabbling for survival by the only means open to them. They are not going to let their children starve just to please some ideological do-gooder living in the protective cocoon of the industrialized societies. It is hard even to criticize the local polititians, who could hardly be expected to enforce legislation which would stop the unfortunate peasants from utilizing what they regard as their own lands. Rightly or wrongly one has to sympathize with the peasant family in their predicament and their attitude. Certainly they will not get much financial help from the rich Westeners, who are loath 'to put their money where their mouth is'. In general they want their cheap coffee beans, cocoa, raw cotton, and vegetable oils, and are not too keen on paying more than the market price for the agricultural produce of the developing countries. Indeed, organizations such as the EEC are often active in keeping such produce out if it competes with their own high-priced internally produced crops and livestock.

Demography

This is undoubtedly the major factor militating against the development of most of the countries of the Third World, and yet even today one comes across the argument, from well-educated people, that there is nothing wrong in the rural populations of the poorer countries of the world having large families: '...gives the family strength...more hands to work the land...an insurance for old age', etc. Yet it is this very attitude that means that there will be no old age, or that one is old by the age of forty. Not only that, it means that the young of today in the Third World have a bleak future ahead of them. In many parts of the world today there is over-reproduction, resulting in a plethora of children, who in turn will produce more children, and no matter what Western theorists may say, nature will remorselessly deal with the overpopulation problem.

Some of the background to this problem is given in Chapter 2, but this issue is so fundamental to progress in the Third World that parts are repeated here to stress this factor's importance. Let us start by quantifying the problem as far as it applies to agriculture. India is presently increasing its population by over twelve million a year, or a million a month – think of this as a food production problem. Each year India increases its population by three times the population of Norway! Kenya has a population growth rate around 4 per cent per year, and is estimated to be doubling its population every eighteen years or so. Quite apart from the food issue, this country has to double, every eighteen years, the number of houses, the number of teachers, the number of buses, the number of pots and pans, just to stand still. This would be quite a challenge for a developed economy. Of course the population problem was at one time exacerbated deliberately by government policy, in the mistaken belief that population numbers meant strength, but the land resources are limited and the subsistence farmers are being squeezed into increasingly marginal lands. As the land is used up under the traditional farming systems so the excess population drifts towards the urban centres seeking any kind of work which will provide them with enough money to feed themselves and their families. In the euphoria of the early days of Independence urban populations were not regarded as a problem; factories could be

constructed to make shirts, bottles, cans, pens and so forth, often
supported by foreign capital, the goods being produced for export
and to a lesser extent for local consumption. Import substitution
was a popular phrase. However, as more and more countries
became independent with more and more factories producing
consumer goods, world markets became increasingly competitive,
and foreign investment more difficult to obtain except at high rates
of interest – debt servicing became a new phrase. Governments of
developing countries found it increasingly difficult to find the capital
resources for job creation as the urban centres swelled with youth
migrating away from the traditional rural life style.

At the time of Independence Tanzania had a population in the
region of 10 million persons. It is estimated that by the year 2000 this
figure will have risen to 35 million, of which 25 million will be rural
and 10 million urban. To provide sufficient urban workplaces for
such a massive number is, quite frankly, beyond the organizational
or financial resources of the country. Britain, itself, has some 3
million unemployed and is not very successful in alleviating the
situation, so it will be even more difficult for an underdeveloped
country with an unskilled population and a limited technology base.
What is more important is that even if they have the skilled workers
it still costs an enormous amount of money to create work places.
Power stations are needed, roads have to be constructed, port
facilities strengthened, heavy plant purchased, etc., and the
workers need houses, sewage systems (unless one is prepared to
accept shanty town conditions), schools, food shops and so on. The
developing countries found that they had insufficient capital
resources to fund their development programmes, and then actively
tried to resettle the unemployed urban population back on the land.
Hence the popularity of World Bank resettlement schemes, transmigration projects, large irrigation projects to provide governments
with a solution to the politically sensitive issue of urban unemployed. But the problem is on a scale beyond even the resources of
the World Bank. They might be able to deal with the problems of
one country, but not 150 developing countries.

An industrial workplace in the UK is valued at thirty to forty
thousand pounds per man. Strangely enough, to establish a
workplace in the middle of the Arabian desert or in Kilimanjaro will
cost more or less the same, or even more. Few developing countries
can move from £100 technology to the £30,000 workplace without
external assistance in one form or another. All one has to do is

multiply £30,000 by 1 million to appreciate the immensity of the task facing the developing countries. The man looking for a workplace in the UK discounts the cost of the power station, the transport system, his previous schooling, etc. African socialism and self-reliance as a policy is quite praiseworthy as an ideal, but sadly it means that it may take a developing country 200–250 years to reach the present level of development in the West – the same period that the West took from the commencement of the Industrial Revolution. However, if we are truthful, it may not be possible for the underdeveloped countries ever to catch up with the West, if they rely on their own 'steam' only, for the simple reason that they have a population problem the West never had.

In this connection it is interesting to note that when 20,000 Ugandan refugees returned to their homes, north of Kampala, after the fall of Obote, they were given £15 per head for tools, seeds and some blankets. How can such a society ever generate enough capital to compete with the industrialized world, a world where a million workers may be backed by £40,000 million worth of investment?

If there had been a gentle increase in population then there could have been an equally gentle drift of population from the rural areas to the towns as workplaces were created. The increasing urban population would have provided markets for agricultural surpluses and both urban and rural sectors would have progressed together. Instead, the population explosion has resulted in governments being more concerned with urban problems and regarding the rural areas simply as a sink for population overspill. This is a recipe for disaster and eventual famine. The poor farmer has a diminishing holding and any surpluses that he may generate above the family needs he has to sell at low prices in competition with cheap imports arranged by the urban sector of the country. He cannot afford inputs and slowly drifts down and eventually becomes functionally landless.

Politics

The previous two sections have tended to lump the developing countries together, equally, but that is not the real situation. The Third World countries differ greatly in their development achievements in agriculture and other spheres. Undoubtedly the extent and soundness of any one country's development, and the well-being of its peoples, depends very much on the character and calibre of the 'rulers'. For many of the developing countries this means one

person, supported by an oligarchy. Most of the developing countries started off their independent lives as democracies, but soon
changed to less democratic forms of government, the commonest
being military dictatorship. The reason for this was quite simple: the
former colonial powers left a power vacuum which had been only
superficially filled by the fledgling political opportunists at the time
of independence. These political organizations had no long history
or experience of government, were internally weakly structured,
and represented a politically naive electorate. There was internal
jockeying for the position of supreme power, constitutions were
quickly changed, and the muzzle of a gun became the arbiter of
power. In many countries military regimes came in not necessarily
because they sought power, but because they were the only
organized, trained, disciplined, large force in the country. Some of
these regimes were benevolent, whilst others were evil, such as
Amin's in Uganda. Where the military governments are stable the
people are able to get on with their lives reasonably independently,
but where there is opposition to military rule the rural population
may find itself liable to attack from both sides.

Further complicating the scene were the politics of the affluent
nations, the power blocs and the international organizations. They
supported regimes which should not have been supported, including the corrupt and evil, for devious reasons of their own which had
little to do with the well-being of the peoples of these countries.
Sometimes they opposed new political philosophies if it suited
them, examples being Kwame Nkrumah in Ghana and Julius
Nyerere in Tanzania. Both these men attempted, benevolently, to
evolve political and development philosophies pertinent to the
circumstances of their respective countries, but they fell foul of
Western economic and banking cartels. Yet in Korea, Singapore
and Taiwan, equally determined men achieved great progress.

On the farmer in the field the political in-fighting had little effect,
except in those countries where armed conflict disrupted the daily
way of life, such as Uganda, Ethiopia, Sudan, etc. For most of the
farmers the only thing that happened was that there was a scarcity of
consumer goods – the disappearance of the bicycle in Tanzania, for
example – or that goods were available but priced beyond the
subsistence farmer's pocket. But for some, life became impossible,
as when they were caught between government and rebel forces.
The rebels expected to live off the land, and the government forces

shot them for helping the rebels, or burned their crops, as is happening in Mozambique at the moment.

Although this section has concentrated on the military powers, in some of the larger and relatively well established countries one can find (I almost wrote, 'come up against') organizations that are political powers in their own right, sufficiently powerful to oppose central government itself. These organizations are nearly always technical ministries, with numerous loyal employees and a strong internal bureaucracy. I am thinking here of Ministries of Water and Power in some Asian countries, which are sometimes so bureaucratically powerful that a government will not risk a confrontation. For example, in Bangladesh, though there is a strong Department of Agriculture, some of its powers are usurped by the even stronger Bangladesh Water Development Board. This body, employing some 70,000 people, has its own Directorate of Land and Water Use, covering soils, irrigation extension and agronomy – even though government policy was that these activities should be integrated within one service.

Technology

This is a section that will have a number of seeming contradictions. There exists in the world the technology to more than feed the present population. Whether there will be pollution problems and major environmental changes is a different matter, but the fact remains that there exist in the world known techniques which would provide all with an adequate diet, and at the same time meet all the primary commodity needs for such products as cotton, rubber, drugs, luxury foods (coffee, cocoa), etc. Even more surprisingly, there exists in most of the Third World countries' research stations sufficient knowledge to meet each country's agricultural needs: the exceptions are the most difficult environments, such as Sierra Leone, Sumatera and parts of the Amazon Basin, where the technology for stable continuous cultivation still does not exist. Not only is the technology known in the research stations of the developing countries, but it is also known by the extension services and often by the farmers. However, for some reason the technologies are not used.

Just why good technologies are not taken up by the subsistence farmers of the world is not widely understood. Educated men, both nationals and short term visitors, tend to put the blame on the peasants – they are conservative, lazy, unintelligent, chronically sick or even simply contrary. If it is not the peasants, then it is the extension services. They are inefficient, idle, lack training, lack proper guidance by senior officers, or don't get amongst the farmers enough. Almost invariably, experts from the industrialized countries criticize the local agricultural extension services for any shortcomings that they see on their field visits. They look no further, and never seem to ask the question why extension services in the developing countries experience such difficulty in extending good farming technology to the subsistence farmers. Grandiose answers are proposed such as the 'Training and Visit' extension methods, which use up a lot of people's time, produce copious but dubious records, and seem to have little real impact on the agricultural scene. Except, that is, in countries that have a strong industrial base.

As an extension worker in Uganda, I considered myself to be reasonably competent, certainly no worse that others, yet I found myself puzzled that the 'message' did not seem to be getting over to the people. The farmers seemed to accept my advice, for example, on how to treble their banana crop yields, seemed to recognize that it was good advice, but did not put it into effect. I pondered over this phenomenon on many occasions, but it took me a while to come up with an answer. As Divisional Agricultural Officer, Mukono, covering the equivalent of three counties, I had some twenty field personnel, agricultural instructors, more or less one for each *gombolola* (sub-county), who were the Department's main extension contact point with the farmers. Most of these instructors had farms of their own within the District and one day I decided that I would visit each of their farms. This caused some consternation, but I persisted and eventually found that the farms of the instructors were 'no better' than those of the farmers they were advising. The cotton was equally badly spaced and the bananas unmulched. The common excuse was that it was the fault of their wives, who kept the farms whilst the instructors were out on safari meeting the farmers. I countered this by saying that if they could not convince their wives of the goodness of their extension advice, what hope had they with the other farmers? However, it was not the instructors who had the problem, it was me, and it took me some time to work out the true answer, which was markets, marketing and prices. Land was not a factor limiting production in Uganda in the 1960s: the energy value of the family generally decided how much land they worked. However, the average farmer could see no value in changing from his extensive production techniques to more intensive methods if there were no markets, or no markets at attractive prices. In the case of bananas the market was small, except around the urban centres, whilst in the case of cotton the return for effort was unattractive. It is interesting to note that the Baganda progressively reduced their acreage under cotton when they found a more attractive crop, coffee, as shown in Table 14. (See also next section.)

Returning to the question of available technologies, it is worth examining their evolution. Up until relatively recent times research examined individual factors, one at a time, in a search for the elusive factor limiting crop yields or better animal production. In general this approach was unsuccessful, apart from disease prevention and pest control. Thus excellent work was done in the inter-war years on breeding for disease resistance, such as virus resistance in cassava in East Africa by Dr Storey, or the selection of cotton varieties with leaf characteristics which made them resistant to jassid attack. It was only after the Second World War that agronomists started experimenting with 'packages' of interacting good techniques. For example, trials on maize, testing the interaction of improved varieties with spacing, time of planting, level of fertilizer, amount of weeding – all these techniques became common, resulting in a 'package recommendation' giving the best combination of a number of interacting husbandry factors. Adaptive research then evaluated these packages in different environments. Probably the best packages that appeared on the world scene were those put out for rice from the International Rice Research Institute in the Philippines, and for the green revolution wheats evolved at CIMMYT in Mexico. Undoubtedly these technologies were a major step forward, but they are not universally accepted by the farmers of the world, and malnutrition and undernutrition is on the increase. The technology exists but it is not necessarily used. The answer to this question is fundamental to the future of the overwhelming majority of the world's population, the subsistence farmers and their families.

On the animal side of agriculture progress has not been as impressive as for crops. In some respects this is due to the departmental division of responsibility for agriculture within the old colonial service. Usually, there was a Department of Agriculture that looked after crops (often including pastures), but which had no responsibility for animals. This responsibility was allocated to the

Veterinary Department, which jealously protected its right to be responsible for all aspects of animal industry apart from pasture management. The background to the development of the milk industry in Uganda is worthy of mention.

After the Second World War a programme was initiated in Uganda to upgrade the local cattle. Milk yields were low, say less than 230 gallons (1045 litres) per lactation, though the cattle had resistance to local diseases and could survive under spartan conditions. Importation of improved breeds was discounted as a policy because the veterinary opinion was that they would need too much attention and care to keep them alive. As a consequence a herd of forty better local cattle was brought together for the objective of producing animals that would be capable of reasonable levels of performance under the prevailing peasant farm conditions. Despite a lack of significant genetic improvement over the years, the statement continued to be made that selection from indigenous cattle was still the soundest long term policy that could be adopted for the improvement of milk production in East Africa.

In the late 1950s Mahadevan and Marples carried out an analysis of the Entebbe herd of Nganda cattle [54] and demonstrated that the genetic improvement per year was very low, being 0.2 gallons (1.0 litre) per year through selection of dams of cows, and virtually nil through the bull selection programme. These findings were included by Mahadevan in a review of dairy cattle breeding in East Africa [55], in which he wrote:

> With thirty years of experimental data from many livestock improve-ment centres now analysed and interpreted, it is possible to state categorically that selective breeding for milk production within the indigenous cattle of East Africa has failed to give any worthwhile results; nor is there any reason to suppose on genetical grounds that it is likely to be any more successful in the future. (p. 321)

As a consequence of changing beliefs, in 1959 a start was made on the planned introduction of exotic European type milch cows into the African farming areas, in particular the importation of high-yielding exotic Friesians from Kenya, capable of giving yields under Buganda conditions of between 600 and 1000 gallons (2725–4546 litres), per lactation. The Baganda farmers took to the breed with enthusiasm and large numbers were imported to supply milk to the Kampala market (where demand previously had been met by daily rail shipments from Kenya). Although the Department laid down rigorous rules about the management of these animals (the farmers had to have available two acres of planted grass per animal, fence the area, and have a cleared strip around the pasture to prevent ticks migrating on to the improved pasture before they could get an import licence), the farmers realized that these animals were capable of giving high and profitable yields of a commodity for which a large market already existed. Several thousand animals were imported from Kenya, much to the surprise of the Department.

The Ugandan experience is of considerable interest as it demonstrates the need for very clear thinking before determining research or development policies. The Entebbe philosophy was entirely based on veterinarian attitudes. They took the approach, seemingly reasonable, that it would be nonsense to bring in high-priced exotics, requiring expensive prophylactics and veterinary attendance to keep them alive. Much better to upgrade the local animals which had acquired resistance by natural selection over the centuries, and were animals adapted to the poor management standards and abysmally bad pastures. In defence of this thinking one must stress that the research philosophy was decided upon when the market for milk in Kampala was not particularly high and its modest needs could be satisfied easily from Kenya (which was also a British colony). But what the Entebbe thinking missed was that even if they had been successful in breeding a herd of local cattle capable of giving milk yields approaching the same level as the exotics, by the time they had achieved this the herd would require the same high inputs as the exotics. If they had taken these improved local animals and given them to the local farmers to keep under their poor management standards on the bare hillsides, with tough old grasses to eat, the animals would have died from the shock just as quickly as the exotics.

For the animal side of the agricultural industry the message is much the same as for plants. Providing one has the capital one can keep high-yielding animals almost anywhere. The cost, however, may be prohibitive in the hot tropics as high-yielding cattle are particularly susceptible to heat stress. An animal producing milk has to convert food (grass and concentrates, usually), into milk and the more milk it produces the more food it has to consume. The food that is consumed is broken down into its constituent parts in the stomachs with a release of heat, and the more food broken down the more heat is released. An animal giving a gallon (4.5 litres), of milk per day may experience only limited heat stress, but take the yield to 2 gallons (9 litres), or even 4 gallons (18 litres), and the animal becomes increasingly stressed. I have seen high-yielding Friesians in Egypt, in temperatures in the high thirties, 'rocking' as they panted trying to get rid of the body heat, with dry cows standing beside them under no obvious stress.

Markets, marketing and prices

These factors are particularly relevant to the development of agribusiness, but they are equally of importance to the subsistence farming family. Although the subsistence farming system can only be marginally improved, because of the farm power constraint, it is possible for most farmers to increase their production by, say, 10 per cent, but even such a small increase may lack a market at an attractive price. It may be very difficult to find a market for that half sack of sweet potatoes, even at a low price.

This aspect has already been mentioned in Chapter 3 as I consider the market problem to be fundamental to any understanding of the subsistence farmer's farming activities, actions and philosophy, and the key to any develoment of that system, both for the individual and the community. If one examines the statistics in the World Bank's *World Development Report* [41] one finds that for the low income economies, that is those with a gross national product per capita of less than $400 per year in 1985, nearly 80 per cent of the total population of 2439 million people is rural. This means that, within such economies, some 1900 million people are, to all intents and purposes, independent as regards their own food supplies. Even more importantly, they live in communities where their neighbours are equally independent. They are in a situation where there are limited markets for their farm surpluses, and even if there are markets, the marketing arrangements are not well developed and the prices almost invariably low. The problem is made clear when one compares the subsistence orientated societies with the industrialized countries. In Britain less than three per cent of the population is involved in agriculture and the remaining ninety-seven per cent are the market. But these farms are very highly mechanized and there are those who would say that agriculture in the industrialized nations is simply a conversion of oil energy into food calories, whilst the subsistence farmer is dependent on the work-energy value of his family and the sun. Some people say, 'Why not give them tractors? That would solve their farm power problems.' But, as we have seen, the tractor is of limited value to them because even if they increase their production by using the tractor, they have difficulty selling the increased production for the reason that their neighbours do not need to buy food.

For those Third World countries which had been colonies before, the euphoria of Independence masked the harsh realities of the independent world. Within a short period of time the new governments realized that they needed foreign exchange to purchase building materials, machines, tools, and skills. They naturally turned to the agricultural industry as a source of funds, for many countries the only source of foreign exchange. The industry was milked by the central governments. (It is interesting to observe that some rural populations reacted to this by creating what are now called parallel economies, with crop prices in the country bearing little relationship to the lower controlled prices.) At the same time as exploiting the established agricultural industry there was a big push to diversify, but in most cases the exercise was not successful as the new producers came into competition with other newly independent states doing the same thing, and the result was a forcing down of commodity prices due to overproduction. To sell the main staple foodstuffs, such as wheat, maize, and rice, the new states had to compete with the surpluses of the industrialized countries, who could, due to economies of scale, deliver foodstuffs, c.i.f., at much lower prices than the local producers. In some cases the problem was exacerbated as the surplus foodstuffs were virtually dumped by the bureaucracies of such organizations as the EEC, with little consideration for the effect on the subsistence farmers. Military regimes were more than pleased to accept subsidized imported foodstuffs as a means of providing the urban hordes with cheap food, not appreciating the fact that they might be discouraging their own rural farming industry in the process.

Pricing policies are equally important as a factor influencing agricultural development. When I was in Uganda there was considerable extension pressure on the small holders to increase their output of cotton. They were encouraged to plant the crop early (which required them to cultivate the land in the dry season, when it was baked hard), rather than late when the soil had been softened by the onset of the rains; to weed the crop at least five times; to purchase sprayers and sprays for insect control; and to pick the crop with care to ensure high quality, etc. At the end of which he would increase his crop by maybe only 25 per cent. This may sound a lot if one is doing all this work by machines, but if one is only cultivating a small plot by hand, then the increased return may not be an adequate return for effort if the price of the unprocessed commodity is low. I once worked out that for the average Muganda farmer the return for growing the crop well would give him a cash return which was less than I would spend on a meal for my wife and myself in the Chinese Restaurant in Kampala. When I was there the price of cotton paid to the farmer for his seed cotton was around 50 cents per pound (in those days there were 100 cents to the shilling and twenty shillings to the East African pound). It took three pounds of seed cotton to produce one pound of cotton lint, which was then exported to Lancashire. There it was processed into shirts which were exported to East Africa and sold for £3, or 60 shillings (and the shirt would only have about a quarter of a pound of lint in it!). There is no doubt that the hand cultivation of primary commodities, such as cotton, is a tedious and not very rewarding pastime. Using hand-power a subsistence farmer may be able to cultivate little more than two acres (0.8 ha) per year (the figure varying according to the environment and the farming system), whilst in the USA this would take only twelve hours using machines (see Table 9). The rural farmers are as keen as anyone to purchase consumer goods, but are very vulnerable to poor pricing policies, and their very independence in terms of food supplies makes them a group that can be given low priority in the urban corridors of power.

To my mind, speaking as an agronomist, it is markets and prices that are the major factor limiting overall agricultural development in the Third World. The technology exists to greatly increase production, as and when needed, but the lack of markets at adequate prices means that the subsistence farmers have no means whereby they can gainfully make use of the new technologies. They can only respond if there are enlightened policies from the top, and in the circumstances of the developing countries this does not always occur. However, even with enlightened market and pricing policies, there still remains the farm power constraint on subsistence orientated farmers.

That small holders will respond to enlightened policies and attractive prices is indicated by the following examples. Many people regard the work carried out in Mexico in breeding the miracle wheats as a triumph for science, and this is so. But it was not only a question of providing the farmers with improved dwarf varieties of wheat capable of standing up to massive dressings of nitrogen fertilizer, plus a package of improved agronomic mea-sures: there was also a change in the pricing policy. The breeders managed to persuade the Mexican government that the new high-yielding wheats and the agronomic package needed to be supported by a guaranteed price for the wheat. This the government agreed to and the farmers, recognizing the value of the new wheats in combination with a guaranteed price, adopted the package and grew so much wheat that the country, once an importer of this crop, became an exporter.

In Uganda in 1955 the government, concerned about shortages of maize, decided to regularize the situation by declaring a fixed and guaranteed price. So much maize was produced by the farmers that agricultural officers had to be brought in from the field to deal with the marketing and storage chaos in Kampala. However, the government was not impressed by the experiment, the guaranteed price was dropped, and maize production declined, returning to the cyclic production of earlier years, where the farmers responded to price fluctuations yearly in arrears. That is, if the price went up because of shortage, the farmers would plant more in the following year, which would result in a slump in the uncontrolled price, so the farmers would plant less in the following year, resulting in a shortage, and so on.

Another aspect of markets and prices relates to economies of scale. An example is the case of dried cassava chips in the Philippines. There is available a quota of some 100,000 tons of dried cassava chips from the Philippines to West Germany which is only 30–50 per cent taken up. However, the price that the exporters can offer the farmers is about 1.50 pesetas/kg of dried chips, which compares to a price of 2.20 pesetas/kg for fresh cassava roots in the local markets. This market can only be met by large producers with economies of scale or subsistence farmers with nil opportunity costs. The problem is complicated by the additional factor that the climate does not make drying easy.

Education

One of the factors that most planners underestimate, or ignore, in planning developments in the Third World is the lack of education. It is a strange fact that educated people assume that they have always possessed the knowledge and skills they have, as if they are an intrinsic part of their being, and seem to forget that their skills and knowledge have been imparted to them through a very

expensive educational system. Highly skilled experts with doctorates may have cost the society in which they live hundreds of
thousands of pounds in training costs since they were the age of five.
The tractor driver will have had a minimum of thirteen years of
schooling, plus technical training. Yet the planners of new developments in the Third World expect partly educated people, with the
rudiments of technical training, to operate sophisticated equipment
in innovative situations. The New Halfa Irrigation Project in the
Sudan, some 400,000 feddan (168,000 ha) in area, about the size of
the county of Surrey, had only one qualified agricultural engineer.
He was a very competent man but the task of keeping all the
equipment operational was rather overwhelming, to say the least.
Just think how many agricultural engineers there are, presently, in
Surrey, and the extent of the back-up repair and service facilities.
No wonder the New Halfa project was bordering on collapse and in
need of rehabilitation when I visited it.

The subsistence farmers themselves are, by my reckoning, an
intelligent group of people, though not necessarily well-educated.
Given equivalent education they have an equal potential, in
general, to become proficient engineers, agriculturalists etc.: it's
just that the massive funds needed for education of the rural masses
in the developing countries are not available. Though lacking in
education, they are, however, highly skilled in the art of keeping
themselves and their families alive, and are able farmers, much
more so than is commonly accepted by the 'superior urbanites'.
Many people confuse their conservatism with unintelligence, not
recognizing in that conservatism an intelligent appreciation of their
subsistence farming system and its limitations. They do not
necessarily reject new techniques because they have not the
intelligence or education to recognize their worth, but simply
because they do not accept that the innovations are applicable or
worthwhile in their circumstances. If the innovation does not work
then it may mean disaster to the family.

The foregoing may be open to the criticism that it infers that the
subsistence farmer is faultless, and that education is overvalued;
obviously this is not correct. There are many ways in which
education could make the lot of the subsistence farmers and their
families a little easier. I see many things being done in the rural
areas that I would do differently, but considering the cost of my own
education and the amount of money spent in transporting me about
the world to visit subsistence farmers in different environments, it

would be depressing if I *couldn't* improve on the system. Seed storage could be improved, better crop drying techniques easily devised, row spacings tightened up, and so on. Of course, if one is in a farming environment where there is relatively low land pressure, as is found in parts of Africa, the farmer may not be bothered about using improved techniques as his present inefficient methods provide him with enough food. But if the farmer is in an overpopulated area of the world, such as Bangladesh, then simple improvements in husbandry methods that bring even small returns are worthwhile. Many of these improvements do not require a cash input and so poor farmers can adopt them; when they require cash inputs there are often no funds available to take up the improved methods.

Education is also important in relation to the farmer's health, and that of his family. Nutritional problems can often be solved by simple extension techniques. I recall that in Uganda, near Kampala, there was a kwashiorkor clinic set up to try and improve the health of the many children who were suffering from protein deficiency. Classically, the uneducated mother breast-fed her child and then, at weaning time, fed the baby on cassava meal. Within a short period of time the baby would show signs of kwashiorkor, typified by ginger hair and general poor health. The clinic used to take the mother into the clinic, treat the child and at the same time give the mother instruction on baby nutrition, based on the use of foods rich in protein that were commonly available in the villages, such as spinaches and beans. Obviously this clinic provided a valuable service in improving the health of the children, but the really interesting thing was that no mother who had been brought into the clinic and taught the rules of simple child nutrition ever returned with a child having the same complaint. Simple rules of hygiene can reduce the gastro-enteric diseases that are so common in the developing countries of the world. People who have been born in villages with polluted water supplies do not necessarily appreciate that the water they have drunk all their lives is harmful. I have often seen rural people using streams as toilets, streams that are also used for washing clothes and household utensils. This is particularly a problem in rural irrigation schemes along the Nile, where gastro-enteric problems are chronic and must have a debilitating effect on the farmer, making his hard work in the fields just that little bit more wearisome.

Infrastructure

According to the dictionaries this refers to the basic structure of an organization, to the stock of fixed capital equipment in a country, including factories, roads, schools etc. Unfortunately, not all expatriate experts from the industrialized nations appreciate just what a constraint lack of infrastructure is for developing countries, mainly because people who should know better discount the enormous contributions of earlier generations to their own economies.

That Westerners, in general, seem to have little appreciation of the contribution of their own forebears to their present state of well-being is a bad fault in itself, but it is an even worse failing not to appreciate the cost in hard cash and human effort of the developments of the past. The presence of these faults in planners is a serious constraint on development in the Third World simply because they result in experts, or consultants, ignoring or under-estimating the capital that is required to bring the underdeveloped parts of the world up to the same standard as the industrialized West. I first became aware of the enormous costs involved in quite modest developments when I participated in a work prospecting assignment in Saudi Arabia. The consulting engineers that I was working for at the time were proposing to put in a bid for consulting services for an agricultural turn-key development project at Wadi Dawasir, some 650 km south-west of Riyadh, and I was involved in a site visit to quantify the scale of the project and obtain sufficient background information in order to submit a proposal document. To all intents and purposes there was nothing at Wadi Dawasir, apart from some artesian wells, so all development would be new. Rough calculations were made of the amount of water that would be available from the deep aquifer, and the amount of land that could be irrigated over a fifty-year period. Included in the costs were estimates for roads, power, houses, schools, mosques, dispensaries, and the total kept on getting bigger and bigger. I found the estimates, as such, meaningless, and as a means of making them more meaningful to me I divided the estimated total costs by, first, the number of hectares likely to be developed and, secondly, by the number of farm families that might be settled. At first sight the estimated costs per hectare and per farm family seemed horrific, but on reflection I realized that the cost per hectare figure was more or less equal to the cost of agricultural land in Germany at that time, which was, if I remember correctly, about £5000 per hectare. The cost per family was between £20,000 and £30,000 and I tried to compare this cost with some related costs in the UK. I found, from the 1984 Blue Book for the UK, that there were 5.4 million employees in the manufacturing industry in the UK, using gross capital stock, at 1980 replacement costs, valued at £195.3 billion, or the equivalent of £36,166 per workplace. The equivalent figure in the construction industry was £12,400 per worker. I came to the conclusion that development in Third World countries was an expensive exercise and seemed to be related to the costs of land and workplaces in Europe. Development was not something that could be done on the cheap. Remarkably, the cost of land in Europe was probably closely related to the development costs over the ages, and the accumulated historical costs of removing the stones from the fields, fencing, or levelling the land and putting in drainage was reflected in contemporary land values.

Since the Wadi Dawasir assignment I have always been some-what suspicious of projects which have a planned input of, say, £100 per hectare. All this means is that the project has little chance of getting off the ground, as one gets 'nowt for nowt'. Sadly, the economists who control the international aid organizations insist on projects having internal rates of return of around 14–17 per cent (a figure that is related to the going interest rates in the industrial states), and to achieve these returns certain inputs are discounted or omitted altogether. Training requirements are reduced to a few weeks' training for key personnel, housing requirements often ignored and put down as a local input, health needs forgotten, roads limited to rough earth tracks, machinery servicing needs sketched over, worker incentives not even thought of, and schools for the workers' children laughed at. 'That is a problem for the Ministry of Education and not the project.' No wonder many projects quietly fail and eventually become the subject of rehabilitation studies.

Tanzania is at present a good example of what happens when the infrastructure is allowed to deteriorate. In that country, now, it is not a question of how to enhance the infrastructure, but how to rehabilitate it. The country had never been very rich but it had some quite well-established agricultural industries at the time of Independence: cotton, sisal, cashews, coffee and tea. However, insufficient attention had been given to maintaining the old traditional sources of wealth, depreciation was not allowed for, and maintenance of primary processing machinery neglected, with the result that exports eventually were more than halved. Also, monetary policies resulted in unrealistic rates of exchange on the foreign money markets. When I was in Tanzania in 1986 the official exchange rate was 15.80 shillings to the dollar, but the unofficial exchange rate, offered quite openly by the touts outside the hotel in Dar es Salaam, was 150 shillings to the pound. There were many opinions on the rightness or wrongness of this grossly distorted exchange rate and for a number of years there had been political resistance to any change in the rate, presumably because this would be tantamount to an admission that the country's economic policies were not working. But the consequence of this artificial maintenance of the Tanzanian shilling's value was that the country's export position became undermined. For example, at the time of Independence some 300,000 tons of sisal were exported per year, but by 1985 the figure was down to about 30,000 tons. There are various reasons for this, but one of the major causes was the exchange rate. Thus, when the sisal was exported the sisal companies had to repatriate the world market value of the sisal, usually in dollars, which was then credited to their local accounts, but converted into local Tanzanian shillings at the rate of fifteen to the dollar. However the number of shillings realized was insufficient to pay the labour or keep the plantations maintained. Sisal estates calculated that they made a 3000 shilling loss for every ton they exported. Of course if the exchange rate had been nearer the true rate of 150 to the dollar they would have received ten times as many shillings in local currency to pay local costs. This imbalance in exchange rates and its effects on export industries is not restricted to Tanzania alone. In Sierra Leone the iron ore industry at Marampa closed down for the same reason. The unrealistic exchange rate has been corrected and I did hear rumours that consideration was being given to the iron ore industry being reopened.

Lack of infrastructure restricts development options in many ways. Absence of health services may make irrigation schemes unpopular in countries where bilharzia is prevalent. Lack of technical schools may mean there are no trained drivers for tractors, or mechanics able to service water pumps. Mass education may be restricted due to lack of broadcasting facilities – Freetown Radio only has a range of 41 miles, and farmers upcountry listen to the news from the BBC and only know what is happening in their capital if it is included in the BBC overseas service!

Statistics

'Statistics' are accorded considerable status in developing countries and much effort is expended in obtaining data about every aspect of national life. Statistical departments are usually well manned, even if not well served with equipment. However, the problem is not so much in the quantity of data but in its quality, and in many developing countries the national statistics have to be treated with caution. There is nothing unusual about this situation, for the very reason that the developing countries are in a developing process. Such countries usually have sufficient background statistics to permit experienced judgement to arrive at adequate assessments of the true situation. However, there are some countries where one has to admit the statistical base is inadequate for any agricultural development planning. This is particularly true of two countries that I visited in 1986, Tanzania and Sierra Leone.

In Tanzania maize production in 1980/81 was estimated by FAO at 800,000 tons, at 1,854,000 tons by Kilimo Ministry of Agriculture, and at 1 million tons by USDA. Quite a difference, meaning that either the yield or acreage estimates are widely out, making it difficult to advise on the agronomy. Are the yields very low, or is it just that the agricultural field staff have not estimated the hectarages correctly? Depending on the answer the agronomist may have to adopt entirely different development approaches. Production estimates for other crops vary just as much as for maize: for example, cassava varied in the same growing period from 1,408,000 to 5,631,000 tons.

In Sierra Leone the position now is so bad that there is no reliable statistical base for development planning in agriculture. The extent of the unreliability is indicated by the Green Revolution document which had been drawn up to cover agricultural development targets for the country for the period 1986 to 1988. In this document there are future crop production targets quoted that are lower than the present estimates of production being quoted in other documents produced by the same ministry a few months earlier.

The fact that there are no reliable statistics available in a country is not in itself a great problem to an experienced agronomist, as there are a number of techniques that can be used to broadly determine the situation in the rural areas, permitting one to come up with reasonably sensible proposals for development projects. The problem is, however, that an agronomist will be part of a team which includes economists, and that the team is answerable to economists in faraway offices. This means that a report written on any development proposal must be put together in a certain way so that anonymous authorities can decide whether the project is economically and financially viable. Consequently the agronomist has to be able to quantify the number of farm families within the project area, the precise area of the crops presently grown in the project area and the present yield levels. That is the 'present-without-project' situation, and this has to be determined before making any proposals for the 'future-with- project' situation. Using such data the economist will then estimate the internal rate of return for the proposed project, using the parameters that have been quoted by the agronomist. Woe betide any agronomist who puts in a vague statement saying, for example, that yields are low. 'They' want to know how low, and if one quotes a figure, there is then a demand to know from where one obtained the figure. Few donors will hand out money for what appear to be urgent and worthy schemes (unless for a disaster situation, as happened in Ethiopia recently): no, they want the benefits to be quantified, because that is the way the industrialized West works. It is only when people see TV pictures of little children starving, with bones protruding, that the entrenched bureaucratic procedures of the developed nations can be relaxed.

Thus, lack of statistics can be a constraint on development in the Third World, because of the Westerner's obsessive kowtowing to the powerful guild of Western economists and their economic and banking theories. Paradoxically those countries that have comprehensive and reliable statistics are unlikely to qualify for basic development aid, for the very reason that they are already well developed, whilst those countries that desperately need help have the worst statistics, and consequently cannot prove their needs. Undoubtedly, this is an area in which international aid could be usefully spent.

Organization and management

The creation of organizations that are functionally sound, and the availability of skilled and competent management to make them work, are aspects of development in which developing countries are particularly weak. This is quite understandable for the simple reason that the countries are extremely short of trained, experienced and able manpower. Many countries cannot afford to pay good salaries to their meagre cadre of trained nationals and one finds them emigrating to the industrialized countries in search of high salaries. In Britain one can find many professional people who were born in the developing countries but are now employed as doctors, engineers, and dentists in the UK instead of meeting their own home country's needs.

The other problem facing the developing countries is that they do not have a sizeable reserve corp or body of professionally trained people from which they can select their senior management personnel. Often what happens is that a person is trained overseas for a particular post and on returning to the country he or she is appointed immediately to that senior post. Technically such people may be quite competent for the senior posts but almost invariably, unless they are remarkable, they lack management experience and, even more important, 'man management' experience. Unfortunately, once such people are appointed it is difficult to get rid of them, if for no other reason than that the developing country has not got sufficient experienced people to recognize incompetence. Also, there is a quite natural nationalistic refusal to accept that a local may not be as good as a more experienced expatriate.

Lack of organizational and managerial skills is one of the major constraints on agricultural development in the tropics, but it is a very sensitive issue. It is in this field that the developed countries could make useful contributions to the development of the Third World countries, but only if the aid is given in an unpatronizing manner, and if the recipient governments recognize that such aid is not a reflection on the abilities of their own nationals. For a number of years I have thought that one of the better ways of helping Third World countries meet their development aspirations would be to provide turn-key support. A developed country offers to fund, establish, and manage a development for a fixed number of years, say twenty-five years, and over that period is responsible for the selection and in-house training of the project's national personnel. At the end of the agreed period the whole project, in a viable state, would be handed over to the local personnel. However, I recognize that national pride does not always take kindly to such propositions, particularly in Asia, with its national sensitivities, but then the donors can channel their aid to those governments that have a more enlightened approach to the acceptance of external aid as a means of improving the lot of their peoples. But the international aid organizations would then have to face up to the true costs of development, which are partially masked by present project planning and project cost estimates.

Bureaucracy

We tend to think of the developed countries as democracies, but in fact as the industrialized nations become richer so they become less and less democratic and more and more bureaucratic. Parliaments become less 'in command of the situation', as national wealth makes the ministries bigger, to the point where individual ministries have political power in their own right, because of their sheer size and the enormous budget allocated to them. A ministry with many thousands of loyal employees is not only a force difficult for a single minister to master, but also a political force able to stand up to government itself. As a consequence the Western democracies are increasingly bureaucracies, at both central and local levels.

Strangely, a similar position exists in the developing world, though for different reasons. In Third World countries where the economies are not well developed the civil service is the most popular source of employment. Salaries are assured, pensions provided, and there are fringe benefits such as car advances, subsidized housing, and sometimes even special food allowances. There are also the fringe benefits associated with bureaucratic powers, such as licences etc., which are a source of supplementary income. In many of the countries that gained independence after the Second World War the ministries are the only organized, disciplined forces in the land, forces which the unorganized rural population cannot stand up against. But, conversely, one finds that there are inter-ministry jealousies and that one ministry's officials will not necessarily cooperate with those of another ministry. Somewhat surprisingly, they will often cooperate with an expatriate consultant or executive, but not with their own kind in another ministry.

There is also a different philosophy regarding management in the Third World countries, which is well brought out by Rangnekar in his humorous book on Indian management [72]. He says that in Europe management is about decision making, whilst in India it is about decision avoidance. I think it is all about job protection. Make a bad decision and it might endanger one's job, so better not to make a decision, indeed to be safe set up a committee to examine the problem. If it is a big problem, within a short period of time the committee will have set up a sub-committee and a decision that should have taken days may take months and even years to be resolved.

International aid organizations

Obviously one has to be careful about what one says about international aid organizations, as it would be easy to cause offence, and that is not my objective. The whole purpose of this dissertation is to be constructive and not destructive. In order to make my position clear this section does not examine the role and place of aid organizations, which are generally classified as charities for tax purposes. The organizations have specific objectives and in my limited experience of them they perform their functions well and sincerely. More than any other aid they help the poorest of the poor, the starving masses, the needy children, and I am not competent to judge them further than that. This section is more concerned with the international development agencies such as World Bank, FAO, Overseas Development ministries of the industrialized nations, etc.

Although I have worked as a consultant agronomist for a number of organizations concerned with agricultural development in the Third World, almost without exception it has been as a member of a team brought together by firms of Consulting Engineers, or for the International Development Agencies themselves. This meant that my development ideas and philosophies had to be adapted and modified to fit in with those of my employer, for which ever project it was that I was assigned to at the time. In the early days of my consulting assignments there were no difficulties for me, as I was engrossed in trying to master a new field of work, the field of consultancy, and the effort of trying to match the peculiar demands of this way of life left me with little time to examine in depth my activities or those of my colleagues. Whilst I am content that I have not participated in any project study in which my conscience was troubled, or where I was not happy with the technical content of my contribution, in recent years I have become concerned whether the activities that I have been engaged on have had any real impact on the way of life of the peoples of the countries that I have been endeavouring to help.

Whilst I have been reasonably happy in my own mind that I have something to contribute, fairly confident that I understand the problems facing the subsistence farmers in the field, I am losing confidence in my ability to persuade other members of the consulting team of the rightness of my approach. It may be, of course, that I am out of touch with the reality of development in the underdeveloped situations, that I am out of touch with modern techniques. But I do not think it is me, I think it is the agricultural experts from the industrialized nations who are out of touch with the subsistence farmers' problems. Specialization in the developed countries has reached a point where the advisers who go to tropical countries do not know what the tropical crops look like in the field; have never worked in the field with peasants; do not know what it is like to dig a plot with a spade hoe using one's hands. We have economists who sincerely think that the problems of the subsistence family can be solved on a computer. All one has to do is to devise a programme, go into the field and ask the locals a few questions, feed the answers into the computer and it will digest them and come up with an answer, usually in the form of an internal rate of return. That the country has overpopulation problems, that its ecology is being irreversibly changed, soils eroded, and even its rainfall pattern changed, is discounted.

I am now close to the opinion that the international development agencies are no longer so able to advise the developing world on its agricultural development problems, for the simple reason that their officers no longer have had any direct practical experience of the farming system of the subsistence farmer. They have no appreciation of the farmers' skills, the reasons for their conservatism, or their mastery of the environment and the delicate balance between survival and disaster. Many of the more recent large scale projects foisted on the rural populations of the Third World, in particular the Integrated Rural Development Projects, have not been soundly based and their main achievement has been to saddle the developing country with greater debt-servicing burdens. The aid organizations usually give their aid, and whilst it may not be well spent, or wasted, at least the aid does not usually involve the recipients in interest payments, whilst the international development agencies usually hand out loans which have to be serviced in due course. Hence the preoccupation of the agencies with internal rates of return in the project feasibility studies. The fact that few projects that are implemented ever achieve the projected rates of return does not seem to matter: as long as the study shows that a good return is feasible then the agency is happy. The agency has got rid of some of its immense development funds, the developing country has got hold of some foreign exchange, and progress has been made – or has it? Monitoring is the 'in' word at the moment, and when done properly it can be useful, but I have been in a situation where constructive comments have been abruptly rejected, and I was told that I was rocking the boat.

In some countries the international aid agencies are actually holding back progress, rather than aiding it. Sierra Leone is a good example of too many cooks spoiling the broth. This is a country that urgently needs assistance in its efforts to solve its many social and agricultural problems, but it is not being constructively helped by the many agencies and countries purporting to provide aid. The problem for this country is that its own ministries, planning departments and other administrative bodies are weak, mainly due to shortage of funds and misdirection. Consequently the numerous organizations, genuinely interested in helping the country in its hour of need, have attempted to give a helping hand. But the help has not been coordinated and each organization has worked in isolation from the others. The result has been chaos, with the ministries unaware of what is being done in the field, having no control over recruitment of field staff or the salaries paid (often there has been poaching of the better ministry staff at higher salaries), and the established field staff have become demoralized and disheartened. Expatriate control over daily paid staff has been poor and overmanning and 'dead men on the books' become commonplace. I was informed by one expatriate worker that there were fourteen agencies who had worked on swamp clearance projects for rice production, and as far as he was aware none of them had ever come together to coordinate their efforts. In wandering around the interior in 1986, looking at the North Central Region, I saw only a few 'improved swamps' growing good stands of rice – generally, the improved swamps that I was shown were not reassuring about the value of the millions of dollars that had been expended on such projects. It may be that I did not see the improved swamps, but in general if there are successful projects the donors and the local officials waste no time in showing them off to visitors, and as I did not see them I assume they were not there to see. Incidentally, I am not talking about a few hectares but about thousands of hectares of so-called improved swamps. However, I am sure the original feasibility studies would have indicated a good internal rate of return for the projects.

At the risk of being classified as old and conservative, I have to make the comment that too much reliance is being placed on the ability of computers to solve the Third World's problems. Organizations such as FAO have mammoth computers which 'crunch numbers'. They demand to be fed, and the feeding becomes an end in itself. I am all in favour of computers as aids to planning, but not as masters. As a small example of what I mean, for one project it was necessary to estimate the present production by some twenty thousand subsistence farmers, but no reliable estimates for the areas of crops grown and the yields were available. In fact more than twenty crops, all mixed together within the same parcel of land, were grown by the individual farmers on their holdings, some consisting of only a few square yards of a crop such as herbs or spinach [44]. In order to resolve the position five major crops were used to represent the probable crop production, which could then be translated into a money value. It was then possible to estimate a 'future-with-project' situation for the individual farmers and by economic analysis to calculate the benefit to the farmer of the new farming system. In some respects it does not matter too much whether the farmer is growing maize or sorghum or rice, for the purposes of the model, but the computer then took the individual holding figures and multiplied them up to produce project benefits. People started asking me what I was going to do with several thousand tons of cassava. My explanation that they did not exist, but were purely for model purposes, seemed to be thin, almost laughable, and it took me some time to get grudging agreement that I was caught in the toils of a computer program which I had not liked from the first, but which had demanded more and more parameters from me and then suddenly in a belch of high speed printing produced nonsense summaries. A case of nonsense in and nonsense out.

Another fault of the international development agencies is that they impose their development philosophies on the developing countries, philosophies which the recipients may not understand, but which they accept because they need the foreign exchange. For example, one agency insists that the development funds should be aimed at improving the lot of 'the target group', which has to be the poorest sector of the economy, or those with the smallest farm holdings, or the functionally landless. Whilst I appreciate the thinking behind the 'target group' approach, I do not agree that it is soundly based. It eliminates help being given to those farmers, at subsistence level, who have demonstrated their ability to make good use of their slender resources, whose husbandry methods are sound and efficient, and whose skills have resulted in the generation of some meagre surpluses to lift their families' standard of living above that of their neighbours. To me there is a case to be made for giving aid to those who have demonstrated their ability to make good use of it. Do not misinterpret this approach: my case is not that aid should go to the rich or wealthy, but that the marginally rich, who have shown an ability to respond and benefit, should be given some priority. The question has been asked as to how one identifies such farmers, but to me, it is not so much this issue that is the problem, rather that they should not be deliberately excluded in the planning terms of reference from the 'target group'.

I may be accused of some inconsistency in the above argument, in that I seem to have indicated previously that I am not convinced that spending money on agricultural development is the better way to help the rural communities, whilst the above arguments seem to infer that I am 'generally' in favour of aid to the subsistence farmers. To explain this inconsistency I have to qualify my approach regarding aid to the rural areas. Where there is no land pressure and the subsistence farmers have available more land than they can work using the available family manpower, then aid may not have any significant effect on the community's way of life. The population can increase and the farmers will just expand horizontally into new lands, as has happened in much of Africa. But if there is land pressure, such as is found in the greater part of Asia, then the situation is entirely different and a case can be made out for aid to increase the productivity per unit area of land to meet the community's needs. In this case there is no opportunity for the increasing population to move horizontally, and there have to be inputs to allow them to expand vertically.

5 The future. Why down? Why not up?

Contrary to popular belief, aid given for the purpose of developing subsistence agriculture in the developing countries, apart from that given for humanitarian purposes during periods of disaster, makes only a small contribution to the development of the rural populations of the Third World. To me, a case can be made that investment of money into the subsistence farming rural sector is a waste of a country's scarce development funds, which would be better spent in the urban sector. I recognize that these are generalizations and contrary to the conventional development philosophies, and that consequently they need some elaboration.

First of all I have to define that part of the agricultural sector that I am referring to in the previous paragraph. I am concerning myself with the great mass of subsistence farmers and their families who are the predominant part of the populations of the Third World countries. I am not considering specialized developments, such as expansions of tea estates, food processing factories for coffee or canneries, or the growing of orchids for export by air, or the impressive wheat and lucerne centre pivot irrigation schemes in Saudi Arabia. Such developments can be analyzed as business propositions, in much the same way as a business development in the industrialized countries of the world. My consideration is more for the hundreds of millions of farm families who independently produce their own sustenance, year in and year out, and whose production is entirely related to, and limited by, the manpower value of the family, with essentially few capital resources. They may have a work ox, or a buffalo, but rarely do they have access to, or own, an engine-powered machine. I am also concerned with those countries where the population is predominantly rural. They are also those countries where populations are doubling themselves in less than thirty years, that is, countries where the population will

*A doon used for lifting water for irrigation of dry season rice crops.
Bangladesh, near Dakha.*

quadruple in an average person's lifetime of sixty years. In Kenya, if
the present birthrate continues, the population could multiply by
eight times in the course of man's lifetime.

If the objective of aid to the rural farming populations is to
improve the lot of the farm families, why do I not accept that aid
given directly to this sector is necessarily beneficial? To me the
problem is one of farm power and markets for surplus produce at
attractive prices. If the farm family has sufficient land to meet its
food needs, then production is directly related to the energy value
of the family unit and we know, without having to go into too much
detail, that it takes a long time for a man to cultivate an acre of land
with a spade hoe (see Chapter 3). Most of the hand labour is used in
meeting the family's food needs and there is only a small surplus of
production which can be sold to meet their necessarily modest
needs – cloth, oil, matches, etc. In general the markets available to
the rural farmer are restricted to weekly markets when traders come
from the towns with goods for sale, transporting back to the towns

the purchased surplus production. However, no matter how large the market is, the farmer's production is limited by the value of family manpower; even mechanization is not a good answer, because family holding is too small. Tractors have what is termed an economy of scale factor and the larger the farm the more efficient and economic the tractor performance: if the plot to be worked is a fraction of an acre the economics are never good. Even if there is a cooperative, a tractor driver may be faced with ploughing several hundred small plots scattered over a hundred farmers' holdings. In some cases the situation is made even worse by fragmentation due to inheritance practices.

So there are major constraints related to farm power, which are difficult to overcome (unless we have nationalization of the land, which is not particularly popular with subsistence farmers and usually not efficient). Even if we can overcome the farm power problem, we still have the question of markets and in general they are restricted in societies where the greater part of the population is rural and by implication already producing independently their food supplies. Thus, if we have a stable community where 80 per cent of the population is rural and 20 per cent urban, then, in rough terms, the farm family uses 80 per cent of its production for survival and the surplus 20 per cent goes to meet the needs of the towns, but this 20 per cent of a farm holding's production is not worth very much in terms of purchasing power to the subsistence farmer's family. Putting it another way, the work inputs of four men produce, under the subsistence system, enough agricultural output to meet the needs of five persons. In the USA four men produce enough to meet the needs of about 140 persons, which means that they are wealthy and can afford the mechanization costs which permit one man to grow enough for thirty-five people.

Obviously the subsistence system lacks flexibility, but, still, that farming system meets the normal needs of the community. There may be malnutrition, some under-nutrition, and fluctuations from year to year, but on average the system meets the needs. (If it does not meet those needs then there will be famine, which can only be alleviated by external aid, either on a short term or long term basis.) Of course if there is a national shortage of food then it would be reasonable to expect the subsistence farmer to increase his production, but he has this farm power constraint, and even if the inexperienced urbanite is right in thinking that his rural cousin is lazy, which is not correct, the amount by which he could increase his productivity is limited eventually by the value of man power. Tractors might be the answer, but we have seen that the economics of using tractors on small holdings are not good, and in any case most developing countries are short of foreign exchange to purchase the equipment and the fuel. In fact, the urban-based government may find it cheaper to purchase food from abroad than set up the infrastructure to service the tractors, especially if the country can obtain dumped food from the EEC, or other sources such as the World Food Programme or Food for Work. It is easy to see that the rural subsistence farmers are very vulnerable to being given low priority in any country's development policies. They are independent, both in terms of sustenance and in their attitude, have no organized political strength, and so are left to fend for themselves whilst the government attends to more urgent problems in the urban areas, whose concentrated masses are more voluble and organizable.

Although the subsistence farmer may receive only lip service in the National Development Plans, central governments are usually quite prepared to support any plans that can increase the number of people that can be settled in the rural areas. Developments of marginal lands, to provide farms for the landless and jobless of the towns, are all welcomed. Irrigation schemes are enthusiastically embarked on, particularly if there is a hydro-power aspect. Transmigration schemes involving the controversial destruction of forests are relentlessly encouraged. But such schemes do not result in any significant improvement in the standard of living of the people living in the rural areas, *rather they result in the rural area supporting more families at subsistence level.* In Tanzania there was a genuine attempt to improve the lot of rural people by the creation of Ujamaa Villages, the expression of a political philosophy which stressed communal organization. Nyerere recognized that it would not be easy to improve the farmers' standard of living whilst they were dispersed on their holdings. If they were brought together in villages they could share community benefits: better water supplies, sewage, schools, dispensaries, shops, social services, etc. The idea was sound, but the cost underestimated, if it was even thought about, and now all that exists are untidy, unserviced villages, only accessible with difficulty along the unmaintained roads. The mammoth costs of urbanization had not been appreciated, or overlooked in the ideological euphoria of independence. Though many people believe that villagization was ecologically unsound in the Tanzanian environment, and this may be correct for the unreliable rainfall areas, personally, I think the major constraint was the unappreciated cost levels of introducing even the simplest of village improvements.

Governments of developing countries will keep on pushing more and more people into the rural areas, both by horizontal and vertical expansion, taking up the marginal lands, and attempting to increase the per acre productivity of the the existing farmlands. Money will be spent on the production of new higher-yielding varieties, money made available for the supporting inputs, such as fertilizers, and so on, but the end result will be simply more subsistence farmers supported at the level related to the energy level of manpower. The only way the government can raise their standard of living is by guaranteeing prices for crops, or providing markets for high-priced crops such as tea, coffee, vegetables, etc., but these are markets that are soon saturated and international competition is fierce.

The inescapable conclusion is that the rural areas of the developing countries of the world will be pressed to accept more and more people, until such time as the capacity of the land to support them under a subsistence, hand labour farming system runs out. Then the urban government will be forced to provide more inputs, fertilizers, etc., in order to improve productivity vertically, and this will depend on the availability of foreign exchange to purchase the inputs. But in a situation where populations keep on doubling every twenty to thirty years, twice the amount of foreign exchange will have been used up just to maintain the previous standards. The squeeze on these countries is intense as many of them have to use more and more of their precious foreign exchange to service the debts entered into many years earlier. Like the farmer in the field who finds that he is still paying the moneylender for a bag of rice that he borrowed many years ago, so the governments are caught in the same trap and some are using over 40 per cent of the country's export earnings to service earlier development loans! (See Table 16.) There is always the possibility of surviving on gifts from the industrialized world, but charity is unpredictable, unreliable and usually has strings attached to it.

The position appears gloomy, but this is not entirely correct. The lands of the tropical developing world are, in general, quite capable of meeting the present and future food needs of the populations, *but not if the farming system is subsistence orientated with the farm power being hand power.* This means that the agriculture of the rural areas in the developing countries can only improve if the urban areas are developed. Urbanization will take people off the land and increase the size of the market for food; at the same time the drift of the population towards the job prospects of the urban areas will result in an increase in the size of the farm holdings, making mechanization more feasible. All this will result in an increasingly healthy agriculture industry over the long term.

My conclusion is that the best way to help the subsistence farmer is to give priority to the development of the urban areas. However, it has to be recognized that urbanization is a very expensive exercise and that it can only be successfully achieved if the developing country can enlist the enlightened financial and technical support of a developed country. African socialism and self-reliance, for example, cannot achieve the development that the emergent nations are looking for, unless, that is, they are prepared to take a very long-term approach to the development in the same way as the industrialized countries.

It would seem to me that the industrialized nations have a challenge before them and that is to bring about the development of the Third World's urban areas, and as a consequence bring about the development of the rural areas. Enlightened cooperation will be needed, but it could be mutually advantageous, although I recognize that for the developed industrialized power blocs the advantage will be less, while for the developing nations such cooperation is vitally needed. Quite frankly, a country such as Uganda, that has good natural resources, cannot progress without outside aid. However, even if the aid is available, if a country is without a government capable of good stewardship the country can only stagnate or even regress. It is difficult to give aid if there is no responsible authority to accept it on the part of the people.

Part II

**The International Agricultural
Development Game and the
Third World**

6 Background to international agricultural development

It is interesting to record that the necessity to set up an organization to deal with colonial affairs was recognized by the British as far back as 1660 (in those days colonial affairs referred to the settlements in North America and the West Indies). At first a Committee of the Privy Council undertook the task, but after a few months its responsibilities were taken over (December 1660) by a 'Council of Foreign Plantations' [17]. An even more fascinating insight into Britain's historical interest in the colonies and their plantations is found in the early history of the Royal Society of Arts. A Committee of Colonies and Trade was formed within a few years of the Society's foundation in 1754, one of its chairmen being Benjamin Franklin.

In more recent times the British government's responsibility for the development of her colonies on a continuing basis was first recognized in 1929 by the Colonial Development Act. Under this Act the amount voted by Parliament in any one year, over a period of ten years, was not to exceed £1 million, equal to some £17 million in 1982 values. Within ten years of the passing of that Act Britain was engaged in a war costing it more than that amount per day.

With the speedy demise of Britain's colonial empire after the Second World War the need for a Colonial Office disappeared and it was absorbed into the Foreign, Commonwealth Relations and Colonial Office. There then followed a period of confusion whilst the British government and the mandarins came to terms with the changed circumstances. In 1961 a Department of Technical Cooperation was established. Then in 1964 the Ministry of Overseas Development (ODM) was set up, which brought together the functions of the former Department of Technical Co-operation and the overseas aid policy functions of the Foreign, Commonwealth Relations and Colonial Office. In 1970 the ministry was dissolved

In many parts of the developing world communications are poor. This is a stick bridge, made out of bamboo, in the north of Bangladesh.

and its functions were transferred to the Secretary of State for Foreign and Commonwealth Affairs. Overseas development work was then carried out by the Overseas Development Administration (ODA). Four years later, in May 1974, the government announced that the ODA was to be, once again, a separate ministry under its own minister. However, in November 1979 the ministry again became the Overseas Development Administration (ODA) as a functional wing of the Foreign and Commonwealth Office.

In 1987–8 British aid, net official development assistance, amounts to £1300 million or an estimated 0.33 per cent of Britain's Gross National Product (GNP).

As an agricultural officer in the colonial service in the 1950s I was isolated from the sweeping changes that were taking place in the world's corridors of power, changes concerning the attitudes and thinking about development and the planning procedures in the underdeveloped countries. Local policy matters were detailed in periodic issues of an 'Agricultural Production Programme' [88], which were produced by the Departments of Agriculture and covered all the crops and their husbandry recommendations. There were, of course, in every agricultural officer's office numerous files in which one could find every policy directive back to the year dot. On taking over a new office one of my first tasks would be to systematically scan every file in the filing cabinets, some being examined in a very cursory way, whilst others might require a few days' quiet perusal. At the end of the exercise I would have a fair comprehension of the agriculture of the district(s), and why and how certain agricultural policy matters had evolved. More importantly, I knew then just how extensive was the range of information held within the office, information that I would invariably need to call upon during my tour of duty in which ever office I was at that time. Furthermore, this background knowledge gave me a fair impression of the level of sophistication of the local agriculture. Similarly, I would have an appreciation of the strengths and weaknesses of the supporting field staff. Office files can be very dull, but they can provide very revealing pictures of the local agricultural situation, not only by what they contain, but even more importantly by what they do not contain. In planning, the negative is equally as important as the positive.

Obviously, the agricultural officer's main preoccupation would be with the whole agricultural situation within his own area of responsibility, but most officers would relate the district situation to the national and regional background. Before the era of 'Planning Bureaus' or 'Ministries of Planning' planning documents were much scarcer, but they did exist, on a scale much larger than is realized by planners today. Planning was often done under the aegis of 'Planning Committees' or, in the case of major policy documents, 'Royal Commissions'. One such excellent report was the 'East Africa Royal Commission 1953–1955 Report' [25], which had impressive terms of reference, as follows:

ROYAL WARRANT

Dated 1st January, 1953

ELIZABETH II

ELIZABETH THE SECOND, by the Grace of God of Great Britain, Ireland and the British Dominions beyond the Seas Queen, Defender of the Faith: to our Trusty and Well Beloved Sir Hugh Dow, Grand Commander of the Indian Empire, Knight Commander of the Star of India, Our Trusty and Well Beloved Sally Herbert Frankel, Esquire,

Master of Arts, Doctor of Philosophy, Doctor of Science. Our trusty and Well Beloved Arthur Gaitskill, Esquire, Companion of Our most distinguished Order of Saint Michael and Saint George, Our Trusty and Well Beloved Rowland Skeffington Hudson, Esquire, Companion of Our most distinguished Order of St Michael and Saint George, Our Well Beloved Daniel Thompson Jack, Esquire, Master of Arts, Justice of the Peace, Our Trusty and Well Beloved Chief Kidaha Makwaia and Our Trusty and Well Beloved Frank Sykes, Esquire, Greetings!

Whereas, having regard to the rapid rate of increase of the African population of East Africa and the congestion of population on the land in certain localities, We have deemed it expedient that a Commission should forthwith examine the measures necessary to be taken to achieve an improved standard of living, including the introduction of capital to enable peasant farming to develop and expand production; and frame recommendations thereon with particular reference to:

(1) the economic development of the land already in occupation by the introduction of better farming methods;
(2) the adaptations or modifications in traditional tribal systems of tenure necessary for the full development of the land;
(3) the opening for cultivation and settlement of land presently not fully used;
(4) the development and siting of industrial activities;
(5) conditions of employment in industry, commerce, mining and plantation agriculture with special reference to social conditions and the growth of large urban populations; and
(6) the social problems which arise from the growth of permanent urban and industrial populations:

and that Our Commission should examine and report on the above matters taking as a basis the general propositions embodied in Part VI of Sir Philip Mitchell's despatch to Our Secretary of State for the Colonies No. 193 of the 16th November, 1951:

and that the Members of Our Commission should hold themselves free to examine, and where necessary comment upon policy in such related fields as, for example, education and public health which appear to them to have a bearing on the problems with which they are primarily concerned; in particular the extent to which existing technical training facilities are adequate to meet the requirements of extensive industrial development;

Our Commission should also consider probable trends of population in East Africa and make such recommendations as they consider appropriate on this subject in relation to the other problems involved:

and that in their deliberations Our Commission should take account of existing obligations incurred by treaty, agreement or formal declaration of policy in relation to the security of land reserved for the different races and groups in various parts of the Territories concerned:

now know ye that We reposing great trust and confidence in your knowledge and ability, have authorised and appointed and do by these Presents authorise and appoint you the said Sir Hugh Dow (Chairman), Sally Herbert Frankel, Arthur Gaitskill, Rowland Skeffington Hudson, Daniel Thomson Jack, Kidaha Makwaia and Frank Sykes to be Our Commissioners for the purpose of, and to make, such enquiry.

And We do hereby authorise and require you with all convenient despatch and by all lawful means to enter upon and to collect evidence respecting the subject matter of such enquiry, and to render a report and make recommendations in accordance with the terms of this Our Commission.

And We do hereby charge and command all whom it may concern that according to their respective powers and opportunities they may be aiding to you in the execution of this Our Commission.

And, for the purpose of aiding you in your enquiries We hereby appoint our Trusty and Well Beloved John Henry Ingham, Esquire, Bachelor of Arts, Bachelor of Commerce, Member of Our most distinguished Order of the British Empire, to be Senior Secretary to this Our Commission.

Given at Our Court of Saint James's this First day of January, One Thousand Nine Hundred and Fifty Three, in the First Year of Our Reign.

OLIVER LYTTELTON

The Commission took two years to complete its work, during which time it received memoranda from 473 different sources and 340 persons gave evidence before it. The colonial authorities may not have been so prolific in producing development reports, but when they did they were usually very comprehensive and thorough.

After the First World War we had the creation of the League of Nations, which was so effective that within twenty years there was a Second World War. This latter war resulted in the creation of the (in theory) United Nations. The United Nations officially came into existence on 24 October 1945 when the Charter had been ratified by China, France, the Soviet Union, the United Kingdom and the United States of America, and by a majority of the other signatories. Under the umbrella of the United Nations are a number of intergovernmental agencies related to the United Nations by special agreements, which as separate autonomous organizations work with the United Nations and each other through the coordinating machinery of the Economic and Social Council. There are fifteen of these specialized agencies which are as follows:

International Labour Organization (ILO) 1914 and 1946

Food and Agriculture Organization (FAO) 1945

United Nations Educational, Scientific and Cultural Organization (UNESCO) 1946

World Health Organization (WHO) 1948

World Bank/International Bank for Reconstruction and Development (IBRD) 1945

International Development Association (IDA) 1960

International Finance Corporation (IFC) 1956

International Monetary Fund (IMF) 1945

International Civil Aviation Organization (ICAO) 1947

Universal Postal Union (UPU) 1874 and 1948

International Telecommunication Union (ITU) 1865 and 1947

World Meteorological Organization (WMO) 1878 and 1950

International Maritime Organization 1948

World Intellectual Property Organization (WIPO) 1974

International Fund for Agricultural Development (IFAD) 1977

One of the first major achievements of the United Nations was the adoption by the General Assembly, on 10 December 1948, of the Universal Declaration of Human Rights, as a common standard of achievement for all peoples and all nations. Of the 30 articles 'covering the promotion of universal respect for and observance of human rights and fundamental freedoms' that the member states pledged themselves to achieve in cooperation with the United Nations, only one, Article 25, concerns agriculture directly. This article reads as follows:

Everyone has the right to a standard of living adequate for the health and well-being of himself and of his family, *including food,* clothing, housing and medical care and necessary social services, and the right to security in the event of unemployment, sickness, disability, widowhood, old age or other lack of livelihood in circumstances beyond his control.

FAO acts as the lead agency for rural development in the United Nations system. The aims and activities of FAO are to raise levels of nutrition and standards of living; to improve the production, processing, marketing and distribution of all food and agricultural products from farms, forests and fisheries; to promote rural development and improve the living conditions of rural populations; and, by these means, to eliminate hunger [22].

The organizational infrastructure was thus set up by the original 51 nations,[1] for the economic and social development of the world, and the various bodies which were established embarked on the expensive business of justifying themselves – most of the work of the United Nations, measured in terms of money and personnel, goes into programmes aimed at achieving economic and social progress in the developing countries, where two thirds of the world's peoples live. Beginning in 1960 the General Assembly proclaimed three successive United Nations Development Decades in order to focus international attention on concrete programmes to aid developing countries.

The strategy for the Third United Nations Development Decade, in setting forth the goals and objectives for the period 1981–90, included:

a 7 per cent average annual rate of growth of domestic product;

a 7.5 per cent annual rate of expansion of exports and an 8 per cent annual rate of expansion of imports of goods and services;

an increase in gross domestic savings to reach about 24 per cent of gross domestic product by 1990;

a rapid and substantial increase in official development assistance by all developed countries, to reach or surpass the agreed international target of 0.7 per cent of the gross national product of developed countries;

a 4 per cent average annual rate of expansion of agricultural production; and

a 9 per cent average annual rate of expansion of manufacturing output [22].

The United Nations Development Programme (UNDP) is the world's largest channel for multilateral technical and pre-investment cooperation. There are 6500 UNDP-supported projects currently in operation, with a total cost, on completion, of $8458.5 million. Of this amount, UNDP is to contribute $3862.9 million and the remainder is to be provided by the recipient countries. UNDP projects, which are aimed at helping developing countries make better use of their assets, improve living standards and expand productivity, involve, amongst other activities, 'carrying out surveys and feasibility studies to determine the availability and economic value of a developing country's natural resources and to assess other potentials for increased output and wider distribution of goods and services' [22, p.III 7].

The United Nations has for many years been concerned over the age-old problem of food shortages and at the United Nations World Food Conference held in Rome in November 1974 the General Assembly was called upon to establish a World Food Council to review annually major problems and policy issues affecting the world food supply. Some thirty countries, with a total population exceeding 500 million, have decided to adopt food strategies, and most have requested assistance from the World Food Council for their preparation. Other United Nations programmes concerned with food aid include the World Food Programme, which it sponsors jointly with FAO and the International Fund for Agricultural Development. The FAO programme uses food commodities, cash and services contributed by United Nations member states to back programmes of social and economic development, as well as relief in emergency situations. IFAD concentrates on rural areas and lends money – most of it on highly concessional or low interest terms – for projects which will have a significant impact on improving food production in developing countries, particularly for the poorest sections of the rural populations. IFAD is particularly interested in aiding small holders (with, say, less that two hectares) and bringing the landless into the development process, thus the Fund is concerned with the impact each project may have on employment, nutrition and income distribution.

In 1960 I left the colonial service and joined Makerere University College, where I lectured in the Faculty of Agriculture for eight years. From Makerere I went to the University of Mauritius as Dean and Professor of Agriculture, staying there four years before returning to the UK where I became increasingly engaged in overseas agricultural consultancy assignments. It was only on leaving the colonial service that I came into contact with the international organizations and their increasing influence in the tropical world. At first it was only with those organizations connected with agricultural education (directly or indirectly) such as Inter-University Council, United States Agency for International Development (USAID), or FAO and UNESCO, but in the late 1970s and early 1980s the contact was extended to other organizations such as World Bank, Kreditanstalt fur Wiederaufbau, Noraid, Asian Development Bank, African

Development Bank, and numerous other governmental or quasi-governmental institutions and bodies. However, the contact with these organizations was, whilst I was employed by the universities, superficial and mainly one way, in that representatives of these bodies tended to come to the faculties for information. It was only when I became involved in feasibility studies sponsored by these international bodies that I started to appreciate just how complex a labyrinth had been created by international bureaucracy. The spending of 0.7 per cent (in theory the amount each country should make available) of the GNP of the Developed Nations had become big business. For example the African Development Bank in 1984 had a subscribed capital (made up of paid and callable portions) of $6.3 billion, whilst IBRD employed 2735 high-level staff with a subscribed capital of $56 billion and its affiliate, IDA, had cumulative usable resources of $30.8 billion. All this is a far cry from the £1 million per year voted by the British Parliament in 1929, although it is interesting to note that in the World Bank Annual Report for 1984 there is a statement to the effect that, in view of the current severe drought conditions in Africa, the Executive Directors approved an exceptional contribution, 'in the equivalent of $2 million, to the World Food Programme', which does not seem over-generous in view of the seriousness of the situation.

My more recent involvement in the 'consultancy game' introduced me to the rather complex ground rules that had become more or less standard for the study and planning of proposed projects in the developing world. Yet, although I say standard, in fact, each organization has its own variations on the rules, its own conventions which have to be observed. Additionally, I came to realize that the job of distributing aid is no easy task for the people whose task and responsibility it is to identify and quantify suitable projects. As one nameless officer once said to me, 'I would like the team to identify suitable projects up to a total cost of, say, $30 million. If it is more then you will get good marks, if less then it is not so pleasing. Of course you could conclude that there are no suitable projects, but that would not be cricket.'

In two phases occupying some twenty-three years from 1950 to 1973, I had been a colonial civil servant in West and East Africa, followed by a period as an academic in universities in East Africa and Mauritius. In 1974 I returned to the UK and entered into the business world, having been fortunate in obtaining employment with a firm of engineering consultants, whose expertise in dams and soil mechanics took them into the associated fields of irrigated agriculture and, hence, put them in need of tropical agriculturalists. During this third phase of my career, I was given the opportunity to familiarize myself, at close quarters, with the thinking and ways of engineers. In previous years I had met engineers, had had discussions with them, and, without thinking too deeply about it, had thought that I knew and understood the function of engineers. I was soon to realize that the way an engineer thought and worked was entirely alien to my way as an agriculturalist. Engineering is a precise science; problems can be defined and precise answers obtained; answers can be presented as figures or drawings on the inevitable drawing board. I came to understand the thinking of Howard Hughes, who called in a structural engineer and not a dress designer to design a bra for Jane Russell. I also came to appreciate that most of the engineers had equally little understanding of the nature of the science and practice of agriculture. Thus, whilst I tended to look upon soils from an edaphic viewpoint, the engineer took the pedalogic approach. I found that I had to be careful when giving agricultural parameters, which I would regard as guidelines and the engineer would interpret as precise statements. This contact with the engineers in their own 'house' was very valuable experience, revealing their strengths and their weaknesses, and was to prove useful to me in later years as agricultural development projects overseas usually have some engineering content.

Apart from the valuable introduction to the engineer's mind and his 'critical path' approach to projects, my time with the consulting engineers was also useful in that I became familiar with the 'work prospecting' procedures. Prior to this phase of my career, I just accepted the presence of consulting firms and their experts working on projects overseas, not knowing how they were selected or got their consultancies in the first place. Indeed, as a person who had been permanently employed overseas, I was slightly suspicious of so-called experts who flew into a country, tore around frantically for a few days making copious notes (apparently picking everybody else's brains), and in a short time produced a beautifully prepared and bound report purporting to provide the answers to problems that I had spent the last twenty years or so trying to solve. At that time I did not understand the function of the consultant, indeed, it was to take some years for me to fully comprehend the experts' role in feasibility studies for projects in developing countries. Many people think that the consultant is a person or group of experts who are particularly knowledgeable within a particular expertise and who initiate or assess new ventures; this is only partially true. Obviously, the expert has to be knowledgeable within his own discipline, but this may be secondary to his expertise in putting together the bones of a project in a way that can be understood by remote financing organizations. He has to be an expert at collecting, interpreting and presenting background information and data, and presenting it in a form that can be understood and used in decision-making exercises in faraway offices. The expert in a consulting team is unlikely, in fact, to be more knowledgeable than the local expert, for example, on the subject of plant protection within the local environment, but he will be more expert at assessing the locally available research findings and incorporating them into a development project study. At the time I joined the consulting firm in the UK all these ground rules of the consultancy game were new to me.

As consulting engineers the firm I had joined had well-established channels for work prospecting and sources of information on contract opportunities with which I had to familiarize myself. The prime example was the *UNDP Business Bulletin* which was published by the United Nations Development Programme, 866 United Nations Plaza, New York, and which provided, monthly, brief details of contract opportunities for projects with participating and executing agencies, e.g. FAO, African Development Bank, Asian Development Bank. To be considered for sub-contracting opportunities, firms and organizations must be registered with the executing agency. Long lists of possible sub-contractors for specific projects are drawn up from a general roster of registered sub-contractors, or by referring to those on the roster who have submitted a 'letter of interest' with regard to a particular project.

The first step in work prospecting in the consultant's office consisted in systematically sifting all notices of forthcoming projects and selecting those for which the firm had in-house expertise and, hopefully, previous work experience. Having decided that the project was one that was within the competence of the firm, was in an acceptable area, and did not clash with other firm consultancy commitments, we would send an expanded 'letter of interest' to the 'executing agency' expressing our interest and drawing their attention to the firm's particular strengths and salient in-house previous experience, which suited it to the job in question.

Two examples of the form in which contract opportunities were notified are as follows:

BURMA: Agriculture,Power, Transport, Industry and Tourism

BUR/74/024 Programme of Pre-investment and Investment Assistance

Work requirements: Specialists on seeds multiplication and distribution, rubber rehabilitation, power, civil aviation, highway improvement, urea fertilizer plant, iron and steel industry, hotel development feasibility etc.

Cost: Not to exceed the equivalent of $2,154,000

Expected to begin: Second half of 1975

Executing agency: World Bank

Expressions of interest should reach World Bank as soon as possible.

IRAN: Natural Resources IRA/74/040 – Integrated Natural Resources Planning

Work requirements: Provision of environmental planners (air, water and soils)

Cost: Not to exceed the equivalent of $24,000

Expected to begin: October 1975

Executing Agency: United Nations

Expressions of interest should reach the United Nations as soon as possible.

Consulting firms would be registered, as standard practice, with a number of different international organizations concerned with aid: ministries, development banks, quasi-government bodies and other agencies such as the British Agricultural Export Council, or the EEC. Firms who concentrated their work prospecting efforts in a particular region, or in one or two overseas countries, would often have an office located in the areas, and senior directors would visit the countries concerned from time to time to maintain personal contact with ministry officials and regional representives of international organizations. Personal contact was considered to be preferable to the impersonal letter of interest, and demonstrated serious interest by the firm.

Having sent off a 'letter of interest', with maybe ten to twenty in the pipeline, one sat back and waited for a telex indicating that the firm had been shortlisted, for which ever project it was, and inviting the consulting firm to submit a proposal document describing how it would meet the terms of reference for the project. Although a telephone commands great respect in an office and people can be seen running at its shrill call, compared to the telex it is of low status. A chattering telex machine will capture the complete attention of a complete office, from floor to floor.

On receipt of an invitation the consultants would, normally, be requested to:

- acknowledge receipt of the invitation by telex and indicate whether or not they intend to submit a proposal;
- conduct a review in the country in which the work is to be undertaken, during which the local government agencies should be consulted; – prepare and submit a detailed proposal for the consultancy services, in accordance with the project brief and the terms of reference.

This proposal was expected to include full details of the man-months of services to be provided, broken down by specialism; the experience of the firm in undertaking work of a similar nature in the past; the curriculum vitae of the personnel to be assigned to the work.

Invitations to submit proposals for a project are, naturally, well received in the offices of the consulting firms, and are normally the stimulus for intense in-house activity and discussions, all directed towards the determination of the best approach and strategy in order to be the successful consultants and obtain the contract for the project. But the preparation of a proposal document is not a straightforward execise, by any means.

The first task will be a line by line dissection of the project brief and terms of reference to make sure that the objectives and requirements of the project study are fully understood and that there are no unacceptable conditions, written or implied. A bad interpretation of the terms of reference and a subsequent ambiguous contract can bankrupt a firm. Having determined the fine detail of the study from the full terms of reference a decision has to be made whether or not to proceed with the putting together of a proposal document. Involved in this decision will be a sensible assessment of the in-house strength to actually do the job, whether other experts will have to be called upon from outside (enquiries will be made to determine if they are available), and whether the job will conflict with other consultancy commitments.

If the answer is, no, then all that is required is a carefully worded letter referring to new work loads, or similar reasons for not taking up the offer – though firms are not too keen on turning down offers to bid for work, and certainly will avoid doing it too often in case they get a bad reputation for rejecting invitations. If the answer is yes, then there are other aspects needing consideration. What is the probable value of the job, how many other consultants have been invited to submit their proposals for the job and who are they, and how serious and strong is the opposition? The level at which the proposal document is to be pitched will depend on the answers to the previous questions.

The short list of consultants invited to bid for internationally funded projects can vary from agency to agency, but will normally be between three and five. To most consultancy firms these are reasonable and acceptable odds, which will justify the spending of not inconsiderable amounts of money in preparing a proposal document. When the odds rise to eight to one, or lengthen into the tens and twenties, then it is increasingly difficult to persuade the directors to fund the proposal preparation other than as an in-house exercise at minimal cost. This is understandable as the cost of a well-constructed proposal, which is a serious and determined effort to win the bid, can be considerable and run into many thousands of pounds. First of all, the project may be so large or complex, and in such an unfamiliar area that the consultants will be unable to put together a pertinent proposal unless they send one of their experts on a site visit. If it is a large multidisciplinary project then it may be necessary to send a small team to familiarize themselves with the background to the proposed project, assess the local situation, and determine the extent of the local facilities. Often the terms of reference will mention that a site visit would be of value and the fact that a site visit has not been made may downgrade the proposal – in the local client's eyes if not with the international body funding the study for the project. It is always reassuring to the client to be able to read in the proposal that discussions have been held with officials in the field or research stations visited. However, to send a small team of experts to a country by air, keep them there in hotels, and hire transport for say ten days can easily cost in excess of ten thousand pounds, without even allowing for home office inputs in preparing drawings, bookbinding, producing thirty copies of the proposal, etc. Costs can soon mount up, and if one has to go through the exercise five times before winning a job then the costs of work prospecting can become a significant overhead expense.

For most major jobs the short-listed consultants send in a team of their own experts for the purpose of getting the necessary background data in order to make the proposal document a demonstration in itself of the in-house consultancy capability and strength, and also to demonstrate to the local client that the firm is acknowledging the importance of the local development plans. The presence of a representative of the firm is in itself flattering, but for some reason or other if there are two (or more) representatives this is more than doubly flattering.

On work prospecting trips of this nature I have frequently dined with the competition, shared transport with them, and even shared background data: all very friendly, though usually not all the cards are put on the table, only those that suit. It should, of course, be mentioned that for these internationally funded jobs the consultants are normally selected from a range of countries, and the competition may be Japanese, Canadian, German, or from one of many other countries, including the developing countries themselves.

The project brief and terms of reference are usually comprehensive and, based on the findings of the original project identification team,[2] provide a good summation of the local background and the study's objectives. Thus, the terms of reference can easily be a document of forty pages or so, detailing exactly how the client wants the job to be done, and may have a table of contents very similar to the specimen shown in Table 15. Care has to be taken in drafting the proposal document to see that all the client's points have been covered and one should avoid, at this stage, any inference that the client has got his terms of reference wrong. It is very tempting to do this, but rarely well received.

Part of the proposal document will be the curriculum vitae section, giving the life stories of all the consultant's personnel who are proposed for the consulting team in the event of the firm being successful in its bid. From a consulting firm's viewpoint the putting together of a proposed team is a tricky exercise, in so far as the client will expect the nominated team to be the actual team on the job if the firm is awarded the contract. This can be a problem as the firm may have their limited number of in-house experts nominated in several project proposals. Changes can be made, but care has to be taken not to do it too often, and the client may reject the alternate if he considers that he is not of the same calibre as the original nomination. A complication in assembling a project team is the start date. Scheduling of staff assignments can be thrown awry by the client's delaying the start date by several months, or even years. Rather inconsiderately, the client will delay making a decision on the award of a contract and then expect the poor consulting firm to bring together again, and quickly, a team that he may have assigned to the project a year previously. However, most experienced consulting firms expect such delays to occur and are skilled at meeting such contingencies. The big problem, though, is the selection of the team leader. In some respects he is the key member of any consulting team and success in winning contracts will depend on the stature and calibre of this one man. Obviously such a person is in demand, particularly for the larger consulting projects, and long delays in the start date may well mean that he is engaged on another assignment and no longer available.

For many agencies or clients it is necessary to submit two proposal documents when making a bid. The first is the 'Technical Proposal', and the second is a quotation for the cost of the services to be provided, usually in a separate sealed envelope. The latter envelope will only be opened after the successful 'Technical Proposal' has been determined, when one firm will be selected for negotiation of contract.

The previous paragraphs describe the classic proposal system followed when selecting consultants for projects that are internationally funded and when the bidding has to be open to firms of any nationality. There are variants, depending on whether the client is a ministry, who might be either the donor or the recipient of bilateral funds, or a private organization or company, but, to a greater or lesser degree, the procedures are likely to be similar.

As a potential member of a consultancy team one has to be careful that the firm's management has not put together a proposal which has been drafted with an unrealistic bias towards the objective of pleasing the client. Thus one can find oneself in the invidious position of having to carry out, in one month, specialist studies which more correctly warrant three months of field work. This is a problem if one is a freelance consultant working for consulting firms, who are not necessarily keen to allow the freelance consultant access to their proposal document until they have won the contract. Alternatively, one may be on an assignment which has terms of reference that have been put together badly by the funding organization, and the flaws in the development philosophy have not been picked up by the consultant's in-house team that drafted the proposal document. It is not always a pleasant situation to be in, in a strange country, having to defend other people's bad concepts –

Table 15 *Specimen table of contents for project brief and terms of referenece*

local experts are no fools and can quickly detect fundamental flaws in the expatriate's development thinking.

This, then, is the proposal system whereby jobs are awarded to consulting firms competing for development projects sponsored by international organizations. The following pages describe in more detail what happens in the field during full feasibility studies for agricultural development projects in the tropics.

Notes

1 The original 51 member states in the year 1945 had a further 107 new member states added to them in the years between 1946 and 1983, of which 40 were former British territories.
2 Before a Project is implemented there are a number of distinct planning stages, such as project identification, pre-feasibility study, full feasibility study, and detailed design and implementation.

7 Feasibility studies for agricultural development in the Third World

SIX PHASES OF A PROJECT

1   Enthusiasm
2   Disillusionment
3   Panic
4   Search for the guilty
5   Punishment of the innocent
6   Praise and honors for the nonparticipants

(A notice on a Monenco office wall in Montreal, Canada)

The client

Usually there will be a minimum of two clients, sometimes more, and the clients may not have identical development philosophies and objectives. This is an interesting complication if one is able to look at it in a detached manner, but it can create an almost impossible project-management dilemma to tax the wits of the team leader. In the field the team leader will have to balance the enthusiasms (or lack of) of his specialist team members[1] with the local client's interests and politics, which may not be unanimous, and with the global dogmas of the international funding body, quite apart from the technical aspects of the project. In some cases the team leader cannot win, and no matter what decision he makes he is going to be criticized by one or other of the parties. His only hope is not to choose a course that opens him to challenge by all parties, including his own team members – in this case a stomach ulcer can become a real possibility.

If the 'field' client is also the funding body, for example, an international company wishing to explore the feasibility of expanding its activities into the field of large scale ranching, then the

Even consultants can have difficulty in visiting the project areas. It took two hours to extricate this vehicle from the mud.

position is fairly straightforward. More often, however, the funding body is not the same body as that with which the consultancy contract is signed. Thus, in the project brief will be a statement to the effect that the international body has made funds available to the government of A to finance the cost of the feasibility study and has (or has not, as the case may be) been asked by the government of A to evaluate submitted proposals and select the qualified firm on its behalf. In this case the 'consulting contract' will be signed between the 'client', who will be a government or a ministry, and the 'consultant', but with the international body controlling the purse strings and the selection of the qualified firm. The influence of the international body is, consequently, considerable, made doubly so by the fact that this is only the study stage and that if the study finds the project to be feasible then the source of funds for the implementation stage may be the same international body.

Contractually the team leader will have one client to deal with and usually the 'client' will nominate a coordinator or a coordinating committee whom the team leader can call upon for guidance and assistance on any matters to do with the study – letters of introduction, resolving of technical ambiguities, making available related government documents, possibly from other ministries, arranging for access to restricted material such as aerial photographs, guidance on local policy matters such as government policy on holding sizes, obtaining advice from higher authorities, etc. Though this all sounds reasonable and what one would expect, in fact the local situation may be somewhat different. The contract may be with one ministry, for instance, the Ministry of Water and Power, but the project may be multidisciplinary, or an integrated rural development project, involving the Ministries of Agriculture, Health, Food, Local Government and Rural Development, and even the Ministry of Finance and Planning. Contacts may have to be established, formally or informally, with representatives at the highest levels of each of these bodies. This has to be done with great care and tact as there may be inter-ministry rivalries of real and serious proportions, indeed officials may refuse to see you, or deny you documents. Then, again, there may be the situation where the coordinator cannot obtain the needed documents, but informal approaches by the consultant may be more successful. Even within ministries there may be antagonisms, and one official will refuse to acknowledge the existence of another in the same corridor. There may also be a Central Planning Bureau, or a Ministry of Planning, whilst the ministries themselves may have their own planning cells, each suspicious of each other. One may even find an Implementation, Monitoring and Evaluation Division in the Cabinet Office.

An experienced team leader will in the early stages of a project make the rounds of the offices of the representatives of the international bodies and in the course of conversation glean a fair picture of the local politics and who the key men are to establish contact with and to meet. An hour with the right man can be very rewarding and get the study off on the right lines from the start. Future personality clashes can be avoided and team members warned of any sensitive areas.

In general, consultancy teams are well received in the developing countries and the local officials are generously helpful and courteous. Indeed they are much more responsive and helpful than people of similar seniority in one's own home country. Of course they recognize that the consulting team is there for the purpose of helping the country in its development planning and they may have received instructions to be cooperative and helpful, but even then it must be somewhat irritating to be plagued by hordes of consultants all asking the same questions and expecting to get instant attention. I know that I used to get irritated, as an agricultural officer, by people ringing up out of the blue and asking if they could come and see me at seven o'clock on a Sunday morning to discuss some matters before they departed by plane for their home office. Unfortunately I have been guilty of exactly the same fault in more recent years – but at least I do not take the local help for granted.

What must be a source of irritation is that some countries have, seemingly, all the technical knowledge and field experience needed to implement the project themselves.[2] I once carefully worded a question in this vein to a Director of Agriculture, asking why they needed us, to which he replied that it was only by this means that they could get the money. This is quite true and pragmatic as people responsible for handing out large sums of 'international funds' insist on the impartial feasibility study approach in order to reassure themselves that the investment is justified. There is also a need for a common yardstick as a means of ranking possible projects within and between countries for the allocation of scarce development funds.

I have stated that local officials are helpful: this is not always so and there are countries in which it is very difficult to carry out consultancy work. The local experts will jealously hide their records and take the attitude that expatriate consultants are highly paid and therefore should not need help from the less highly remunerated local staff. Indeed some of them will only part with information, such as rainfall records that are freely available in most countries, on payment of a 'dash'.

Whilst this can be annoying to the expatriate consultant, it is not necessarily correct to regard such practices as corruption. As one American put it to me, with regard to the practice of paying for information in one country which is notorious for this locally accepted custom, 'Civil servants do not get a salary in this country, they get a retainer. This gets them to the office and if you want any more out of them then you have to give them a gratuity, bonus or local supplementation.'

The consultants

In the past, communities and their institutions evolved naturally, depending on the mood of the moment rather than any preconceived and approved plans, and often on the strength of will of one man to lead others to do things in the way he wanted. Most of the world's finest legacies are objects, social institutions or laws that at one time were concepts in one person's mind, or in the minds of at most a small group of influential people. Nowadays society is organized and regulated in a democratic manner. There are rules and more rules and controls and bye-laws, all making inspired innovation increasingly difficult. With progress life has become more complex, so much so that it is now impossible for one person to be a master of all trades, with the inevitable emergence of the specialist and the consultancy profession.

In the UK most professional institutions have within their constitution clauses relating to consultancy and its practice, which were at one time rigorously upheld. Consulting firms were partnerships with unlimited liability – that a consultant could be a limited liability company was inconceivable and obviously raised doubts about the consultant's own confidence in his expertise. Certainly no consultant should have any financial relationship with any company, firm or organization, or carry out work in fields outside his own competence. Nowadays, in the past few years, the codes of professional conduct have been rephrased to permit such relationship, providing it is not prejudicial or inconsistent with the consultant's duty to advise the client impartially. These changes are mainly a response to pressures from UK firms or companies offering consultancy services overseas,[3] who found themselves in the strange position of not being able to quote in their brochures that they were members of the relevant professional body in the UK.

Most of the international organizations that make use of consultants recognize that there are in the world various forms of consultancy firms, and providing the circumstances of the relationships are stated and they do not conflict with impartiality, the funding bodies are quite happy to make use of their services. Obviously, the standing and status of a consulting firm is of concern to the international funding organizations, if for no other reason than that the recommendations of the consultants may lead to the implementation of projects incurring the expenditure of hundreds of millions of pounds, and as a consequence the funding bodies have laid down principles and guidelines governing the employment of consultants or consulting firms. Guidelines for the use of consultants usually take the following form:

General. The consultants must be competent for the task and should come from UN member countries.

Consultants employed by the funding organization. The funding organization can use consultants for technical assistance programmes, for projects where the organization is the executing agency, or where the organization wishes to supplement its own staff.

Consultants employed by the 'client'. The funding body may require the recipient to select and engage consultants, but the funding body usually needs to be satisfied that the consultants are competent for the task. The employment of domestic consultants either alone or in combination with a foreign firm is often encouraged, and, all things being equal, may be given preference.

Kinds of consultants. Firms of consulting engineers are most frequently needed and, in general, fall into one or other of the following classes:
- firms of independent consulting engineers;
- firms which combine the functions of consulting with those of contractors, or who are associated with or owned by contractors; and
- firms of consulting engineers affiliated to manufacturers, or manufacturers with design offices offering consulting services.

Functions of consulting firms. The functions of a consulting firm used for projects include:
- preliminary investigations and reports at pre- and full feasibility levels, economic and financial justification, model design, estimated costs, scheduling and related aspects;
- detailed design, specification and contract documents and analysis of bids; and
- supervision of construction and sometimes initial operation. The guidelines will also include notes on selection procedures to be followed when selecting the consultants.

In general consulting firms are long established and, within the fraternity, well known for their particular brand of expertise and area of work. They will have in-house personnel covering the key disciplines involved in their field of interest, and, often, associated experts whom they can call upon from time to time, depending on the particular needs of any particular project. Thus, for example, a project may have a forestry component which has to be examined and assessed within a broader study: however, few consulting firms can afford to maintain a forestry expert within their own organization just on the off chance that a job will turn up calling for his services. Where a proposal calls for the inclusion of a forestry expert the firm will either associate with a firm specializing in forestry consultancy, or call on the services of an individual who is available to any firm requiring his services on short term assignments. Sometimes the consulting firm will have a panel of retained experts whose names are included in the firm's general work prospecting publicity brochures.

New consulting firms appear now and then, but they normally experience difficulty in obtaining work as they can quote only limited previous work experience in their job proposals, which puts them at a serious disadvantage compared with the established firms that can quote a number of previous jobs.

The consultant's objectives

Ostensibly, the consultant's objectives are to meet the client's wishes as described in the terms of reference. The consultant will take great care in preparing the proposal document to convince the client that the firm is the best choice, that it has had considerable experience in similar jobs, that the proposed team is an amalgam of expertise which other consultants will have great difficulty in matching, and, finally, that the fees quoted are very reasonable. To do such proposal exercises in style costs money and a not inconsiderable percentage of income will be allocated to work prospecting. The firm, if large enough, will have its own print room and staff capable of producing high quality publications, with glossy covers, colour photographs, and very fine graphs and figures. Senior personnel will make regular visits to the head offices of the international organizations. Staff will attend and participate in international conferences, seminars, meetings of professional bodies, and so on. All these activities result in considerable overheads that have to be met each month, on a regular basis, and for large, well-known firms these overheads will easily amount to several hundreds of thousands of pounds.

The objective of the consulting firm's head office is thus quite simple: it is to obtain a steady stream of consultancy work to generate sufficient income to meet the overheads. As most consulting jobs are relatively short term, by the very nature of the consultancy studies, this means that management are continually occupied with the task of work prospecting. Having put together the team for the project, funded the work prospecting exercise, and calculated the fees (each step requiring an expertise of its own and considerable experience in contractual matters) and having won the contract, management will hand over the project and its management to the team leader and the team.

The consulting firm will, of course, expect the team to perform the task in a professional manner, in accordance with the firm's in-house standards and style, with the objective of producing a competent, professional study report in line with the terms of reference. Strangely enough, the larger and more established the firm, the more professional and stereotyped the report, with the dullness of a series of textbooks following a standard format. This is, as a consulting technique, impressive and intimidating, as each report takes on the status of a reference work and becomes a source text for other studies. Unfortunately the completeness and sheer professionalism of the report can conceal the fact that the study has not got to grips with the fundamental technical, social and economic aspects of the study. Stereotyped professionalism may be all right when carrying out a study for a highway or a bridge, but may not be the correct approach when dealing with integrated rural development projects.

The controversy over whether consultants should be innovative in their reports or stick strictly to the letter of the terms of reference is discussed later in this chapter.

The team leader and the team
Normally the team leader will be a senior in-house person who is familiar with the consultant's house style and the firm's day to day financial procedures (including how to make irregular payments without incurring the wrath of the accounts division, who can become very petty about minor accounting innovations when the job is finished). He will be a man who has the confidence of the senior partners in his ability to do the job and protect the good name of the firm. Nothing is more disastrous for a consulting firm than for a job to go 'wrong', for there to be serious errors in the technical detail, for the planning concepts to be badly conceived, or the terms of reference left unfulfilled. This exposes the consulting firm to serious criticism and damages its hard-won reputation. Whilst the study is being carried out in the field the team leader represents the firm, and in some respects is regarded as the firm; the firm's future standing is in his hands. The team leader is like the captain of a ship,

an absolute master abroad, but accountable in the 'home port'. Consequently the firm takes some care in selecting the team leader, as an unsuitable person can cause severe problems for the team members in the performance of their own specialist studies and also for the firm in its relationship with the client.

As stated earlier the team leader is, almost invariably, one of the consulting firm's permanent personnel. Indeed the funding organizations are not happy when a firm has employed an outsider to fill the position. The criticism is that the outsider has no commitment to the firm and may possibly be less concerned about the successful outcome of the study than a permanent employee whose future status within the firm may also be at stake.

For large projects the team leader may have no other responsibilities than the direction of the study, and – an important 'and' – the writing of the main report. This latter responsibility means that the team leader must involve himself closely in the job descriptions of each member of his team, which are written up before the commencement of the field studies, and keep himself up to date with the daily progress of each team member's work in the field. This is no easy task and requires the team leader to have a good comprehension of each of the disciplines represented in the team. This comprehension has to be sufficiently deep for him to be able not only to incorporate the individual contribution into the text of the main report, but also to be able to direct, when necessary, the individual team member in his role and keep him in line with the other team members. It is easy for individuals to go off at tangents, which may be interesting but are completely irrelevant to the project study. No matter how interested or sympathetic the team leader may be in side issues that have been raised by a team member, his main concern is to fulfil the terms of the contract, and that may be difficult enough without any distractions. On a rehabilitation study for a large irrigation project, involving 26 team members, one of the aspects that had to be examined was the question of health. The medical officer who was assigned to the team to cover health aspects managed to convince most of the team that one of the major constraints to development was the pollution of the domestic water supplies by nearly every known water-borne disease, with the consequent gastro-enteric disease incidence amongst the population representing over half of the registered known morbidity. Although I accepted the medical officer's findings without reservation, there was little I could do but draw attention to the situation when I came to write the main report, as his recommendations, and the estimated costs, were outside the terms of reference for the project. The aim of the study was to examine the existing situation and come up with recommendations for the rehabilitation of the agricultural project, which if accepted and implemented would generate the income needed to support improved water supply systems. It was a question of priorities, and it was the team leader who had to keep the team on target, both individually and as a group.

Quite apart from the logistical problems encountered by a team leader, the most difficult task is to guide the team members without controlling them. They are acknowledged experts in their own disciplines and their opinions have to be treated with respect, but when put into a multidisciplinary team they can become moody, irrational, excitable and demanding. Even the best of team members can suddenly explode over some issue or other, not even to do with the task in hand. The team leader has, thus, to be an expert in gentle man management. In my experience there is always one passenger in every team, and usually one who is an awkward character.

Consulting firms of any standing can usually field a team composed of their own personnel, who are tried and trusted employees and whose abilities are known. Under these circumstances the team works smoothly, each member knowing the role and strength of each of his colleagues. However, for big projects, or when the consultant's in-house strength is stretched by overlapping projects, the firm may have to call upon outside assistance. In this case the study may not proceed so smoothly, though this may not mean that the study is any the worse for the internal dissension; it may even result in a better report being compiled.

Although the previous paragraphs imply that the field study is left entirely to the team leader, this is not quite correct as the usual practice is for consulting firms to include in the fees for the study an element for head office inputs and airfares for site visits. As far as the team leader is concerned head office inputs and visits are an unfortunate necessity. Head office participation allows the team leader to procrastinate in the field, to refer awkward issues as being beyond the authority of the team leader's brief. It also gives the team leader the opportunity to involve the head office in any contentious matters. One colleague once informed me that he always sent one or two telexes to head office whenever he was abroad. 'It makes them feel that they are contributing and part of the study; it makes them feel needed.' But on the negative side is the inevitable 'helpful' interference by the visiting director or partner. No matter how unintrusive they are ('Don't worry about me, just carry on as usual'), there are the questions and suggestions that cannot be ignored, often well meaning and pertinent, but still additional strain on a team leader under stress. It may be thought that team leaders should be above stress, but in my experience this just means that it is disguised as it is almost impossible for a team leader who is doing his job properly not to be under some stress or other. There are those who enjoy being under stress, and are at a loose end when there is no stress.

All that has been written in the previous paragraphs might lead one to think that consultancy projects in developing countries are smoothly run operations, the result of careful planning and preparation. In my experience this is rare, and in practice the projects never go as planned. Logistical as well as technical problems have to be overcome by the team leader. At the time of preparing the proposal document priority is given to determining the technical background of the project and presenting the consultant's approach to the study, and consequently there is little time available for considering the logistical aspects. It is taken for granted that suitable accommodation will be available and that the question of transport will not be too difficult to resolve in the event that the proposal has a successful outcome.

What actually happens is that the project does not commence on the original planned date. The proposal may have become just a file number when suddenly it springs to life, negotiations are completed and there is a frantic mobilization exercise. Team members' planned holidays are postponed, replacements for team members, now on other assignments, are found and approved by the client, flights are booked, injections obtained, and so on. Usually all this takes place within a month of contract signature, which is not long if one has to mobilize a large team. When all the travel arrangements have been finalized and the documentation aspects dealt with, the team leader will proceed to the field to make the arrangements to receive the team members as they arrive. Travel arrangements can be complex as team members will have differing lengths of assignments for their inputs in the field. Some may have to complete their studies before another expert arrives: thus the soils studies, for example, will be completed before the agriculturalist arrives. Some experts may make an input for only two weeks whilst others may be on site for several months.

Depending on the scale of the project he may arrive a week or more before the arrival of the experts. In that period of time he will have to make the accommodation arrangements, hiring a house or houses, booking hotel rooms, or checking the accommodation provided by the client. This is always a difficult exercise as the locals are not slow in realizing that they have been presented with a golden opportunity. How difficult the exercise may be depends on the country in which the project is located and where the project offices are situated. Sometimes there may be two offices, one in the capital and another within the project area. The mere fact that the country is a developing country in itself means that the accommodation is not likely to be good. Oddly, the choice may be between international cuisine at £100 a day or rooming houses at 2 shillings a night. On one job I took over one complete floor of a rooming house, paying over the odds for it, on the understanding that it was reserved for myself and the team members, whether the rooms were occupied or not. I also required that the rooms be given a thorough cleaning, some additional furniture acquired, and that the number of beds in each room be reduced from four or more to one.

Having settled the accommodation problem, which will seldom please all the team members, the next issue will be the provision of transport. According to the wording of the contract this may be a responsibility of the client or provision may be made for the consultant to make his own transport arrangements. I have yet to decide which is the lesser evil. Undoubtedly, if it is a long term study then the consultant will be better served if he makes his own arrangements. The drivers are more amenable, the service to the individual team members more reliable and flexible, and provision can be made for the team members to have access to the vehicles outside office hours, often by private arrangements with the drivers, which keeps both sides happy. For short term assignments it is better to make use of the client's vehicles, though they may not be so reliable, the drivers recalcitrant and sometimes alarmingly lacking in driving skills. Another alternative is to have the vehicles provided by a local associate, but this is not necessarily a good arrangement either. The issue has to be played very much by ear, but it has to be solved satisfactorily otherwise one has expensive consultants sitting doing nothing and planned itineraries ruined.

Whilst the logistics are being attended to, the team leader will also be checking on the office accommodation and facilities, checking that the typewriters actually work, that the typists can type in English at a rate of more than one page per day, that the office has drawing pins and squared paper, etc. If the team requires drawing office facilities this can be a major exercise for the team leader, although the equipment is usually brought out by air from the home office. All sorts of permutations are possible in the exercise of mobilizing in the field.

In any spare time the team leader will be making contact with the client's officers, briefing them on the consultant's programme of work for the next few months or so, and generally making courtesy visits to all the people who may be involved in the team's activities during the study. If counterparts are to be made available by the client, then initial arrangements will have to be made for their release and allocation to the individual team members.

The team leader may also have to familiarize himself with the geography of the capital, determine where the ministries are located, who the key officials are, where their offices are to be found, run down supplies of simple aids like street maps, names of suitable eating houses, where the book shops or chemists are, and so on.

At the same time the team leader, if he or she has not been in the country before, will be collecting as much background information as possible: this will be needed to draft the final report and also to give guidance to the team members as they arrive.

The composition of the team will vary according to the nature and scale of the project, but will be in line with the provisional staffing schedule suggested in the terms of reference for the project. As an example, for a large project, involving, shall we say, sixty man months of studies, there may be some twenty-five experts assigned to the study covering the following disciplines:

soil science	environmental pollution
hydrology	agricultural engineering
irrigation engineering	civil engineering (buildings)
agronomy	civil engineering (roads)
entomology	domestic water supply
animal husbandry	power
forestry	agricultural economics
health	economics
sociology	organization and management.
marketing	

For each of these disciplines there will be a team member, sometimes more than one, or one expert may cover two or more related disciplines. Each team member will be allocated a precise number of man months for his assignment. Sometimes the assignment will be split between the field and the home office, this being the cheapest arrangement as it involves less accommodation and daily allowance costs; however, not all clients like this arrangement and may prefer all the project work to be done within the country. This does have the advantage, of course, that local counterparts can be directly involved in the preparation of the annexes covering each of the disciplines, which are normally appended to the main report.

The team's objectives
There has to be an assumption that the team leader and the individual team members, whilst not missionaries, have a certain dedication to their work and are genuinely interested in playing a part in the development of countries overseas. Furthermore they will usually take pride in their own expertise, often reacting volubly to any suggestion by the team leader or other team members that their discipline is of secondary importance. A good team member will be 'pushing' the team leader, and not the other way round. Experts who need prodding by the team leader, who are not innovative in their thinking and their work programme, are a nuisance to team leaders, and whilst they may not be dropped from the study they may find difficulty in being accepted on future projects. The dedicated individualist who works in isolation from the rest of the team, and who will not accept any extra-curricular project responsibilities, can be equally tiresome, but provided the task is fulfilled there is not much that can be done about it.

As individual team members they will have the task of obtaining all the relevant background information, in their discipline, which will be needed for their contribution to the larger study. Having obtained the information, which may consist of a review of existing data, results of a sample survey or maybe just interviews with farmers or local officials, the information then has to be interpreted, analyzed and presented, with the expert's conclusions and recommendations if required. Usually the reports of the individual experts, which may be voluminous, are presented as annexes. Additionally the expert will be required to provide the team leader with a summary report which will be used by the team leader when the Main Report is compiled.

When all the experts have completed their technical inputs, and have agreed on a team approach to the project recommendations, cost estimates will be prepared and given to the project economist who will then, following international rules, calculate the internal rate of return.

There can be no denying the need for economic appraisal of proposed projects in developing countries. Equally desirable are the existence of common techniques and yardsticks for the presentation, analysis and interpretation of the financial and economic aspects of a proposed project. What is not so desirable is for the economic appraisal to assume overriding importance, to the extent where the technical and social aspects of a study are subservient to cold numerical calculations. As far as I am concerned I accept economic analysis as a tool to be used in appraising a project, which if implemented could lead to the expenditure of many hundreds of millions of pounds of scarce public sector funds,[4] but I become uneasy if obtaining an internal rate of return between acceptable and predetermined percentages becomes the overriding objective of the consultant and the client.

The client's objectives: the developing country's perspective
We have seen that there may be two clients; the funding organization and the recipient or developing country. They may not necessarily have the same objectives. This section is concerned with the objectives of a newly independent developing country, 'newly' in this case meaning any country that has become independent since 1945.

Naturally, the developing country's government wishes to appear to the people of the country as the initiator of development, actively engaged in ushering in a new era, continually examining ways of improving the well-being of the people at large. Whilst development is an easy subject to pontificate about at a dinner table, in parliament, or to a village group, unfortunately the actual achieving of soundly based development is not so easy. That there might be difficulties in achieving development was not so evident to the leaders of the young nations; they were full of the euphoria of Independence, often actively encouraged by experts from the developed world who had an equal naïveté when it came to understanding the problems of development in an underdeveloped context. The Americans thought that one could drive bulldozers up the beaches leaving a trail of development behind them, the

Russians thought that the same could be done using snow ploughs, whilst the inexperienced ministry official purchasing a hundred tractors found that one had to purchase ploughs as well. And these were problems applying to the whole spectrum of development, not just agriculture.

The fundamental problem was the lack of infrastructure to support accelerated development. There was also the question of national pride. Developments were planned which included provision for expatriates to manage the development during the early establishment years, but this was often unacceptable as national pride demanded that the top jobs should be allocated to locals. The lack of trained and experienced manpower to occupy posts at all levels was and is a serious constraint on development. To purchase a tractor is a simple exercise, to use it is more difficult. People, particularly those who live in developed countries, are remarkably unappreciative of just how much training may have to be imparted in order to pass on skills which in developed countries are taken for granted. A tractor driver in a developed country may have received fifteen years of schooling and institutional training, costing several thousands of pounds, and will be proficient in diesel and petrol engines, ploughing, plough settings, seed drilling, combine harvesting, machinery maintenance, and so on. In a developing country one may be lucky if an applicant for a job of tractor driver has a driving licence. This lack of trained and experienced manpower is also a constraint at the top. I recall that Makerere University College's record performance was from student to Permanent Secretary in three years, a situation that speaks for itself. There is a tendency, because of national pride, for newly qualified locals to be given top jobs almost immediately on qualifying. Whilst these accelerated promotions are understandable, it does mean that a senior post is now filled by a young, untried person, and if he proves unsuitable for the position it may take years to get rid of him, whilst he sits there blocking progress.

Quite apart from the lack of manpower, there is usually a lack of physical infrastructure – roads, service facilities, spares, minor training institutes, housing, fuel, and so on, all making development difficult to achieve. There is little doubt in my mind that insufficient attention is given, both by the authorities of the developing countries and the funding organizations, to these infrastructural deficiencies. However, meeting the infrastructural needs is an expensive exercise and if the full costs are included this would result in a very low internal rate of return.

One way round some of the problems is for development projects to be planned on a turn-key basis. The whole project is planned and implemented right up to the stage when the engineering works are completed, the machinery installed, the staff recruited and in-house job training given, and the project is fully operational. At that stage the project is handed over. Unfortunately there is a tendency to hand over such projects to trained but inexperienced top management, and within a few years rehabilitation studies are being conducted. Of course, inexperience is not the prerogative of underdeveloped countries alone; many highly trained and experienced experts from developed countries may also prove to be inexperienced under developing country circumstances. I recall being most impressed by the expertise of three gentlemen from Arizona who were implementing a large centre pivot project in Egypt, and who assured me that they had no time or need for feasibility studies as they had experience of similar conditions in their own home state. I was somewhat cynically amused to learn five years later that a feasibility study was being belatedly carried out.

The previous paragraphs are concerned more with the negative side of development planning rather than with its political objectives. That there are difficulties in achieving the rate of development as laid out in a Five Year Development Plan (a universal planning document nowadays) is not easily admitted within the developing countries. It is, politically, not good news to the ministers and consequently shortcomings in the implementation of projects are not dwelt upon, or just ignored. Anyone who raises awkward questions is accused of rocking the boat and of not thinking positively. There is, thus, a political need for there to be a number of development schemes in the pipeline in order to reassure the population in general, and the opposition in particular, that the government is actively engaged in the task of good stewardship. Unfortunately, the very fact that the country is developing means that it is short of funds for development. This puts its rulers in the invidious position of having to seek external funds for development projects, but, fortunately, or maybe unfortunately depending on one's politics, there are numerous multi- and bilateral sources of funds. Obviously, if a developed country has a Ministry of Overseas Development, or an international organization has development funds, then these organizations will have within them officers whose specific duties are to find, identify and even initiate projects to which the organizations' funds can be allocated. The officer will be judged on his ability to find good projects to sponsor – nothing pleases a minister more than to be identified with a project that is going to help the less fortunate peoples of the world, or to cut the tape at the opening ceremony. The problem facing officials responsible for aid disbursement is to find a country that is politically acceptable, has a stable government, contains a number of potential development opportunities, and is amenable to accepting aid. All a country has to do is show itself to be a good receiver of funds and all the officials responsible for aid will come streaming to the door. Various countries have had this favoured position, such as Sri Lanka for its Mahaweli Development Project, a massive power and irrigation development, and Bangladesh with its population and periodic catastrophic flooding problems. Many other developing countries could also qualify for aid on a large scale, such as Uganda, but there is no stable government for the aid officials to talk to, and even if they do find somebody to talk to it is difficult to recruit experts who are experienced in tropical development to go to the country in question.

So both the donor and the recipient have a political need of development, but there is also a genuine wish to have development as a means of raising the standard of living within the country, or as a means of alleviating urgent problems, such as food shortages. Unfortunately aid is not an unmixed blessing, and may bring in its train unwelcome side effects. Not all aid comes as gifts, and many programmes are funded by loans which need to be serviced as debts. If the aid is too great, or given too fast, then the country's economy can become unbalanced, as can be observed in South America. The extent of public debt and the debt service ratio is shown in Table 16.

For some countries aid may be the source of the greater part of the country's foreign exchange and under these circumstances there may be strong local pressures exerted on the consultants and their personnel to present the results of the feasibility study in the most favourable light. As an agronomist I found such pressures usually taking the form of pressure to estimate the present crop yields as low as possible and to estimate future-with-project yields at the maximum research station level, in order to make the benefits and justification of the project as high as possible, as a means of convincing the funding body of the suitability of the project for investment. Very few target yields are achieved in practice when the projects are implemented.

Table 16 *External public debt and debt service ratios for selected countries for 1985*

Country	External public debt in millions of dollars	Interest payments on external public debt in millions of dollars	Debt service as percentage of export of goods and services
Ethiopa	1,742	35	10.9
Bangladesh	5,968	89	16.7
Burma	2,947	70	51.4
India	29,743	1,066	12.7
Sri Lanka	2,914	113	14.7
Kenya	3,263	127 (1983)	20.6 (1983)
Pakistan	10,707	308	30.0
Egypt	18,501	970	33.6
Ivory Coast	7,100	413 (1983)	31.0 (1983)
Turkey	18,180	1,277	32.1
Malaysia	17,966	1,461	27.5
Brazil	91,094	7,950	34.8
Mexico	89,010	9,436	48.2

Source: World Development Report 1987 [41]

The client's objectives: the funding organization's perspective
No matter what may be said before or during the feasibility study, when the final reports are submitted it is the funding organization that will be seen to be the real client. And this client will expect the main report to present an unbiased and impartial statement of the proposed project. The main report will be taken to pieces and the supporting annexes examined in detail. Statistical inaccuracies will be spotted, technical parameters challenged, suggested project components queried, the development philosophy questioned, all much more thoroughly than by the local client. All this for the purpose of deciding whether the project is worthy of investment and implementation, and woe betide any consultant or team leader who has bent to local pressures and fudged certain unfavourable aspects. My experience is that the funding body's appraisal team will, by some instinct or other, soon pinpoint any weakness, flaw or inaccuracy in the feasibility study findings and recommendations.

Having appointed or approved the consultant the funding client will expect the consultant's team to carry out the feasibility study in an accepted and professional manner, according to their guidelines.

Table 17   *Investment estimate accuracy*

Project planning stage	Investment estimate accuracy range in %			
Identification selective decision	-30%			+30%
Prefeasibility selective decision		-20%	+20%	
Feasibility investment decision		-10%	+10%	
Project implementation phase		-3% +3%		

Source: International Centre for Industrial Studies [90].

Most international agencies will include in the terms of reference a model table of contents for the main report, and will, additionally, have generally available guidelines for the preparation of feasibility studies [31, 90]. Normally the consultant will have worked for the international body before and will be aware of its procedural requirements, so there should be an awareness of the international body's general requirements in the conduct of studies in the field. The acceptance by the international body of the consultant's consulting ability will be demonstrated by the offer of further contracts. In carrying out the feasibility study the funding client will also expect the consultant to firm up the estimates of project costs, in line with Table 17.

As a general rule, when reporting on feasibility studies the consultant and his team leader can rarely be right all the time. Thus the team leader may have ensured that the team sticks entirely to the letter of the terms of reference, yet at the time of appraisal he may be criticized for not having used his initiative over some issue or other. However, he will probably be criticized in the next project for examining issues which are considered to be outside the terms of reference. The answer is always to satisfy the terms of reference and, if some unexpected issue arises, then get approval in writing or by telex to vary the study to meet the contingency.

Another generalization: you can never fully satisfy the wishes of both clients (quite apart from the conflicting advice from the consultant's senior partners) and so make sure before having to defend your main report and its conclusions that you have complete confidence in them, otherwise everyone will criticize you.

Notes

1 The 'experts' in a consulting team are a further complication for the team leader, each of them having tunnel vision and regarding their own specialism as the most important, and often taking sides in the fundamental policy arguments.
2 Whilst it is correct that the technical knowledge is available in some, but not all, countries, what are often and more importantly lacking are organizational and management skills.
3 Constitutional codes of professional conduct applying to consultants in overseas countries are not so exacting as those that had become accepted as conventional for the long established professional institutions in the UK.
4 In fact, scarcity of funds is not the major factor limiting development. The greater difficulty is to identify possible agricultural development projects which are suitable for study and hopefully eventual international investment.

8 Project field work and report assembly: some wrinkles and reflections

General

Whilst we may accept that suitably qualified persons who work in developing countries on feasibility studies may be called experts, specialists, or consultants, we cannot assume that they are equally entitled to be termed 'planners'. Thus the civil engineer, whose expertise is in the field of site investigations for dams, may be the wrong person to be involved in the exercise of drawing up a national dam construction programme. Likewise the entomologist, who specializes in the control of white fly on cotton, may be misused if his assignment involves him in the exercise of overall project planning, irrespective of his own opinion or the validity and worth of his views on the broader agricultural problems of the developing world. Almost invariably experts in a narrow specialism, who know more and more about less and less, are guilty of the conceit that because they are respected, often internationally, for that narrow expertise, then they should be equally respected for their views on a wide range of other matters about which they know very little. The conceit is worsened by the expert confusing respect for his specialized knowledge with respect for the quality of his mind. Whilst there are people with exceptional minds, minds whose brilliance takes them to the frontiers of knowledge, most specialists are only exceptional for their narrow specialism and not for their other qualities. Indeed their very specialism has ensured that they have a blinkered approach to the rest of life that goes on around them. One expert once told me that, 'The biggest problem for African agriculture is the nematode. Until they solve the nematode problem they will never improve their agriculture.' In making such a remark he had written off all the other social, environmental, educational, medical, political, economic, and other human problems constraining the development of agriculture in Africa.

A rich farmer(!) with two oxen and a wooden plough on the Asian subcontinent. Replacing his oxen with a tractor won't necessarily benefit him or his village.

Having made the point that the specialist is not necessarily the person most fitted to be responsible for the broader aspects of planning agricultural projects in developing countries, one has to make the further observation that it is usually this cadre that is made responsible for planning and policy making. Thus the international agencies, the Ministries of Planning, and the consultants are dominated by doctorates, and the more specialized and qualified, the higher one goes. Obviously one has to be careful as to what one says about this situation, as one can easily be misinterpreted, but it must be recognized that over-specialization in the upper echelons may be disadvantageous when it comes to planning matters relating to the broad spectrum of life. And this cannot be more applicable than when planning agricultural developments for communities engaged in subsistence farming.

Slowly this section is drawing us to the general question of training and its suitability for a particular employment. The former colonial services had their own in-house training procedures, more or less in the form of an apprenticeship, for their 'A' Scale officers. They required of their general service officers that they should have a first degree, presumably as a sign of having been reasonably well educated, and then gave them two further years' of probationership, followed by a further three years in the field before they were confirmed in their appointments. The post of agricultural officer was considered to be a career in itself and the salary scale was devised accordingly. Promotion to the higher administrative ranks within the agricultural service would only be considered after many years' service in the districts – twelve years' service before promotion to the rank of Senior Agricultural Officer was quite normal. It was also normal for officers to be moved around the districts and divisions at frequent intervals, as a deliberate policy of broadening their experience. No matter how good, an officer who had stagnated in one place was unlikely to be considered for higher posts. With the demise of the colonial service the 'apprenticeship' system of training ceased abruptly and with that cessation the source of widely experienced, professional, tropical agricultural administrators dried up. Many of the former agricultural officers drifted into other occupations or joined the international agencies, though these bodies were not too happy about employing such men as they had a colonial stigma attached to them. But many of them found there was a demand for their services as freelance consultants and continued to play a role in the development of the tropical world. However, these men are now in their sixties and seventies and becoming increasingly thinner on the ground.

It would be nice to think that the creation of a cadre of similar men was now the responsibility of an international organization, such as FAO, but in general these organizations are composed of specialists who have had only superficial contact with the farmers of the tropical world in their own environment.

One of the reasons for the lack of well-educated generalists in the period after the Second World War has been the increasing influence of the North Americans in the world in general, particularly the impact of their ideas and attitudes on higher education.

The attitude of the British to university education was nicely summed up in the 1964 Hale Report on university teaching methods, a report of the University Grants Committee [39]. Before considering the wider question of teaching methods, Hale and his committee, with nice logic, defined their understanding of the aim and nature of an undergraduate course. The following are extracts from their report in the section on 'General Considerations'.

> The challenge to the present-day university teacher comes not only from the increased numbers of students and the diversity of their social and educational backgrounds, but also from the growth in the volume and complexity of knowledge. One effect of the growth of knowledge is that first-degree courses tend to become overloaded with fact. Attention has been drawn to this tendency in successive reports of the University Grants Committee as well as in that of the Committee on Higher Education. The danger is that the student will spend too much of the limited time at his disposal on memorizing facts, and will have insufficient time to master the principles underlying his subject and to develop his power of thought. If, as we believe, the most important purpose of a university education is to teach the student to think for himself, this is a serious danger, and it is one of which we believe that the universities are becoming more widely aware. (p.8)

> If this tendency [increased post-graduate work] continues, as seems likely and desirable, undergraduate courses might come to be designed and taught merely as a preliminary to work for a higher degree. We should deplore this. In our view the essential purpose of the first-degree course is to give to the student a preparation for his professional life which does not depend for its value on the addition of a postgraduate course. The practice of proceeding to further degrees in science as a preparation for outside professional work as well as for academic work does not in our view make this principle any less applicable to science courses. The aim and nature of the undergraduate course seems to us to be quite distinct. *This should be not only or even primarily to equip the student with knowledge, but also, and more importantly, to teach him to think for himself and work on his own.* (p.9)

The British system was to educate in the first instance and to follow this up by training. The American system, to me as an outsider, seemed to be orientated towards training rather than education. Thus the Americans that one met in the 1960s were better trained than their British counterparts, but not as well educated. Whilst I was at Makerere College in Uganda an American arrived to join the faculty in order to teach and strengthen the Animal Science Department. I informed him that he would have to give an introductory course on the role and place of livestock in East Africa to the first years, but to my surprise he said that he could not do this, as he only knew about poultry, and even in the field of poultry he was rather restricted as he was only really familiar with broilers. However, let there be no doubt, he knew more about broilers than any of the British lecturers.

Another characteristic of the American experts who were appearing increasingly on the scene was an almost fetish-like devotion to academic qualifications. Seemingly the aim in life was to attend courses, pile up credit hours and get more and more higher qualifications as one became more and more specialized. Unfortunately this preoccupation with higher qualifications was passed on to the developing world.[1] This is not necessarily a bad thing but there is a tendency for the top jobs in developing countries to be filled by highly qualified specialists,[2] rather than well-educated generalists.

Planners are made, not born, and the creation of a good planner depends very much on how he is educated and trained, and how and where he obtained his experience. Possibly the best example of the value of good education and wide experience in creating the man is that of Sir Winston Churchill. A good planner may have a specialism, but this must be reinforced with a good education followed by broad-based field experiences if he is to be able to meaningfully contribute to the development of the peoples of the less developed areas of the world. Yet, the future of the developing countries are in the hands of specialists, or people who have insufficient breadth of experience.

Most of the developing countries have inherited their educational institutions and conventions from the West, and in general they have remained fundamentally unchanged. Only President Nyerere of Tanzania has attempted to introduce changes to make the ways of the higher educational institutions match the needs of the poorer masses of the country. That the traditional structure of the Western style universities may not be ideal for the developing countries has been highlighted in an address by Herbert Farbrother to the Tropical Agriculture Association [33]. The title of his address, 'How to make irrigation work: the view of the agriculturist', is interesting, in that Farbrother was a highly specialized cotton plant physiologist in the 1950s and 1960s and has now arrived, through the years, at the point where he is happy, presumably, to consider himself a generalist. Maybe he has realized that highly trained specialists are only 'tools' to be used by generalists, and that what the developing world needs more than anything else is a corp of able generalists.

In his paper on irrigation and its problems, Farbrother discusses the many requirements of workable irrigation schemes, starting with a reference to the Queen of Sheba and the construction of vast dams by the Sabaeans at Mirab in biblical times. Interesting as his paper is in general, it is his comments on education that are particularly of interest in the context of this section:

Desirable changes in education

Admittedly, there is no immediately available alternative to the multi-disciplinary approach; but this need not prevent us from discussing long-term strategies for improving the operation and management of existing large-scale irrigation schemes.

As I see it, the only hopeful route lies in a series of fundamental changes to university and technical college training policies in each of the Third World countries concerned. The main change would be to acknowledge that irrigated agriculture deserves to be recognised as one, single, undivided and specialized professional responsibility in its own right. Hitherto, the responsibilities for irrigated agriculture have been shared, somewhat arbitrarily, between irrigation engineers and agri-culturists; and friction at the interfaces between their various spheres of interest has been identified as the most common single cause of poor overall scheme performance. Existing Faculties of Civil Engineering and Faculties of Agriculture would be unlikely to welcome the creation of a new and specialized hybrid profession, as the prestige and status associated with playing the dominant role in irrigation still continues to be a major issue in Third World countries. Nevertheless, the concept of setting up *comprehensive Faculties of Irrigated Agriculture* would be far more appropriate to present and future manpower requirements, than simply retaining the pattern of university traditions that we have here in the United Kingdom, or elsewhere. Undergraduates could then antici-pate a broad mix of *all* the relevant subjects in irrigation (engineering and agricultural) over a common five year degree course; with specialization into, say, research, 'design' engineering, economics, natural resource allocation, etc., coming in at the post-graduate level. (pp.3-4)

If Farbrother's paper was an examination of the broader prob-lems of making an irrigation scheme work, in amongst this wider approach we nevertheless find the mind of the 'planner' at work. Thus the exercise of examining a subject in its broadest context revealed a fundamental flaw in the training approach for the professional officers concerned with the management of irrigation schemes. Once the fundamental problem had been identified, a solution was found. This is what planning is all about: the marshalling of facts, identifying the key problems, and then proposing an approach, or approaches, to the solving of the problem. Having come up with an acceptable approach to the problem one can devise a solution, which, in the case of our agricultural feasibility studies, may be a development philosophy, or a project development strategy. Once the fundamental development philosophy has been decided then the roles of all the other disciplines involved in the study become clear. Their technologies can be fitted into an agreed plan, strategy or development philosophy.

This, then, is the nature of the planner, a generalist who may or may not have been a specialist at one time or another. He will have had considerable experience in different walks of life; he will be able to converse with people of other disciplines and fully comprehend what it is that they are trying to express.

When I was an agricultural officer I knew, almost precisely, what were my duties and responsibilities. On taking over a post one would receive detailed notes from the previous officer in charge, and there were always by one's side the standing orders and financial orders, which contained somewhere in their sections orders and guidance covering almost every possible event that could be regulated. Thus there was guidance on the length of string that was required to be attached to a cork, and in turn attached to a specie box when it was being transported across water, or one could find out the daily allowance for keeping a camel.

On leaving the colonial service and joining the university world, I also knew exactly what my responsibilities were, though in this case the job description was one of the briefest I have encountered. Universities can be rather flattering in the wording of the duties of an appointment, in that they are so brief that the only possible inference is that lecturers are of a calibre not requiring to have their job spelt out. My own duties were stated to be, 'to take part in the teaching of Crop Husbandry, to assist as may be necessary with the teaching of special or postgraduate students, and to do everything in your power, by research and otherwise, to increase the knowledge of your subject'. After leaving the university world I joined the business world, the world of consulting engineers. At first I thought I understood what my function was, but with time I have come to realize that my understanding of my function was not as clear-cut as it should have been, and that in fact my interpretation of my duties was slightly confused.

I had always regarded myself as a crop husbandry man, or, in later years, as an agronomist, and sometimes as an agriculturalist. However, I tend to avoid the latter term as it implies an expertise in livestock husbandry, of which I have only a working knowledge, and that only in so far as it relates to the integration of crops with livestock. So, in my mind, it was as an agronomist that I participated in consultancy work overseas in developing countries, yet I had difficulty in pithily describing my expertise in my curriculum vitae. It took me some time to realize that, for many studies, I was actually involved in two separate functions, which although appearing to be more or less the same were in fact separate exercises. One function was as a straightforward, specialist agronomist, whilst the other was as a broad-based agricultural planner.

My confusion over my function was also complicated by the fact that consultancy jobs relating to agricultural development can be of widely differing types, and at differing levels of study. It may be said, of course, that my job as an agronomist should have been easily describable and confined to clear-cut husbandry issues, but in practice I rarely found this to be so. In order to examine the husbandry of individual crops and devise workable rotations, I found myself almost inevitably involved in an examination of the national agricultural system, the research facilities, and the strength of the Departments of Agriculture and their extension services in the field. I needed the background information in order to relate my narrow agronomic recommendations to the national scene. No doubt other team members may have wondered why I was interested in the number of people in a country and in what they ate, when my terms of reference asked me, for example, to examine the feasibility of irrigating crops other than rice. To me the broad study seemed to be the natural precursor to the detailed look.

Having completed a number of pre-feasibility and feasibility studies, presumably not disastrously, or I would not have been engaged for other assignments, I found myself describing the assignments as jig-saws. My first task in any new assignment is to obtain all the pieces, without having a clear idea of the final picture. Consequently I become an obsessive collector of any background information that seems to have the slightest bearing on the project in general and its agriculture in particular. As a standard practice I visit every bookshop and supplier of government publications, information departments, banks (who produce very good economic reviews), central banks (who produce annual reviews of the economy of the whole country), Departments of Statistics (a fertile source of background data), departmental libraries, USAID libraries (usually an excellent and generous source of information), and any other institutes or bodies that produce literature on the local agro-socio-economic scene. Some of these sources of information are hidden away and have to be ferreted out. I will also make early visits to all the relevant research stations and peruse their journals and bulletins, quite apart from meeting the research workers. All this activity is purely for the purpose of making sure that I have all the pieces of the jig-saw. I become very concerned that I might have missed some point, some key factor, the lack of which will make my agricultural report fundamentally invalid. And these key factors are not necessarily agronomic. For example, a lack of knowledge about land inheritance and fragmentation of holdings may invalidate proposals about cultivations.

Usually, having obtained all the background information, the pieces of the jig-saw, I will then spend some time trying to put them together to form a picture, on which I will be able to superimpose the project. Having mastered the fundamentals I find that the more specialized agronomic aspects fall rationally into place in the proposed scheme of things. The following sections examine in greater detail some of the background aspects that have to be determined in carrying out a feasibility study for a development project in developing countries in the tropical parts of the world.

Geography, mapping and photography

Before going to a country that is new to me I will attempt to garner as much information on the country as I can, either from my own library or by the purchase of books on the country. As an example, before my first visit to Bangladesh on a study of small scale irrigation sector projects, I purchased B.L.C. Johnson's book on the geography of that country [45]. Books such as this make excellent reading on the plane, and quickly introduce one to the salient characteristics of which ever country one is concerned with at the time, giving a researched report on the politics, the people and the economy, the physical environment and natural hazards, the agriculture, industry and communications, etc. Then there are the international reports, such as the *World Development Report* [41], produced by World Bank and Oxford University Press, which provide one with the basic parameters, giving one a yardstick whereby one can judge the development status of the country in comparison with other developing countries. Other publications such as *The Statesman's Yearbook* [68], or general statistical publications of the Food and Agriculture Organization, are also worth perusing. I will also familiarize myself with the pertinent sections of any relevant technical publications that I may have, such as the Interagency Project on Agroclimatology reports, produced by FAO, UNESCO, and WMO [64, 95].

On arriving in a new country one of my early tasks will be to visit the local bookshops, or ideally the local university bookshop, and purchase any publications that may be of use to me in the feasibility study. Often I am told 'not to bother, they have nothing', but this may only mean that the person making the comment has not had the eyes to see the useful publications, or does not know where to look. It is surprising how often one will obtain a dusty, old, but extremely useful publication, to be told, later, by a local official that he has never seen it before and where can he get a copy? The local counterpart does not realize that there is also a value in finding out what is not available, its very absence a factor to be taken into account in assessing the strength of the local agricultural scene. For the same reason I make it a point to stop, when touring, and visit town markets or weekly roadside markets. People think, I am sure, that I am making use of the opportunity to be a tourist, often wondering why I should be so interested in a heap of vegetables lying on a mat on the ground. But the range and quality of the produce can give me a few more pieces of the agricultural jig-saw. It is also a place where one can quickly obtain information on market prices. A man selling rice will be flattered that you have stopped to look at his stall and will be only to happy to tell you which are his best rices and their prices.

At the same time as trying to assess the level of the local agricultural technology (on the assumption that the more developed the agriculture, the greater the number of publications there will be available,[3] I will be exploring every avenue in an endeavour to obtain maps. It is one of the strange facts of life that people in developing countries do not understand maps, cannot read maps, and quite often do not appreciate the value of maps. And this is so for quite senior officers. Yet mapping is an important part of any feasibility study – if the boundary of the project cannot be agreed upon then there are bound to be conflicts between the various experts at the time of writing up their reports, and the economics may be invalidated. It is surprising how often one expert will carry out his study on one area, say 50,000 ha in size, whilst another expert is studying an area of say 67,000 ha. Not only are there differences of opinion about acreages, but experts may even differ in their opinions as to in which districts the project area lies.

Even the local counterparts may have differing ideas. Confusion often occurs because the boundaries of provinces, districts or smaller administrative units have been changed because of internal governmental reorganizations, or because the local government boundaries are different to those used by other government departments.

All countries have Survey Departments but access to their maps may be difficult, for the simple reason that the Department often comes under the Ministry of Defence. Consequently maps can be restricted documents, and if the maps are not restricted then the aerial photography usually is, especially to foreigners. On one project it took me three months before a set of aerial photographs were released to me. However, no matter how long it takes to get hold of them, I consider it well worth while persisting in the exercise as I regard aerial photographs as one of the more valuable tools when it comes to the planning of large scale integrated rural development projects. Unfortunately, the value of aerial photographs is not appreciated by local officers, for the simple reason that if they have difficulty with maps then aerial photographs are impossible to understand.

Ideally I will have a good road map of the country, at say 1:1,000,000 scale or one inch to sixteen miles, and a 1:63,360 scale or one inch to the mile map of the project area. These will be general maps, but I will also endeavour to obtain copies of soil, topographic, climatic, population or other maps that are available. Maps at a scale of 1:15,000, or 4 inches to the mile, are useful but normally only needed for detailed planning.

Naturally, soil maps are essential: they will either already be available or the consultant will conduct his own soil survey of the area. I find all the different scales used in mapping somewhat confusing and so I usually have with me a very useful specification sheet which was drawn up by the Land Use Division in Colombo, Sri Lanka, part of which I have included in Table 18. I find soil maps, with fine mapping units, difficult to interpret, and I allocate one or two evenings to colouring them by hand. Usually a pattern will appear that was not obvious before, or I will bring out some feature that requires further investigation. For some unknown reason or other I find such exercises best done by myself and not allocated to others. For the same reason I like to analyze data myself, otherwise certain patterns, irregularities or inconsistencies may be missed.

Having located and obtained copies of the available mapping, I turn to the question of the aerial photography. As I have said, it may be difficult to obtain copies, but the exercise is well worth while, and the issue should be taken right to the top if there is any bureaucratic obstruction – to be done with care, of course, as one does not want to create antagonisms or involve one's counterparts in inter-ministry disputes. Depending on the job, photography should be available at scales not greater than 1:30,000, and more often 1:15,000 or 1:10,000, with, hopefully, semi-controlled mosaics. There should be sufficient of these to permit them to be used in the field and have lines drawn on them as working documents. I find them useful for revealing agricultural features on the ground which cannot be immediately interpreted and will need ground verification on a field trip. As one does not have much time to spare for field trips, the aerial photographs can mean that the available time is more usefully spent, rather than traversing an area looking for one-knows-not-what. It can be very satisfying if one finds 'it' on blind excursions into the field, but it is much more efficient to have an aerial photograph in one's hand when one does it, and even that simple exercise can appear mystifying at times to those who are not familiar with such aids.

Whilst I am tremendously impressed with Landsat remote sensing, and have used it to advantage in countries like Bangladesh, I find it more applicable to National Land Use Planning, in view of the lack of supporting facilities within the developing countries. False colour photography can be useful for studying time-of-planting patterns etc. but expertise and sophisticated facilities are needed to make use of the photography. However, new technology and equipment will make Landsat photography increasingly impor-tant in planning exercises in the developing countries. Equally valuable is infra red photography, in fact, I think it probably the more useful for detailed planning, but, like the Landsat facilities, its potential is not yet fully understood by the governments of the developing countries. Indeed, there can be rejection of, and almost disbelief in, the idea that a few colour photographs can be of any real value in planning. Strangely enough, I have also encountered disparaging attitudes to their use by team members who regard them as toys, so the officials in the developing countries are not necessarily alone in their 'head in the ground' approach. It always seems a pity to me, however, that governments of less developed countries should permit any new technology,

Table 18 *Kinds of soil survey and their specifications*

Kind of soil survey	Purpose of soil survey	Published scales of soil maps	Mapping units	Minimum number of observations
1 Exploratory soil survey	Broad national resources inventory	1:250,000 or smaller scale	Great groups, phases and associations of great groups, etc.	Variable
2 Reconnaissance soil survey	Resources inventory; regional level planning; project identification and siting	1:50,00–1:250,000	Great groups, sub-groups or families, their phases and associations	1 per 5sq km (2 sq miles)
3 Detailed soil survey–low intensity	Detailed resources inventory; feasibility studies; preliminary project planning	1:25,000–1:63,360	Series, phases of series, complexes of series, associations of series and undifferentiated units	1 per 50–70 ha (125–175 ac)
4 Detailed soil survey–medium intensity	Detailed project planning and irrigation planning; land use planning	1:10,000–1:25,000	Series, phases of series, complexes of series, associations of series and undifferentiated units	1 per 10–20 ha (25–50 ac)
5 Detailed soil survey–high intensity	Research stations; pilot projects; urban use; farm layout	1:10,000 or larger scale	Series, phases of series, complexes of series and undifferentiated units	1 per 0.5–5.0 ha (1.0–12 ac)

Source: Land Use Division, Irrigation Department, Colombo, Sri Lanka, May 1977

which could help them and is often freely available, to lie idle, buried in entrenched bureaucracy, but it happens. Most frequently, it occurs in countries with military regimes, who are usually rather suspicious of cameras, binoculars, and foreigners who want aerial photographs. This is particularly so if the project is located near an international border. One also has to be careful in such cases that one does not unintentionally cross the border, which may not be marked. Once, in Dinajpur, in the north-west of Bangladesh, I asked a group of local farmers, who had accompanied me to a project site, whether an isolated mango tree in the near distance was in Bangladesh or in India, whereupon there was quite a bit of discussion and it was eventually decided that it was most probably in India. I decided to keep well away from it, being cautious and not having my passport with me at the time.

The environment

Having located myself, and having cajoled the rest of the team into accepting my first estimate of a project's area and boundaries,[4] I next direct my attention to the environmental aspects. This is an important aspect of any study, and data may be required on the environmental aspects by several different disciplines – for example, hydrology, irrigation engineers, dam designers, agronomists – though each may be looking at the data through different eyes. The environmental aspects that will have to be covered will vary from country to country and project to project, and one of the very real problems that will face the planner is that he may only be in the country for part of the year and, yet, have to be able to picture the farming environment over a complete year. Examples of the environmental factors that will have to be considered include topography, soils, climate, and river levels. The pertinence of these factors in planning exercises is elaborated upon in the following sections.

Topography

To the casual observer a locality may be flat, gently undulating, undulating, hilly or mountainous, and he will be quite happy to describe the area in those terms. Whilst this may be adequate for the tourist, the planner will have to assess the topography in more detail. He will need to know the extent of the catchment area, the percentage slope and the soil characteristics, and relate these to the total rainfall, the rainfall intensity and the rainfall run-off. Using such data he, or one of his colleagues, will be able to predict the likelihood of flooding, or the amount of water that could be stored in a reservoir for irrigation use, decide on the need for water and soil conservation measures, or recommend cultivation practices, or examine any other topographic factors that may be relevant to a particular scheme or area.

In the not too distant past, topography was a relatively unimportant factor in tropical agriculture; the soil had a reasonable cover of forest and shifting cultivation, with its short period of arable cultivation and long period of regeneration, did not do much damage to the land. When I was an agricultural officer in Bombali Circle (an agricultural division comprising two districts), in the Tonkolili District of Sierra Leone one could still find forested areas which had had twenty-five or more years of rest following three years of shifting cultivation. I returned to more or less the same area, around Bumbuna, twenty-five years later and found most of the hillsides denuded of trees and covered with grass. Interestingly, there was a period not so many years ago when one school of opinion scorned any suggestion that the removal of forest would alter the environment; it was said that there was no scientific proof that the felling of forests brought about any change in the climate. Personally, I was uneasy at large scale destruction of forest, particularly if the watersheds, the hilltops and the river banks were denuded. However, I had no positive proof that the practice was environmentally bad, and, though I was disturbed at what I saw, I also recognized that I may have been guilty of self-interest, in that I wanted to protect an environment that I liked. My sense that there was something wrong was balanced by an awareness that there were subsistence farmers in the world who, because of rising populations, had no other resource to exploit other than a forested, steeply sloping hillside. It is very difficult to persuade them that they are doing anything wrong, and even if one could persuade them, they have no alternative course to follow. Circumstances made them bad farmers.

That the removal of forest may result in a long term change in the environment was brought home to me in the early 1970s during a trip with agricultural students to Kenya. Arrangements had been made by the Kenya Department of Agriculture for us to visit a village in a dry arid area, just to the west of Nairobi and on the edge of the escarpment looking down on the floor of the Rift Valley. To me the area was typical of an environment that was only marginally suitable for arable cropping – poor soils, low and unreliable rainfall – supporting a mixture of poor maize and sorghum plants, but still densely populated. If one wanted to be a subsistence farmer then this was not the best of environments in which to attempt it. While talking to one of the elderly locals I found out that he had spent all his life in that village and so out of curiosity I asked him what the area had been like when he was a young man. To my surprise he informed me that the dry arid area, which was all around us as far as the eye could see, had been forested when he was a young man, and he pointed to a small gully set in gently undulating cropped land and said, 'In there was a spring that always flowed. It hasn't flowed for many years, now.' In fact I could detect no trace of a spring ever having been there.

In Indonesia at the present moment forest is being felled to make way for transmigration schemes, taking people from densely populated areas (Sumatera Island has an overall population density of 51 persons per sq km compared to 687 persons in Java), and resettling them in less densely populated areas. I have seen some of these schemes, which are many thousands of hectares in size, and still do not know whether to be full of praise or horrified at their audacity. I find myself having to recognize that the speed with which the tall forest climax vegetation has been removed, the land cleared, farms laid out, houses built, and families installed, is very impressive, but I find myself alarmed at the lack of knowledge of how best to manage these lands, with their high rainfall and erodible soils, in order that there may be a stable arable agriculture. Most of these areas are best suited to tree crops, hence the farmers' lack of experience in continuous arable cultivation. The dominance of tree crops in a typical high rainfall, humid and tropical environment, in association with rice as the main food crop, is shown in Table 19, which gives the areas under the main crops grown in North Sumatera. The paddy crop is, of course grown mainly on level and bunded *sawah* lands, and is the main food crop as shown in Table 20. The typical agriculture can thus be described as the production of perennial tree crops and wetland paddy, with a small area of conventional upland arable (*palawija*) crops grown on suitable areas near to the housing (*kampongs*) and the mixed fruit tree areas. The yields of the perennial tree crops and the paddy are good, but by world standards the yields of the *palawija* crops are poor. This is partly explained by the fact that little research attention has been given to the cultivation of rainfed upland annual crops in these environments in the past. It is only now that population pressure is forcing the people into annual crop cultivation in unfavourable environments that there has been an increased research input. Research into the technology needed to change from a shifting cultivation system to a system of continuous production of annual crops in the humid tropics, usually on acid infertile soils, has only recently been initiated, having had low priority for the allocation of scarce research funds. Outstanding in this area of research is the work being done by J.J. Nicholaides and his colleagues working in the Upper Amazon Basin [62].

At the other extreme of topographic environments we have the example of Bangladesh. We tend to think of the Delta as being within Bangladesh, but in fact Bangladesh is in the Delta: the point being that it is an incredibly flat country within a very large Delta (it is some 143,998 sq km in size with a population of 92 million). Because of the flatness and the fact that three major river systems, the Ganges, the Brahmaputra and the Meghna, come together with a combined peak flow of 5 million cusecs, it is an area where disastrous flooding occurs from time to time. When one realizes that Sylhet, about 150 miles from the Bay of Bengal, located in the north-east of the country, is only 10 feet above sea level, then one can appreciate that differences of only 3 feet in land levels can be of great significance in this country. With increasing familiarity with the agriculture of Bangladesh I have come to realize that what appears at first sight to be a relatively simple rice orientated agriculture is actually one of the world's more complex farming systems. The Bangladeshi farmer is a very skilled person who has a complete understanding of his complex and rather unfavourable environment, and who has a finer understanding of the importance of topography than other farmers in the world, and yet he is in a flat environment.

To the agriculturalist topography is a factor that has to be examined in conjunction with rainfall (both total and intensity), the nature of the soils, and the proposed cropping pattern for the future. This examination will lead him to certain conclusions about the need for water and soil conservation measures.

It will be noticed that I have referred to 'water and soil conservation measures', and have not expressed it in the more conventional way as 'soil and water conservation'. This may seem a rather minor point, but it is, actually, of great importance as to which way the concept is expressed when talking to farmers in the

Table 19 *Areas under main crops in North Sumatera, 1981*

Crop	Area (thousands of hectares)
Rubber	483
Wetland rice	477
Dryland rice	114
Oil palm	270
Coconuts	120
Roots	46
Coffee	37
Maize	31
Cloves	19
Grain legumes	17
Tea	11
Tobacco	4
Cocoa	7

Source: Kantor Statisk Propinsi Sumatera Utara Dalam Angka, 1981.

Table 20 *Production of major food crops in North Sumatera (000s of tonnes)*

Paddy	Maize	Cassava	Sweet potatoes	Peanuts	Soya beans
1980	67	354	196	14	4

Source: Kantor Statisk Propinsi Sumatera Utara, 1981.

field. Traditionally, extension workers would go out into the field and harangue the small holders about the need for 'soil' conservation measures, forecasting future disasters if bunds, or other recommended measures, were not put into effect. The response from the individual farmer was usually lukewarm, for the simple reason that he never saw his farm being eroded. When the torrential rain came down he retreated to the shelter of his hut, and when he came out after the storm the farm seemed the same as it was before. Soil erosion is rarely dramatic; it is a slow insidious happening, taking many years for the true calamity to reveal itself. Consequently the subsistence farmer does not respond particularly well to soil conservation advice until it is too late. Personally, I did not talk about soil conservation on my extension safaris; rather, I concentrated on water conservation. Farmers found this a much more understandable approach. They can understand that plants need water to grow, and that if the rainfall runs down the slopes as surface run-off,[5] then it will not enter the soil where it can be taken up by the plants through their root systems. What is more, the effects of water shortage can be visually demonstrated. In Buganda I frequently pointed out to farmers growing coffee on unbunded sloping land that their trees were showing signs of water stress, whilst a farmer on the other side of the valley, whose coffee shamba (farm) was bunded, had trees which showed no signs of wilting. It was relatively easy to persuade the farmers that the reason why their trees were not so healthy looking was because they had less available soil water than the other farmer. If the farmers then followed up my extension advice by constructing bunds at three feet vertical intervals (the standard recommended spacing for bunds in that area) then they would get increased yields and I would have achieved a further benefit of conserving the soil at the same time.

Topography, and its related aspects, are, thus, of considerable importance when planning agricultural developments, particularly in relation to water and soil conservation, though unfortunately it is not necessarily acknowledged in an economic appraisal.

Soils

Most feasibility studies have a major soils content, and a lot of effort is put into surveying, describing and quantifying the various soil groups and, leading on from these studies, producing land capability maps. These studies are fundamental to any natural resources study, and for most agricultural development projects, but some engineers either do not accept the need for such studies or will attempt to have the input scaled down. In some respects the soil scientists are themselves partly to blame for this attitude, in that they may make their studies too pedalogic, and thus difficult for laymen (including myself) to understand. Producing numerous tables of figures of obscure soil parameters, in parts per million, may mask their true worth unless they are related to the edaphic aspects. Having said that, I have to say, also, that I find well-done soils reports most useful as a fundamental background for any planning exercise. Good mapping,[6] which has been planimetered, is equally valuable on field visits, when the present land use can be related to soils which have been demarcated on paper – patterns of land use can appear, which otherwise would be difficult to explain, or might even pass unnoticed.

I mentioned earlier that because soils maps can be quite complex I find that it is worth while colouring them, which will bring out any geographical and cropping patterns. Having taken the trouble to colour soil maps I usually find that specialists of other disciplines are keen to have a look at them, which reassures me that the effort was worth while.

There are many general textbooks covering all aspects of the soils of the world [32, 76, 91, 96], and most countries have their own textbooks or other publications [67] that can be referred to for the general background of the soils in the country under study, and so it is not intended to go into any detail here. However, it is necessary to make the comment that soils are not static and, moreover, can not only be degraded but also created. It is generally accepted that bad crop husbandry techniques in the tropics can result in the degradation of a soil, for example, by continuous cropping without returning any nutrients or organic matter to the soil, or by the absence of water and soil conservation measures, but what is not so readily accepted is that good husbandry methods in the tropics will, over the years, result in an improvement in the soil fertility. Whilst the long term beneficial effects of good husbandry were recognized in the temperate farming areas of the world, the same techniques were not thought to be equally effective in the hotter tropics – the higher temperatures resulted in a rapid disappearance of any added organic matter, or so ran the usual explanation. Yet at Serere, in Uganda, long term fertility experiments were detecting significant and positive responses to the application of relatively small dressings of farmyard manure at levels as low as 5 tons per acre (12.3 t/ha), a rate so low that it was difficult to apply evenly.

The most convincing proof I have seen that good soils can be created by good husbandry techniques was demonstrated by a Mr Streeter in Uganda. He, quite simply, set out to master the techniques of growing crops of high-yielding tomatoes for the Kampala market. He nearly bankrupted himself in the process, but in the end he was producing yields of 25 tons of saleable fruits per acre (62 t/ha), grown in the field in the open. This was something that had never been achieved before in that part of the world, and led him into the business of growing vegetables for export by air to the UK, a relatively new venture in those days. Whilst I was impressed by his technological achievements, what impressed me more was the transformation in the fertility of the soils that had taken place under his cropping regime. Soils that had previously been typical, lifeless, tropical, reddish brown sandy loams had become almost black in colour and, remarkably, full of earthworms. I was once told that if a soil looks good, smells good and feels good, then it is good, and such was the soil that Streeter had created as a by-product of good husbandry techniques. Another sign of a good soil is that if one takes a handful to examine and then drops it, the hand will be clean: this was also a characteristic of Streeter's soils, compared with the structureless, reddish brown soils, typical of the area, which would leave one's hands dusty and dirty after handling them. The previous comments are, of course, edaphic in nature, whilst most soils reports are pedalogic.

As mentioned in the previous section, the planning team will need soils maps (see Table 18), but they will also require advice on many other aspects of soils, such as:
- soil physical characteristics: organic matter, soil structure and porosity, particle sizes, soil depth;
- chemical characteristics: soil reaction, cation exchange characteristics, salinity, toxic substances;
- mineralogical characteristics: minerals, carbonates, gypsum;
- soil-water relationships: infiltration rates, hydraulic conductivity (permeability), soil water availability, water quality.

Using this data the planning team should be able to determine the best land use option(s), and even predict future pitfalls that may be likely if the present land use pattern is changed. For example, the team will be able to advise the planner on the needs for drainage in an irrigation scheme, necessary to prevent the adverse salinity effects of rising water tables. It may seem strange that the introduction of irrigation into an arid area may have to be balanced by the provision of drainage facilities, but it is so. A good example of the problems that can be encountered when the traditional farming pattern is changed, is that of the agriculture of the Egyptian Delta. The construction of the Aswan High Dam permitted an increase in the cropping intensity from one to two crops per year, both crops having to be irrigated as Egypt has no significant rainfall. However, what was not anticipated was that the increased application of irrigation water would also result in a rise in the water table with consequent soil salinity problems.

Having drawn one's conclusions about the best agricultural development options for a project area, the land capability maps will be used to quantify the benefits when determining the economic viability of the proposed scheme. It will be appreciated that there may be several land use options within a specific project area, each related to the prevailing soil and topographic conditions.

Climate

More time may be spent collecting and analyzing climatic data than in satisfying any other project parameter. This is particularly so if the project is an irrigation scheme associated with a hydro-power project, but even on non-irrigation projects considerable attention will be paid to climatic aspects.

It is a useful generalization that in environments where rainfed agriculture is practised the climatic data is of descriptive value. It allows one to explain why crops are planted at a particular time in relation to the rainfall pattern; why crops fail in a certain year (or series of years) can be demonstrated on rainfall distribution curves; why certain crop varieties will only grow at certain times of the year can be explained in terms of mean monthly maximum temperatures. Thus, the climate can be numerically defined, either as cold statistics or as graphs, as part of the project's environmental background. As a resource the climate cannot easily be changed on a grand scale. We can calculate whether supplementary irrigation would be beneficial, and how much would be needed, but apart from that the climate is an unchangeable factor. It can, of course, be changed on a micro-climate scale, by the use of overhead shade, windbreaks, mulch applications, plastics, mixed cropping, etc. Trials to initiate rainfall by dropping silver iodide, or dry ice, on clouds have been carried out, but with no real success.

It is in the context of irrigated agriculture that climatic data is of greatest importance, because it is in this case that the deficiencies of the climate, in particular rainfall, are to be made good by irrigation. As irrigation means the regulated application of water to crop land, there must be some way to calculate the optimum use of a scarce resource, water, and this needs data. Sometimes, water is not a scarce resource, for example irrigation using abundant run-of-the-river flow, but more frequently the amount of water available for irrigation is limited, especially if it is groundwater.

There are many publications covering the various aspects of crop water requirements and irrigation [8, 23, 24, 59, 93], for it is a complex subject, and strangely imprecise. No two irrigation engineers, hydrologists or irrigation agronomists seem to approach the problem in the same way, and every one of them can find something to query, criticize or fault in the studies of other specialists. However, one thing they have in common is that all of them require the calculation of evapotranspiration (ETo) and a knowledge of crop coefficients. There are various ways of calculating reference evapotranspiration but most of them depend on combinations of the following climatic data: mean temperature, mean relative humidity, mean maximum relative humidity, total windrun, mean daytime windspeed, mean actual sunshine duration, and mean radiation.

Having determined the above data, by following a standardized calculation procedure such as the Penman Method, or the Modified Penman Method, one can calculate the reference evapotranspiration.[7] This estimate can then be used with the crop coefficient to determine crop water requirements, and if one knows the effective rainfall then the irrigation requirements can be determined.

The crop coefficient is determined from the following information: the date of sowing, the length of the total growing season, the duration of the initial stage, the duration of the crop development stage, the duration of the mid-season stage, and the duration of the late season stage. In practice there are standardized tables of crop coefficients that can be used, covering most tropical crops, and under two humidity and wind levels.

On feasibility studies of irrigation projects, the agronomist will automatically be assumed to be an 'irrigation' agronomist and may be required to advise the team on the water requirements of crops. However, on large projects there may be hydrologists and irrigation engineers as well, each having his own approach. If there are two irrigation engineers and one is French and the other British, there will be, inevitably, misunderstandings and argument, each following different methods of calculation. Under these circumstances there has to be an in-house meeting to come to an agreed approach and demarcation of responsibilities.

As an agricultural officer and lecturer in Crop Husbandry I never had to worry too much about climate, apart from its value in a descriptive sense, and as part of the environmental background. This was because I had always been stationed in areas where the agriculture was rainfed. Of course, I knew about Penman calculations, crop water requirements and irrigation techniques, but in an academic, remote way. It was only when I became involved in consultancy and feasibility studies that I became personally involved in the practical problem of determining irrigation water requirements. I soon realized that every irrigation scheme is different. The simplest case, from the point of view of calculations is when there is no rainfall at all; matters become more complex when there is a dry season and a wet season, where the irrigation requirements may range from full to supplementary. All this has to be related to the soil characteristics and the proposed cropping pattern. Fundamentally, the purpose of this rather complex mathematical game is quite simple – it is to provide a reasonable estimate of the peak water requirements of an irrigation programme so that the irrigation engineer can calculate or determine the size of the canals, structures, and field distributory systems to meet that requirement. The other, quite simple purpose of the calculations is to provide an estimate of the total amount of water that will be required in the field to meet the proposed cropping water requirements. Knowing the capacity of the reservoir, or the safe yield of an aquifer, one can determine the size of the irrigation project. This is an oversimplification, naturally, and in practice a number of models will be proposed and analyzed, crop ratios will be changed, times of planting staggered, rotations rearranged, etc., before the best fit is obtained.

It is an interesting exercise to obtain copies of all the other irrigation studies that have been conducted by various consulting firms in one country and to compare their various estimates of water requirements for the different crops and for a whole irrigation project. The variation can be considerable and the cause of alarm, if one is not prepared for it. Somehow or other no two studies will have the same estimates of effective rainfall, of percolation losses, of infiltration rates or crop coefficients.

Quite apart from the question of irrigation requirements, the agronomist and the planner will need to look at the climatic data in order to understand the present agricultural performance and also to set up parameters into which any new proposed cropping patterns will have to be fitted. Usually, rainfall and temperature data will be available for most districts, but maybe for only a few years, and sometimes the data may not be entirely reliable. Rainfall data for Galiraya, a remote village in the north of Bugerere Saza, in Buganda, was once analyzed for the purpose of preparing a Manning's 1:1 Rainfall Confidence Limits and it was noticed that it never rained on a Sunday, and that storms often occurred on Mondays. Sunshine records may also be kept, and more rarely wind speeds.

When I am in a project area I will collect rainfall data from as many stations as possible, particularly if the project is located in an area with varying altitudes. In many environments, rainfall will be

Table 21 *Monthly rainfall data at Panchagar, Dinajpur District, Bangladesh in mm*

Month	1972	1973	1974	1975	1976	1977	1978	1979	1980	1981	1982	1983	10 yr av.	19 yr av.
Jan	1	1	0	0	0	0	0	1	0	0	0	3	0	1
Feb		13	0	0	0	0	0	3	7	0	0	0	2	5
Mar	0	0	5	0	0	0	7	1	5	4	30	29	5	8
Apr	51	23	28	8	10	173	113	36	17	117	117	29	64	49
May	**236**	97	41	86	32	109	82	74	160	**430**	122	**369**	123	134
Jun	**414**	**485**	163	**295**	**349**	**288**	195	97	**408**	**296**	**302**	**764**	**240**	**357**
Jul	**700**	**283**	**930**	**593**	**408**	**606**	**1123**	**694**	**932**	**879**	**1067**	**1168**	**728**	**872**
Aug	109	**338**	**539**	160	**845**	**719**	136	**465**	**666**	**423**	27	**616**	**432**	**582**
Sep	**376**	**239**	**361**	**287**	141	48	**440**	**526**	82	**521**	**472**		**312**	**268**
Oct	38	122	48	25	53	**234**	0	**338**	16	0	30		87	97
Nov	0	0	0	0	0	50	0	3	0	0	0		7	12
Dec	0	0	5	0	0	4	0	29	0	8	0		2	12
Total	**1924**	**1597**	**2114**	**1505**	**1840**	**2230**	**2091**	**2285**	**2678**	**2175**				

Source: Panchagar Meteorological Station.
Note: Rainfall greater than 200 mm in bold type, see text.

closely related to altitude, the isohyets following the contours. The character of the rainfall will also change with altitude, the intense tropical storms being more typical of the lower altitudes, whilst the rainfall at the higher altitudes, say 7000 feet (2133 m), tends to be gentler and more prolonged. In some stations it is possible to obtain average yearly data; this is useful as a pattern, but it has the disadvantage that one cannot discern the variability within and between years. Consequently, I prefer to have the data as monthly records over a period of at least ten years. Examination of average rainfall data may lead one to the conclusion that there is adequate rainfall to meet the needs of a particular crop, but closer examination of the monthly data may reveal that due to the unreliability of the seasonal and monthly rainfall, moisture stress may occur from time to time in, maybe, two years out of five (see Table 21). Rainfall data is also very useful in explaining the local time-of-planting dates for different crops, and equally important for indicating the best harvesting times, from the point of view of crop drying, etc.

In his classification of agroclimatic zones, L.R. Oldeman [64], uses 200 mm/month (8 inches) as a guideline for adequate precipitation for wetland rice production. Further, he states that rainfed rice requires a minimum of three consecutive wet months to cultivate one crop and at least five months for two crops, providing the first is sown prior to the onset of the rains. Examination of Table 21 explains why most farmers in the Panchagar area of Bangladesh grow only one crop of rice per year, whilst farmers further south in better rainfall areas can grow two crops per year.

Temperature data is generally more consistent and reliable, although one still has to be on guard for the thermometer with the broken mercury column. In the case of this parameter the average monthly data is the more useful, especially with regard to the suitability of crop varieties for a particular time of the year. For example, in Bangladesh there are local Boro rice crop varieties which are cold tolerant, and can be planted over the winter period, whilst many of the improved varieties do not have this cold tolerance. At the other extreme tomatoes will not ripen at very high temperatures, over say 30°C, and there may be problems if wheat is planted too late, involving maturation during the hotter months of the year.

Rainfall patterns and temperature data are fundamental to any planning exercise, in both broad and specific aspects, and few proposed projects are likely to be of value if the climatic parameters are not given due cognizance. In some respects this is why the Tanganyika Groundnut Scheme failed. The average rainfall per year at Dodoma for the period 1920 to 1949 was 23 inches (584 mm), a quite reasonable rainfall for rainfed crops, including groundnuts, but what the planners overlooked was that the minimum over the thirty year period was 8.7 inches (221 mm), and the maximum was 42.63 inches (1083 mm), in other words the reliability of the rainfall for the area can only be classified as poor. However, all was not lost. Tanganyika got a port and a railway out of the project and it was the beginning of an excellent livestock scheme.

Another factor of some importance is day length. Obviously, this is a fixed factor, and it cannot be altered under subsistence farming conditions, but it can and does have a great influence on the choice of crop varieties, their time of planting and the sequence of crops within the rotation. This factor is of greatest importance in the rice based farming systems of the tropical world, where there may be one to as many as three crops per year. Rice is photoperiod sensitive and may be 'date fixed' for the period of maturation or 'period fixed'; thus the first group will flower on or about a set date, almost irrespective of planting date, whilst the second group will take a set number of days to mature from the date of planting.[8] Plant breeding has resulted in a number of high-yielding varieties, which are usually photoperiod insensitive and can be planted, more or less, at any time of the year. In many countries the traditional names for the seasons, or the cropping slots, are still retained, but with the proliferation of new crop varieties, each having different responses to climatic factors, it is easy for a visiting agronomist to become confused: what he sees in the field may not, necessarily, agree with the textbook accounts. Thus, on a day trip in Bangladesh it is possible to see plots of paddy being transplanted, plots just flowering and crops being harvested, which can be confusing if one is attempting to slot what one sees neatly into the formalized seasons. It can be even more confusing if one comes across a patch of groundnuts growing quite happily in the middle of an irrigated paddy field. All that is proved is that although one can attempt to formalize cropping sequences for planning purposes, in practice the farmers have much more flexibility.

Sunshine hours per day can also be important when irrigation facilities are being introduced. Traditionally the crops will be grown during the rainy season when it will be overcast and there will be fewer sunshine hours. Irrigation will normally be provided during the dry season, and because this is usually a period when there is little cloud cover, crop growth will be enhanced and yields correspondingly higher, compared to similar crops grown during the wet, and overcast, season.

Windspeeds are not normally too important, except as a factor to be included in Penman calculations. However, having said that, strong winds can be of importance if they coincide with the hot dry season, and they can push up the daily water requirements significantly. Rotations may have to be phased to avoid such periods, in order to reduce the costs of the irrigation structures. If the project is in an area prone to cyclones, then the choice of crops may be limited because of this factor. The classic example is Mauritius, which will have several cyclones each year as a normal occurrence (if the cyclones do not come then there will be a shortage of rainfall). Gust speeds of up to 80 mph (129 km/hr), are quite usual, but it is only when the speeds exceed 100 mph (160 km/hr), that there will be serious alarm.[9] Such windspeeds make the growing of tree crops almost impossible. The gusty nature of the winds and the fact that the wind direction changes through 180° as the centre of the cyclone passes through the island, results in a corkscrewing effect on trees and will literally twist small shrubs out of the ground. It is because of the cyclones that sugar cane has become the main cash crop of the island, it being the only crop that will tolerate cyclones. The other cash crop, tea, is also a crop that will tolerate cyclones, though only just, because of the flat plucking table which is a characteristic of the crop's husbandry.

The only other interest that one may have in windspeed is if it is high enough, and regular enough, for windmills. Windmills, like solar power, are always of interest in developing countries as a source of cheap power, but usually the wind speeds are not high or constant enough to make them a practical proposition. Minimum windspeeds for windmills to be feasible will be about 4 m/sec or 14km/hr.

The climatic environment has, thus, been shown to be of great importance in planning studies. As a subject it is vast and can be examined at macro- and micro- levels. It involves consideration of the seasons, the latitude and the altitude, and the interaction with the soils and the topography. Yet whilst the planner will have to explore the subject carefully and in depth, it is a subject that the subsistence farmers understand instinctively,[10] and their farming practices, no matter how strange to the outsider, are the result of generations of contact with that very environment. This is particularly true of the subsistence farmers in a rainfed agricultural environment, who have devised stable farming systems to match the environment.[11] The planner who proposes changes in the traditional farming systems has a tremendous responsibility to ensure that nothing that he proposes will result in future instability. It must be noted that faulty agricultural planning concepts may take years before they are detected, by which time the consultant will no longer be remembered. *We must always appreciate that what may seem to be a simple change in technology, an interesting exercise in innovation, to the specialist, may be a question of survival to the subsistence farmer and his family.*

Where the proposed changes involve the introduction of irrigated agriculture, then the position is somewhat different. Providing the irrigation scheme has been well conceived, then the project, if implemented, should eliminate risk, and the farmer will get an assured return from year to year, unless a reservoir is not filled or an aquifer recharge fails. However, we meet again the requirement that the climatic parameters be well studied if the irrigation scheme is to be well conceived and stable. It is surprising how often some factor is miscalculated or overlooked in the original planning – for example, the rate of siltation of reservoirs[12] or the effect of removal of silt from the Nile waters by the Aswan High Dam on the downstream river banks.

River levels

As an agronomist or planner I rarely had to consider the question of river levels, apart from the question of flooding incidence and the need for flood protection, until I worked in Bangladesh. I have said earlier that my original impression of the country was that it was essentially flat and the agriculture was basically simple. It did not take me very long to realize that the agriculture was very complex and one of the more interesting that I have had the privilege to become involved with in my consultancy assignments.

On flying in to Bangladesh from Calcutta, looking down, providing there are no monsoonal clouds, one can observe that there is no part of the land surface that has not, at some time in the past, been a meandering river now silted up and cultivated. The dissected meanders are clearly visible, many of the farmers' fields having boundaries that seem to follow the old river courses. On the ground one can drive from Dhaka to the northern border and as far

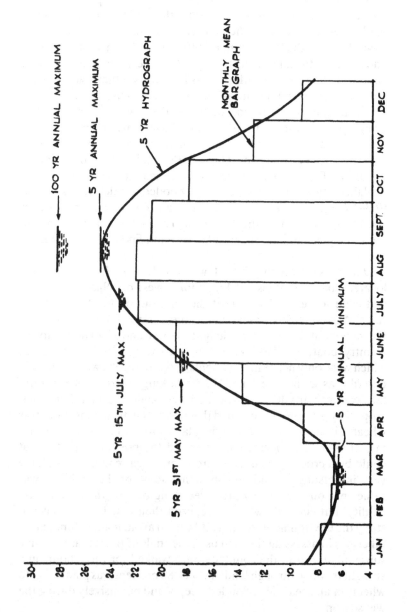

Figure 1 *Typical Hydrograph For Bangladesh River Station 361 (based on Survey of Bangladesh Datum (SOB)).*

as the eye can see the land is essentially flat and, depending on the time of the year, everywhere one looks there will be paddy growing. And when one gets to the border at Tetulia and looks across towards India, the land continues off into the distance, still flat until one comes to the hills of Darjeeling. Then one has to realize that the Ganges-Padma, draining the waters from the southern slopes of the Himalayas, the Brahmaputra-Jamuna, draining the waters from the whole of the northern side of the Himalayas, and the Meghna bringing down waters from Assam[13] have a maximum combined flow, between June and August, of more than 5 million cusec (141,583 cumec), carrying about 2000 million tons of sediment annually. This amount of water is difficult to conceive, but it explains why a third of the country is flooded to a depth of 1–15 feet (0.3–4.6 m), in a normal year. Then try and conceive farming where one can grow wheat in the winter (dry) season and then go back to the same piece of land six months later and find it under 15 feet of water.

One sub-project in which I was involved in Bangladesh was located about 40 miles (64 km), north-west of Dhaka and I was fortunate in being able to visit the area during the height of the rains. Accompanied by several members of the Bangladesh Water Development Board, after a delightful three and a half hour trip in a country boat, which took us through extensively flooded areas which were only negotiable by boats,[14] we arrived at what I can only describe as a sizeable lake. Whilst talking to some of the local farmers in their village (on raised levee lands) I asked them what crops they grew, to be informed that one of the dry season crops was wheat. I looked at the surrounding lake with its 12–15 feet (3.6–4.6 m), of water and instinctively rejected the possibility that wheat could be a crop for such an environment. 'Oh really,' I said, 'how very interesting. Could you show me some of the grain?' I was rather put out when they produced a big bag of wheat: not good quality, but certainly wheat. I realized then that I would have to study the environment carefully if I was to avoid making fundamental errors in assessing the land use potentials of project areas. On a subsequent visit to the country I once walked for three hours in a straight traverse through land of which 80 per cent was planted up to wheat, in an area which flooded deeply and extensively during the wet season.

Because so much of Bangladesh's farming lands are flooded each year, as a normal environmental feature, over the centuries

Table 22 *Varietal characteristics of selected paddy varieties in Bangladesh*

Variety	Season	Maturation period (days)	Height inches	(cms)
Chandina	Aus	115–120	32–36	(81–91)
	Boro	145–150		
Biplab	Transplant			
	Aman	140–145	38–40	(97–102)
	Boro	170–175		
IR8	Aus	130–135	40	(102)
IR5	Transplant			
	Aman	135–145	46	(117)
Pajam	Aus			
	Boro			
	Aman	120–130	50–60	(127–152)
Habiganj Boro VIII	Boro	150	55–57	(140–145)
Kataktara	Aus	100–105	56–58	(142–147)
Latisail	Transplant Aman	150 a	58–60	(147–152)
Nizersail	Transplant Aman	165 a	60–62	(152–157)
Habiganj Aman IV	Broadcast Aman	230 b	72–96	(183–244)
Habiganj Aman V	Broadcast Aman	240 b	108–144	(274–366)

a Photoperiod sensitive and their date of sowing is assumed to be mid-June.

b Photoperiod sensitive and date of sowing assumed to be April.

Source: Bangladesh Rice [7]

hundreds of rice varieties evolved, each adapted to a particular depth of flooding. One has to appreciate that a farmer may have, within his holdings, land at several levels, ranging from, say, 5–15 feet (1.5–4.6 m) above sea level, and he will grow several different varieties of paddy, each suitable for different flooding regimes and for different times of the year (see Table 22). In order to

to comprehend the individual farmer's cropping choices, and the cropping pattern for the whole community, I found myself becoming
involved in river levels and mean monthly water levels (hydrographs
– see Figure 1). Using the hydrographs and hypsometric curves for the
land levels, I was able to show graphically why farmers followed
particular rotations and when were the ideal times for planting
different varieties of paddy. Furthermore, and this was very important
to me, I was able to check that any new cropping proposals actually
fitted in with the predicted water regime. Of course, nature is
unpredictable and will keep on producing unseasonable weather,
flooding or droughts, and it is to alleviate such eventualities that the
Bangladesh Water Development Board is actively engaged in flood
protection, drainage and irrigation projects.

To put the hydrograph in Figure 1 into perspective, one has to
visualize a farmer having land at, say, 12 and 20 feet (3.7 and 6.1
m). In a normal year his land at 12 feet (3.7 m) will be flooded to 10
feet (3.0 m), so a 3 feet (0.9 m) rice variety would not survive, but a
12 feet (3.7 m) variety will survive, though once in a hundred years
even the deep water rice may be drowned. His land at 20 feet (6.1
m) will, however, be suitable for the higher-yielding, but shorter-
stemmed, rice varieties.

Statistics

Whether one likes figures or not, they will constitute a large part of
any report, if for no other reason than that the proposed project will
have to be costed and the benefits quantified. This means statistics
will be needed; indeed, the project economist will insist on them
being provided, and if there are no local sources then the team will
have to carry out its own surveys. Usually a study will make use of
locally available statistics, such as population data, district records,
areas, and so forth, but with the proviso that their validity will be
checked. This is not necessarily a separate act, rather the individual
team members will as a matter of routine be querying all data that
comes before them, checking for inconsistencies and errors.

That there will be errors in the national and locally available data
is a certainty, not because of any particular inefficiency, but just
because of the lack of trained manpower to collect and assemble
statistics. In fact Departments of Statistics are usually staffed by
dedicated individuals and if one comes to them with a problem they
are normally only too pleased to be able to help. One of the big
problems with national statistics is that they are often 'smoothed' or

'adjusted' as they progress up the normal channels. The field survey officer will make a genuine assessment of the local situation for any particular item of information and hand his findings on to his immediate superior. The superior will compile tables bringing together data from several field workers and in the process may well decide to 'smooth' any little errors that he thinks he has detected. There are also opportunities for adjustments in response to local politics, as the figures pass upwards on their way to the central bureaus. Central government itself may also correct 'irregularities'.

In Uganda, whilst I was there, there were two methods of estimating crop acreages. One was the Buganda method and the other was the Eastern Province method. In Buganda the acreages of all crops grown in a representative square mile[15] were measured twice a year, and the acreage per taxpayer (within the square mile) for each crop was determined. These estimates were then used to provide an estimate of the area of each crop within a *gombolola* (sub-county), by multiplying the known number of taxpayers in the *gombolola* by the sample estimate of crop acreage per taxpayer. This system of acreage estimation depended on the ability of the agricultural instructors to measure small plots of land by pacing and simple triangle geometry, so there were some inaccuracies. For example, not all instructors' paces are a yard, although they were often assumed to be so. However, the method was adequately accurate and excellent for determining trends in acreages. The Eastern Province method consisted of an assessment of an average plot size for each crop in a representative area, and then multiplying these estimates by the number of plots of each crop planted within the sub-county. The problem with this method was that the chiefs were required to submit returns of numbers of plots planted each month for each crop, and in order to impress ministers and others (with the good work they were doing in the districts in encouraging the farmers to plant more and more of the crops that government was interested in), the chiefs would inflate the figures. As a consequence *gombolola* crop estimates could be double the true figure.

In other countries I have seen series of figures for total crop production which appear to be normal until one realizes that they have been calculated using the same crop yield figure for the past ten or twenty years. This will only be detectable if one divides the gross production by the corresponding acreage estimates (often done in order to determine whether there are any yield trends), when one will find that one has a constant yield, meaning that there has been no assessment at all.

In a paper entitled, 'An assessment of the accuracy of the official agricultural statistics of Bangladesh' [in 15], Carel E. Pray 'shows that the official series of acreages under HYV crop varieties have been found to be highly misleading because of early underestimates of the rice acreage under HYVs and more recent underestimates of the wheat acreages under HYVs'. He also refers to the inaccuracy of jute statistics and the misleading impression that such inaccurate data can give. The following is an extract from his paper regarding jute statistics:

> The yield per acre series shows a substantial drop in yields which scientists have sought to explain in a number of different ways. This turns out not to reflect a decline in yield (or if there was a decline in yield it was simply a coincidence), rather it is a reflection of the Bureau of Agricultural Statistics' discovery that the official yields in the 1950s and early 1960s were far above the actual yield. (p.2)

Having found out that the yields were too high the Bureau's officers attempted to correct the data over a period of years rather than make a once and for all adjustment, hence the confusion amongst the scientists.

If there are no reliable statistics then the consultant may have to conduct his own surveys, such as crop cutting yield determination exercises, socio-economic exercises, farm surveys, time of planting studies. Sometimes they may be included as a study requirement in the terms of reference for the project, or have been proposed by the consultant in his proposal document, or the need may have appeared as the study progressed, in which case it would have been necessary to obtain approval for additional studies.

Obviously, statistics are an important background to any development study, and a great deal of effort will be given to collecting and interpreting the available data. Personally, I try to get series of data for a minimum of ten years, as this gives me the opportunity to determine trends, or the absence of trends. As a generalization, there are few countries nowadays that do not have copious statistics, as compiling statistics is one of the 'in' things to do. However, not every country knows what to do with the statistics once they have them. From the individual consultant's point of view, analyzing statistics can be a very rewarding and revealing exercise, but it does have its dangers, in that conclusions may be reached that nobody wants to hear. Then one is faced with the problem of whether the release of the conclusions will be constructive or destructive. There is no value in being negative or destructive if it is not going to achieve any positive results, and under those circumstances the consultant may be advised to leave well alone. However, it is a matter of fine judgement as to whether the findings will be constructive or not. Sometimes issues should not be ignored just because they are likely to be ill-received, and if the expatriate consultant won't raise the issue then nobody will.

The social background

It is important to remember that all development schemes are concerned with people, and when we talk about agricultural development schemes we are usually talking about rural people. They are no different to anyone else, no more or less intelligent, often with the same aspirations as the town dweller, though to me their values, their attitudes to other human beings, are often finer and more humane. The farmers in their homes are people to be respected, to be talked to as equals and never patronized. Yet though the farmers have every right to be respected, in fact they are rarely accorded that respect by the city dweller. Many times I have been informed by the urban professionals that the peasant is lazy, idle and unintelligent; I was once told, 'If they only worked as hard as we do in the towns, there would be no food problems.' Of course the subsistence farmers do have something the urbanite is very jealous of, and that is their independence and the fact that they have the security of their holdings. But this very independence and rural security means that they have few material possessions and limited access to services. Their water will be, even in these sophisticated times, from a well or polluted stream, sewerage is non-existent, medical facilities concentrated in the towns, communications sketchy, schooling limited and leisure facilities rather simple. Yet, although the farmers' lives may appear hard to the town dweller, they, and the community in which they live, can still enjoy life in their own way, there can still be laughter. I remember having the privilege of being taken round a Harijan village in Tamil Nadu, and being struck by the amount of impish jollity amongst the children. It is when there is no laughter that one knows that things are not so good.

This then, briefly, is the social environment of the subsistence cultivators: a house of sorts, a small farm, hopefully a full belly in most years, but few material possessions and limited access to community services. These are the true 'clients'. There are others, even more important in some respects, who also need help, and they are the rural landless or functionally landLess. These are people who, through no fault of their own, may have inherited a part of the father's or mother's farm which is too small to be a viable unit, or are people who have become indebted and have been forced to sell their farms. Indebtedness is a major factor in stultifying development by the individual, and for many of the poorer rural communities indebtedness is a normal condition. They may have to part with half of their harvest to pay off debts, and then half way through the year have to ask for food on credit to last them until the next harvest. Once in this cycle, it is difficult to get out of it.

A tenet of faith of many aid givers, that seems somewhat illogical to me, is that aid should be directed to the poor, sometimes the poorest, in the community. The illogicality is best demonstrated by example. In Tamil Nadu we, a group of 'aid givers', were taken to visit an outstanding farmer who, on 5 acres (2 ha), had levelled his land, put in irrigation channels, purchased fertilizers, planted high-yielding varieties, and become a model farmer. Everybody was proud of him, but one of the party I was in, said, 'Yes, this is all very impressive, but this is not the kind of farmer we want to help. He is rich, and can afford to purchase inputs. We want to help the poorer farmers who cannot afford to purchase fertilizers, etc.' This, to me, is a trite comment, a hackneyed approach, that whilst appearing altruistic may in fact be a wrong approach. Obviously, we all want to help the poor, but it is debatable whether concentrating aid on them is the best way to help them. It may be that such aid is purely palliative, relieving but not curing, and further aid will be required in the near future. It is possible to argue that the 'good' farmer on his 5 acres (2 ha), who has demonstrated his ability to use new technologies, is the man who should be assisted. He is the man who is likely to make best use of aid, who is more likely to generate employment for the functionally landless. By all means help the poor but do not overlook the need to help the farmer with proven ability. Also do not forget that the 'good' farmer on his 5 acres (2 ha), in a less developed country is still a relatively poor man by Western standards.

The wish to aid the unemployed and landless, whilst entirely justifiable, can result in real problems in the early establishment phase of irrigation schemes. If hitherto unused barren lands are opened up to arable farming by the provision of irrigation (and irrigation schemes are nearly always large) then the sensitive issue comes up of who are to become the tenants? Governments immediately think of the unemployed in the towns, but if these people, who have already demonstrated their inability to succeed in their urban environment, are granted tenancies it is highly likely that they will be unable to succeed in the innovative environment of a brand new irrigation scheme. Training facilities for the new farmers might overcome this difficulty, but training costs money, needs trainers (who might not exist), and in any case would have to be included in the project costings and make the internal rate of return not so attractive. Whilst I am no advocate of large farms, a quite convincing case can be made for 'master farmers' who employ labourers, though this is considered rather capitalistic in the egalitarian world of the poor. As has been said, cynically, in the past, 'African Socialism is equal shares of less and less.' It is easy to substitute 'egalitarianism' for 'African Socialism'. Unfortunately, egalitarianism is a popular tenet amongst the wealthy 'aid givers', but they do not necessarily have to live with the results of egalitarian policies.

Another aspect of the social environment that has to be considered when looking at the local agricultural background is the whole subject of land inheritance. It may be patrilineal or matrilineal, or both, and if the sons (daughters) are entitled to equal shares of the deceased's land holdings (there may have been more than one holding) then fragmentation is inevitable. In Kigezi in Western Uganda the 1966 Agricultural Census revealed that there were an average of 6.2 blocks of land per farm. The smallest block consisted of one tree. Fragmentation is also a problem in Bangladesh, as shown in Table 23. A schematic distribution for one farmer's plots in Bogra, Bangladesh is shown in Figure 2.

Although fragmentation can be a major constraint on development (for example, consider the social implications of trying to lay out a field canal system for an irrigation scheme served by a deep tube well), it is one of the most difficult features to correct. Many agricultural officers who attempted to introduce land consolidation have been chased by angry farmers. It is a very sensitive issue, and whilst every farmer agrees that land consolidation would be a good thing, that is only if he is allowed to keep the better parcels of land

Table 23 *Fragmentation of holdings in Bangladesh, 1977*

Number of farm holdings	
One fragment	163,000
Two to three fragments	943,000
Four to five fragments	1,222,000
Six to nine fragments	1,607,000
Ten to nineteen fragments	1,700,000
Twenty plus fragments	620,000
Total number of holdings	6,257,000

Source: Bangladesh Agricultural Survey, 1977 [9]

and discard the less good. The only country I know where land consolidation was successfully accomplished was Kenya, but that was during a state of emergency in the Mau Mau period.

Another constraint on development, which I shall include in the social section for convenience, is the shortage of skilled and trained technicians, at all levels (including graduates). I personally think that the training element in projects should be strengthened, and that most consultants understate the need for basic training. Unfortunately, this is partly because the 'clients' in the field do not recognize their own deficiencies in this respect, quite naturally not wishing to acknowledge that their training facilities are inadequate or understaffed. The problem is also compounded by the fact that many of a country's nationals who go abroad for training or further training do not return. The following is an extract from a review of Sudan in *The Times*, 10 January 1978:

No one knows exactly how many Sudanese are now working abroad. But some rough evidence exists which may shed some light on the scale of migration. According to the Bank of Sudan late last November, remittances by Sudanese expatriates will this year reach $300m against only $10m for 1977 and less than $1m for 1976. Furthermore, recent customs returns have said that of the 9000 motor cars cleared at Port Sudan between 1976 and 1977, more that 6500 accompanied Sudanese returning on holiday from Saudi Arabia.

In 1971 there were 41 Sudanese graduates, 174 technicians and about 1400 skilled workers in Saudi Arabia. Kuwait had only 51 Sudanese with work permits in 1973 while Libya's 1974 figure was 4500. According to the latest estimates, Saudi Arabia now has about 137,000 Sudanese teachers, agricultural technicians, builders, drivers, craftsmen and office staff. Last year's estimates say that there were 20,000 Sudanese workers in the United Arab Emirates, 8000 in Libya and 2000 in Kuwait....

About 12,000 Sudanese are receiving higher education in the United States, Europe, Egypt and other countries. And if most of them return home after completing their training, the supply of skilled and managerial staff will be improved. But there are serious fears that large numbers of such people may prefer to remain abroad. Justification of these fears comes from the fact that about 70 per cent of those who qualified in medicine degrees abroad in 1976 have not returned home. (p.11)

Undoubtedly, health is another major constraint on development, but shortage of money and the reluctance of highly trained medical staff to live in the bush make it a hard problem to solve. It is a little difficult to believe that many of the less developed countries still have such very low life expectancies (see Table 24) and this must be a reflection on the health position and the world's socio-economic priorities.

Table 24 *Life expectancy and population per physician*

Country	Life expectancy male, 1985 (years)	Population per physician, 1981
Guinea	39	17,110 (1980)
Sierra Leone	39	19,300
Niger	42	47,640 (1980)
Chad	43	38,790 (1980)
Uganda	45	24,500
Bangladesh	50	9,700
Indonesia	53	12,300
India	57	3,700
Egypt	59	760
Turkey	62	1,530
USSR	65	270
Singapore	70	1,100
Jamaica	71	2,700
United Kingdom	72	680
United States	72	500
Switzerland	73	390
Spain	74	360
Norway	74	460

Source: World Development Report [41]

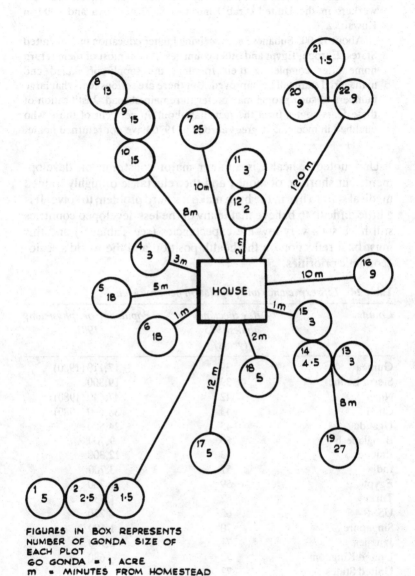

FIGURES IN BOX REPRESENTS
NUMBER OF GONDA SIZE OF
EACH PLOT
GO GONDA = 1 ACRE
m = MINUTES FROM HOMESTEAD

Figure 2 *Spatial distribution of a farmer's plots in Bogra, Bangladesh (22 plots totalling 1.336 ha).*

The agricultural background

As an agronomist I naturally feel that the agricultural section of this treatise should be the largest, but in fact many of the agricultural aspects have already been touched upon in previous sections, which simply confirms that agriculture is a multidisciplinary subject. However, before going on to consider the question of individual crop husbandry, time of planting, rotations and yields there are some agricultural background matters that are pertinent to the circumstances in which the cultivator finds himself carrying out his daily round.

The farmer in the UK, within the Common Market, is part of a highly evolved and complex marketing system. A dairy farmer can produce 1000 gallons (4950 litres) of milk per day, put it into a stainless steel tank and sit back and wait for the cheque to be paid into his bank account. He does not have to worry about markets or marketing, or delivery rounds; that is all taken care of by somebody else. A farmer producing 1000 gallons (4950 litres) of milk in the north of Bangladesh would not know what to do with it. Whilst I was Lecturer in Crop Husbandry at Makerere University College in Uganda I devised a crop rotation for the university farm at Kabanyolo, which included the growing of thirteen acres of sweet potatoes. The crop grew very well but the farm manager, Hugo Barlow, had immense difficulty in finding a market – eventually he managed to sell the greater part of the crop to a hospital at 3-5 cents per pound.[16] We also tried growing sweet corn on a large scale, but once again ran up against the market and price problem.

It must also be remembered that the subsistence cultivator in the tropics, in a predominantly rural population, has limited funds at his disposal for high inputs. This situation is well illustrated by the story of the Egyptian tomato cultivator. Yields of field grown tomatoes are not very good compared to world standards. Thus in Itsa District, Fayoum Governorate, yields averaged over 1979–81 about 6.16 tons/feddan,[17] whilst the national figure was 7.55 tons and the estimated potential yield 26 tons (according to a report on a Presidential Mission on Agricultural Development to Egypt prepared by USAID in 1982). One consultant was rather critical of the Egyptian farmer and quoted the tomato yields as an example, saying that in the UK yields of over 70 tons per acre were standard. I pointed out that, in fact, the Egyptian farmer's performance was very good, particularly in his circumstances, where his main energy resources were his bullock for the *saqiya* irrigation, his mule or camel, and the family labour. He could sell his tomatoes at £E 250 per ton and his family labour input was around £E 350 per feddan – not too bad a return at 6.16 tons per feddan. Not that he would have a feddan of tomatoes, the average farm size being 2.15 feddans per family. If we compare this situation with the UK tomato grower it does not seem too good until we examine the costs of growing tomatoes in the UK. An acre of glass will cost some £100,000, plus another £50,000 if services have to be laid on. Heating can cost £20,000 per acre, water may be £500, and labour £20,000 for a long term mono-crop. Yields have to be 100 tons/acre to cover costs, anything less than this and the grower is in financial trouble. No doubt the yields of tomatoes in Egypt could be brought up to those of the UK, but at an unimaginable cost, and certainly a cost well beyond the resources of any less developed country or even the World Bank. It is pertinent to quote from Makhaijani and Poole's book on *Energy and Agriculture in the Third World* [56] :

> India's entire development budget for almost 600 million people is considerably smaller than the expenditures of US consumers on electric household appliances; it is about equal to sums spent on dogs, cats and other pets in US homes. Public investments in the underdeveloped countries are often in the range of $10 to $20 per capita per year. (p.9)

So efficiency may be judged in several ways and it is not necessarily the farmer with the highest yield who is the more efficient in terms of the best use of natural resources. Unfortunately I no longer have the reference, but in the 1960s I read an article on energy inputs in the production of crops which stated that the subsistence farmer produced, more or less, 7 calories of food energy for every calorie of energy work. If he used oxen then the ratio went down to 3–4 calories per calorie input (the oxen also needing to be fed), and if he had a tractor then the ratio was more or less one to one. I have discussed this on occasions with agriculturalists in the UK and their opinion is that the ratio may be less than one to one, if all the energy inputs are allowed for – the energy needed to manufacture the tractors, the ploughs, the combine harvesters, the driers, the stores, plus the oil to run the machines, the aerial sprayers and so on. So who is the more efficient? It is not questioned that if every farmer in the world used oil at the same rate as the farmers in the Western hemisphere the world's oil reserves would be used up very quickly – although the actual energy used in the field operations, such as planting, ploughing and harvesting may be less, the total energy requirement in making the machines, and for ancillary equipment, will be more. In 1977 Bangladesh had 3454 tractors,[18] whilst the number in the USA for the same year was just under four and a half million; the United States Agricultural Industry also made use of three million trucks, compared to a total number of 9757 for the whole of Bangladesh.

Returning to the question of the agronomic input into a feasibility study, the first priority will be to determine the standard crop husbandry practices for the present range of crops being grown in the project area, plus any others that might be possibilities in the future. Usually there are local reference books or Ministry of Agriculture publications available which will give the basic background, and all one has to do is check that the data given in these publications is relevant for the project area. Surprisingly, there will be inconsistencies in the published material, or generalizations which do not fit in with all the environments encountered within a country. Planting dates may vary by as much as a month between the north and the south of a country; seed rates will vary; crops will be grown on the flat in some areas, but in others on shallow ridges with different soils or rainfall regimes. The reason for this is that farming is not a precise science and each farmer is an individual with his own way of doing things. That is why no two farms are the same: each will vary according to the interests and abilities of the farmer; some will prefer crops and some will have a liking for animals. If one wants to have a splendid example of the way in which small uniform plots can be worked in many different ways one has to go no further than a group of allotments in the UK. If one examines a number of agricultural annexes to feasibility studies in a country, but by different consultants, each annex will contain varying agronomic parameters. This is not a reflection on the efficiency of the agronomist in the collecting and compiling of his data, but purely an indication of the wide variation in local practices even within quite small areas, variation that is too great to be contained in a project study. In fact, examination of agronomic practices in too much detail can be counter-productive, creating unnecessary confusion when attempting to formalize a model project for analysis. However, to find a fault in a consultant's background data gives many people satisfaction, even if the detail is relatively unimportant in terms of the project's objectives. I once knew an engineer in West Africa who always worked on the deliberate mistake theory. His theory was that if he put in a deliberate mistake then head office would find it and take great delight in informing him of the error that they had detected, requesting him to amend the drawings (or whatever) that had been submitted. Letters would pass back and forth and eventually the item would be approved. If he did not do this, he said, then head office would come up with some modification of their own, a suggestion for consideration which they thought might improve the proposed work, but which was usually alteration for alteration's sake. The problem was, however, that sometimes head office would not spot the deliberate mistake.

Having 'mastered' the individual crops and their environmental peculiarities,[19] one can turn one's attention to the question of time of planting, and its corollary, time of harvesting. A good example of a cropping calendar is shown in Figure 3, which is a stylized presentation and most useful in any planning exercise. It must be appreciated, however, that as a stylized presentation it does not cover all the regional and district variations. For example, paddy varieties may differ by as much as 100 days in their growing periods. Care has to be taken over crop growing periods as the quoted data may not always refer to the same circumstances. Thus a rice variety may be classed as a three and a half month variety, but is this from the time of transplanting or the time of sowing the seed? Where there is doubt I prefer to refer to the growing period as 'seed-to-seed' in number of days. The number of days that a crop takes to come to maturity may also vary depending on the time of year that the crop is planted.

Depending on the nature of the project it may be necessary to devise a new rotation. Of all my consultancy tasks I find this the most challenging and enjoyable. There is something satisfying in producing a rotation that will meld together well, will meet the farmer's needs and which will be implementable. I prefer to prepare the rotation in a form that can be implemented by the individual farmer, rather than in the form of cropping patterns which apply to the whole project and which may not be implementable by the individual farmer. An example of a model rotation is shown in Figure 4.

Having put together the husbandry, time of planting and rotation aspects of a project, we then come to the issue which causes me most trouble in a feasibility study. That is the question of present and future crop yields. Yields are such a sensitive subject because they are a fundamental component in the determination of the economic and financial viability of any project. A slight adjustment of the yields upwards can change an unimpressive IRR of 12 per cent to a

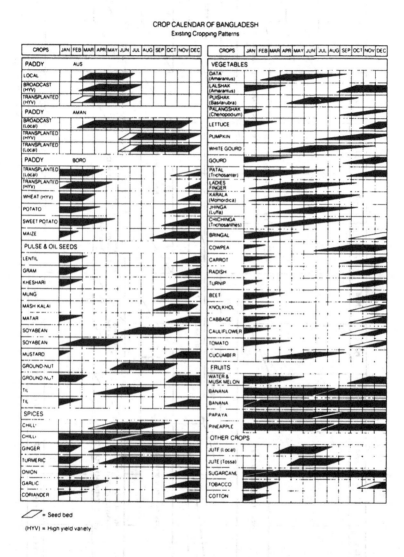

Figure 3 *Crop calendar of Bangladesh – existing cropping patterns*

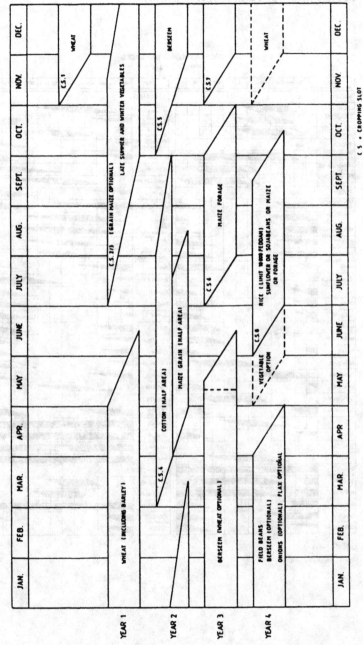

Figure 4 *Model rotation – Fayoum Governorate, Egypt*

healthy 17 per cent and vice versa. Frequently I have been challenged by a local client who regards my future yield projections as too low and consequently not putting the proposed project in a favourable light for international financing. The international agencies' obsession with the internal rate of return as a yardstick for judging possible projects is mainly the cause of the local client's concern over yield levels and the wish to have them estimated on the high side. Personally I do not think that agricultural projects which have the objective of improving the food security position of a developing country should be judged on the basis of international interest rates, especially when those rates are usurious.

The other reason why I run into trouble over future yield projections is that few people understand basic statistical theory. Let us take the example of a proposed irrigation scheme in an area where traditional irrigation schemes already exist, possibly supplied with irrigation water from small tanks (centuries-old reservoirs). Records will be available for the estimated yields of paddy from the existing traditional schemes, which could be, say, 3 tons per ha per crop (with possibly two crops per year). But research station yields of 7–10 tons per ha may be quoted as having been achieved for high-yielding varieties using recommended inputs. Pressure will be exerted to get the consultant agronomist to use the research station yields as the potential future yields for the project, but these are yields obtained under ideal conditions, with the whole of the resources of the Department of Agriculture supporting a handful of expensively trained and motivated research workers. The research station yields cannot be used as target yields for projects for the simple reason that they cannot be regarded as averages. If we are contemplating a 10,000 ha irrigation project there may be up to 10,000 individual farmers settled on the scheme and the eventual project yield will be the average of the yields obtained by 10,000 farmers. If we assume for the purposes of this argument that the distribution of the paddy yields is normal, and not skewed, we can also say that half the farmers will achieve yields that are less than the project average and half will achieve yields that are higher than the project average. It is quite possible that the better of the 10,000 small holders on the irrigation scheme will achieve yields approaching those which were obtained on a research station, but the possibility of half the tenants achieving yields greater than the research station yields is a statistical impossibility (unless the research workers are no better than the average farmer).

Thus the use of potential yields which are based on research station achievements can be misleading as they represent the upper limits of a yield distribution curve obtained under conditions of maximum inputs, with the full technical resources of the Department of Agriculture involved. They do not represent the average yield that can be achieved by a mixed bag of farmers, with varying interests, environments, resources and levels of inputs. As a move towards more pragmatic targets the term 'field potential yields' is being increasingly used.

When working on feasibility studies it is important to remember that the 'target group' is composed of relatively poor subsistence farmers, and what may seem an exciting innovation to the visiting consultant may be fatal to the farmer and his family if it does not work. I always try to produce agricultural proposals that are workable by the farmer with his simple resources, and which will be to his benefit, but it is not always easy to devise such proposals in a way that will appeal to the people controlling the purse strings.

Organization and management problems

The first and essential component for any proposed development project, if it is likely to become successful when implemented, is that the original concepts be sound. This is not as easy as might be thought, especially in an innovative situation. There is an assumption that if a group of highly educated men put their heads together they will come up with a soundly based project. That this is not so, is demonstrated in the West by the number of companies that fail, ideas that do not take off – for example Concorde, the Sinclair electric 'car', the VC 10, all near misses. However, the fact that some ideas are not successful is quite normal and acceptable in a situation where there is a constant source and trial of new ideas. Those that are good ideas will succeed and those that are not quite so well thought out, or badly implemented, will fade away. One of the problems in the developing world is that the international agencies like to think big in their planning, preferring a few multi-million dollar projects. There is a readiness to consider projects that will involve the expenditure of $10 or a $100 million, but less enthusiasm for the $100,000 project. One international agency official once told me, in a roundabout way, that small projects could become an accounting problem, and it was neater to have one big project to concentrate on. The problem with the 'big project approach' is that once the planning gets to a certain stage there seems to be no way to stop it, even if doubts are developing about the soundness of the initial concepts. Individuals who ask awkward, but constructive questions, are accused of rocking the boat and not being helpful. Personally, I would prefer to see a million dollars spent on ten projects, in the hope that three will be successful and grow on that success, rather than the whole amount being spent on one project where the soundness of the original concepts has still to be proven. I appreciate that for some developments, for example those involving hydro-power, it is not possible to adopt the 'small is beautiful' approach, but the general principle of initiating lots of small projects is still valid and attractive.

Usually, the project philosophy or concepts, and the associated planning strategy, can be expressed in a few paragraphs, and this leads to the misconception that the exercise of thinking up the basic concepts is something that can be done without too much thought or effort. Unfortunately, for many terms of reference the project philosophy has been inadequately thought out, presumably because insufficient time has been allotted to the task of thinking. This is not particularly a problem if one regards the purpose of the terms of reference as being to define the question and the project 'boundaries' in their widest senses, but it can be a problem if the consultant does not, himself, confirm the validity of the project concepts implied in the 'question'. Some consultants are wary about examining the client's project philosophy as it can lead them into some rather 'treacherous waters'.

If one has got the basic concepts right then the ensuing background studies are rationalized and a good technical base for the project emerges. Of course in the process of assembling the technical base for the project, findings may be made that indicate a need to modify the fundamental project philosophy.

When the concepts are right, and the technical base for the project has been established, there remains the question of organization and management. This is a very sensitive issue, and one can easily offend national pride. However, lack of oganizational and management skill is a weakness in the developing countries, whether they are prepared to admit it or not. This is, though, no reflection on the country's managerial class, being a perfectly understandable consequence of the country's own nationals having had no long experience of organization and management. Independence meant accelerated promotion for anyone remotely able to occupy senior positions, and these people, in order to mask their inexperience, took refuge behind bureaucratic procedures. This meant that they avoided making decisions. Unfortunately their own supporting juniors quickly sized up the situation and they in turn would make no decisions.

Thus, one of the greatest constraints on development is bureaucracy. Ministries or development boards can be so big and so entrenched that they become almost more powerful than the government itself. This is quite understandable as each ministry has a concentration of the country's trained manpower, which is disciplined and loyal to it. In a country that is developing and has few disciplined organizations, any organization that is large and well disciplined has considerable political clout. It is a force that other ministers will hesitate to challenge.

Oddly enough, in my experience, it is the countries which lean towards Marxism that have the most stifling bureaucracies. In one such country in which I had an assignment with the Ministry of Water I was clearly informed that I was to have no contact with the Ministry of Agriculture officials. When I said that this was not acceptable to me I was informed, quite nicely and matter of factly, that even if I went to the Ministry of Agriculture the officials would not receive me. If I had any questions then I should put them on paper and they would be sent up to the Minister who would transmit them to his opposite number, who would in turn send them down through his organization to the officials concerned, who would then give me the data or information required through the reverse channels. I learnt later that the officials of both ministries were hesitant about meeting me in case I quoted them and what they had said met with disapproval from above, which might result in disgrace.

In some cases, though not always, local high officials will privately acknowledge that there should be an expatriate management level input during the period of implementation and for some years afterwards, whilst local counterparts receive training both on the job and overseas, but would not be prepared for their views to be made public. In this case the consultant has to present such a suggestion tactfully – it is very easy to be patronizing about such issues and this can easily offend the local officials and the client.

It must always be appreciated that it is much harder for a local to be a manager than an expatriate. Employees will accord the expatriate a respect that they will not give to their own kind. For example, in Sierra Leone when I was there in the 1950s as an agricultural officer, I was always treated courteously and with respect even though I was young, but life was more difficult for an African agricultural officer of the same age. The village elders were not going to have a young African telling them what they should be doing on their farms, indeed not. And the same applies now to young local project managers, plantation managers, sugar factory managers; they have more difficulty in managing their own people.

Whilst I think there is a need for expatriate inputs during the establishment period of any new development venture which has international funding (if there was no management weakness in the country then such ventures would have been initiated internally), I acknowledge that life may be difficult for the expatriates who take up such posts. They may be exposed to questions about their presence in the local press; locals will ask them if they cannot obtain work in their own countries; so any proposal to include a semi-permanent expatriate input during any phase of a project has to be planned with care.

The economic background

'The poor have a right to receive what the rich have a duty to give,' goes a local saying in Aceh Province, Sumatera Island. There were times in the late 1950s and early 1960s when the USA was producing too much food and actually dumping milk powder and dried eggs in the Atlantic (this was before the US government came up with the idea of paying its farmers not to grow crops), yet there were countries in the world that were short of food. Somehow or other it seemed to me that the world was badly ordered when food could be deliberately destroyed in one place whilst there were people who were short of food in another place. I realize that it is a complicated issue, that food aid can have its disadvantages, and that the provision of an adequate diet for all the peoples of the world would be a mammoth logistical and organizational task, but I was unprepared for the unfeeling, complacent attitude of economists to the problem. I recall asking an economist how it was that food could be destroyed in one part of the world and people be dying from shortage of food in another part, to be told, quite bluntly and confidently, 'They cannot afford to buy it, so they will die.' From that time I have always been suspicious of the ethics of well-fed economists, and I have a similar suspicion about the general validity of the internal rate of return as a yardstick for the justification of an agricultural development project in the Third World.

I have no objection to economic yardsticks being used as tools in the evaluation of projects, as a means of quantifying varying and diverse benefits and converting them to a common denominator (money) so that the respective merits of different types of projects can be compared and ranked. But I do object when 'money', or other economic yardsticks, become the main criteria of a project's worth. Yet to many international organizations concerned with development the internal rate of return is not just an aid but the ultimate raison d'être of a feasibility study. A project is judged on whether the IRR is 17 per cent or not, or whatever the desired figure is at that time. However, the use of such a criterion in an essentially subsistence economy may not be valid. How can Western 'Monopoly game' interest rates, applicable to a society that will pay £1 for a cup of coffee, be applied to development projects in areas where thousands are dying of hunger, such as Ethiopia, or where the main source of farm power is the farm family? What is the economic value of a full belly?

Whilst, repeating what I have just said, I acknowledge the usefulness of economic analysis in feasibility projects, they must have the status of a useful tool and no more. To judge everything on whether it makes money or not may be perfectly valid in the developed world, but is of dubious value in the developing world. Personally, I would prefer to see more 'good stewardship' values in project evaluation.

What do I mean by good stewardship? When I was an undergraduate studying agriculture we were taught that 'a farmer should endeavour to hand his farm on to the next generation in a better condition than he himself received it'. That to me is good stewardship, whereas nowadays it would seem that there is a rider, to the effect that one does nothing to a farm if it does not make money. Fields become larger to make money; hedges are removed to make money, not because their removal improves the farm; the pig is tethered by a body belt to the floor to make money, not to improve the pig's quality of life but to reduce its intake of maintenance food and hence increase the profit. Maybe these are values that work in an accountant/economist dominated world, but they may not be the correct values in the developing parts of the world.

Piassava, the fibre used in scrubbing brushes or farmyard brooms before the advent of man-made fibres, was an important export from Bonthe in Sierra Leone and farmers in the 1950s were paid about £70 per ton for the retted fibre. The Department of Agriculture conducted trials on methods of retting in the course of which they found that they could not produce the fibre at under £170 per ton. In those days we accepted that the subsistence farmer would sell produce below production cost because he had no alternative sources of cash, which he needed to pay his poll tax and buy his few manufactured necessities of life which he could not make himself (such as pots and pans). In later years the economists became more prominent, in the process creating their own guild jargon, and I was informed that it was all to do with 'opportunity costs'. As I mastered one new term so they introduced more; the gold standard was abandoned for opportunity costs, gross margins, linear programming, cost benefit analysis, discounted cash flow, internal rates of return, shadow wage rates and sensitivity tests. Probably all this jargon and these 'rules of the game' amount to a useful contribution to the Western world's way of life (though the present economic chaos does little to reassure one that it is meaningful), but its relevance to the rural subsistence communities in the developing world is problematical. One sympathizes with the Nkrumahs and Nyereres of this world who at least attempted to challenge and change the Western-inspired rules.

To me the two important factors constraining natural agricultural development, that is development which would occur without any outside aid, are markets and prices. Technically, there are no agricultural problems that cannot be solved, indeed there is no need for new technology, just the application of existing knowledge. No, it is not the lack of technology, it is the markets and prices that are the problem. Let us examine the history of the green revolution wheats which were so brilliantly evolved in the CIMMYT programme in Mexico. There can be no question that the new wheats were good – indeed, they swept round the world in the same way as the IR 8 rice – but one of the reasons why the Mexican farmers originally took up the new wheats, plus the associated input package, was that the Mexican government agreed to introduce a guaranteed price and market for wheat. If there had been a guaranteed price before the release of the miracle wheats it is possible that the farmers growing the old varieties would also have responded by increasing production. In the year prior to my transfer to Uganda in 1956 the Uganda government had decided to guarantee a minimum price for maize grain (if I remember correctly it was about 12 East African cents a pound – or 24 shillings for a 200 lb (90 kg) sack). The result of this was that the farmers planted a greater acreage than ever before. Unfortunately the department's officers had not detected the increase and when the crop was harvested the government was suddenly embarrassed by a glut of maize grain in the market. All the go-downs were full and agricultural officers were pulled out of the field to assist in the marketing of the crop. The guaranteed price was abruptly dropped, the market disappeared and the price declined to about 9 cents per pound. Presumably the farmers had found the guaranteed price of 12 cents attractive, but when the price returned to normal the incentive disappeared.

Maize production in the adjoining country, Kenya, was different in so far as there was, in addition to the small holders, a European settler farming community who farmed on a business basis. Farming was more developed, husbandry standards better, and yields per acre correspondingly higher. Also, marketing and markets were well developed, with associated marketing organizations (Uplands Bacon Factories, for example), and prices for maize were substantially higher in Kenya than in Uganda. Indeed, smuggling of grain across the border could be a lucrative game, though strictly prohibited. Under these circumstances the production of maize grain was fairly constant over the years. However, the environment for growing maize was very varied, from sea level to say 9000 feet (2745 m),[20] and from 12 inches (305 mm) of rainfall per season up to more than 25 inches (635 mm). This meant that the returns from maize production could vary considerably from environment to environment. Obviously, in some areas growing maize would be more lucrative than in others, and as the environment became more and more unfavourable so the crop would be less and less financially attractive to the farmers. The interesting thing about this situation, which may have parallels in other countries, is that if the government used price as a means of regulating the gross production of maize grain, for example by pushing the price up, this did not necessarily mean that the existing maize farmers (who might have fixed cropping patterns related to machinery resources and rotations, etc.) would necessarily increase their production (though they would have a better gross margin), rather one found maize production being extended into areas where previously, because of environmental constraints, the growing of maize resulted in a loss or breaking even. With the increased price the production of the crop became more attractive and would support, if needed, increased inputs to correct the environmental deficiencies. Adjusting the price upwards would result in the existing farmers making more profit from the crop and allow farmers in more marginal situations to take up the crop. Yet as far as the national average production costs per acre were concerned the position might remain more or less static (because of the increased input costs of the new marginal producers who had taken up the crop because of the increased price). In the same way a decrease in price would knock out the marginal producers.

Markets and prices are thus very important to farmers. In developed countries the markets and prices are well established and regularized, but this is not the case in the less developed countries. I have often thought that the best way of assisting developing countries would be to provide them with guaranteed markets for their exportable agricultural products at reasonable prices. A fair price might be a more attractive proposition, than a low price and the possibility of 'strings attached' charity given at the whim of the donor nations. However, being pragmatic we have to accept that the world does not look kindly on such marketing arrangements as the commonwealth sugar agreement, or butter agreements.

Assembling the jig-saw

If it is a three month assignment, I will spend the first two weeks stripping the capital's store of information, follow that with six weeks, or so, on field visits to the site, the research stations, etc., and then complete the writing up of the first draft of my annex to the main report in the next fortnight. I will then have fourteen days left for revising, amending, and polishing the text, with the objective of handing over the completed annex to the team leader about three days before completion of the assignment. The last three days are for emergency alterations to the text, or for additions or expansions of material suddenly found to be urgently necessary. These are ulcer-generating days and there is always a certain relief when one gets on the plane. I find the exercise of writing technical reports to be exhausting, late-night work, as I may have to revise the text several times before I have eliminated all the ambiguities, spelling errors, inconsistencies in table layouts, incorrect references, random use of imperial and metric units, etc.

If I am team leader then I will also have the responsibility of putting together the main report, which is a bringing together of all the salient points of the annexes into one condensed but comprehensive report. To do this well is not an easy task. One must include all the technical points, the benefits and justifications, highlight the key features, and clearly present to a reader, who may not even have visited the country, the project's philosophy, and its relevance to the country's development needs. And all this has to be done in not more than forty pages of single spaced text. One of the problems is that the team leader has not only to summarize the work of all the other experts, he also has to be able to understand what they have said and be able to absorb the key phrases of their respective jargons, for he will have to defend his main report (and the annexes), before the client's own experts. Their attitude is quite simple: you wrote it, therefore you must be able to defend it. Knowing this, one takes great care to write nothing that one does not understand or make sure the 'expert' accompanies you to the meeting.

In writing the main report and the annexes it is important to remember that one of the tasks of the consultant is to assemble, interpret and present all the background and facts relating to a proposed development project in an internationally accepted form. This is in itself an expertise. Of course there has to be technical competence as well, otherwise the reports have no substance, but many people do not appreciate the skill needed to present a technical proposal on paper. And if a project cannot be presented on paper then it cannot be implemented.

Notes

1 It is interesting to observe how quickly the Presidents of newly independent states acquire the qualification of Doctor.

2 Often acquiring this post-graduate training in universities in the developed and industrialized countries, a training that is not always relevant to the subsistence orientated society of their homelands. Sadly a number of these highly trained persons do not return to their own countries, but use their specialism in other countries where they can obtain higher salaries.

3 As a general rule, research workers cannot resist writing up their findings and publishing them at every opportunity, and as their standing in the research world depends on other people knowing about their work, their papers will be freely available, providing they are quoted in one's reports. This is so except in some Moslem countries, even in internationally known research institutes, where research papers are produced and then locked away. To get these papers out of locked cupboards requires a lot of tact and skill.

4 Sometimes it may be necessary to refer the issue back to the client, particularly if it turns out, on closer study, that the area as defined in the terms of reference is ambiguous. This can be an important issue if the consultant is responsible for conducting a fixed cost survey, e.g. soils or socio-economic, and the area is not clearly defined.

5 Rainfall intensities, that is the rate at which rain falls, usually measured over short periods of time, can be as much as 13 inches per hour (33 cm/hr), but soils may only have a rainfall-acceptance rate of 3–5 inches (7.6–12.7 cm) per hour (variable depending on the slope, soil cover, condition of the soil, extent of saturation, etc.). Where there are no water conservation measures it is quite possible for 30 to 50 per cent of the rainfall to be lost as surface run-off, with a consequent reduction in groundwater recharge.

6 The Russians have a good rule of thumb: that there should be one or two observations per square centimeter of map.

7 The rate of evapotranspiration from an extensive surface of 8–15 cm tall green grass cover of uniform height, actively growing, completely shading the ground and not short of water.

8 In Bangladesh the traditional Aman varieties are period fixed or day length sensitive, whilst the Aus varieties are photoperiod insensitive.

9 Up to 80 mph (129 km/hr), damage is linear, but above that speed damage will be increasingly geometric. Cyclone Carol in Mauritius exceeded 125 mph (201 km/hr) (that was the recording when the anemometer snapped), and at such speeds trees will be uprooted and lives lost.

10 The traditional farming practices are well proven survival techniques that have been handed down from generation to generation, from father to son.

11 Unfortunately, this is no longer true as population increases have brought about instability. This point has been made before, but it has to be repeated again in this context.

12 The Khashm el Girba Dam on the River Atbara, providing a storage capacity of 1.3 milliard cubic metres to be used for the irrigation of 400,000 feddans, was completed in 1964. Sedimentation, a serious problem in Sudan not only for this reservoir, had reduced the live storage to 0.775 milliard cu m in 1977 and is expected to be reduced to 0.500 milliard cu m by 1997.

13 Where rainfall can exceed 700 inches (17,500 mm) per year.

14 Boats are very much a feature of the Bangladesh scene and every family will have a boat – even in central Dhaka itself people will be using boats during the rains.

15 An area of approximately one square mile, which was considered to be representative of the agriculture of the whole *gombolola*, was selected for each sub-county, and once chosen was used for acreage determination each year.

16 At that time there were 100 cents to the East African shilling, and 20 shillings to the pound.

17 One feddan is 0.42 of a hectare or 1.038 acres.

18 To put the number of tractors into perspective, in 1977 there were 6,852,558 farms in Bangladesh using 7,271,874 wooden ploughs, 5,723,788 spades, 12,218,108 sickles, and 8,342,157 weeding hooks.

19 An agronomist may have to examine the husbandry of only a few crops in any one study, but each study will have a different range of crops to be studied, which may tax the wits of the best of agronomists. There is a strange belief that agronomists have an encyclopaedic knowledge on all crops that grow in the tropics, including horticultural crops, flowering shrubs, and forest trees.

20 I have seen very healthy maize plants growing at over 8000 feet (2440 m) in Kenya, but they may take over a year to mature.

9 Recapitulation, conclusions and recommendations

This book is not intended to be a textbook on famine or on the development of agriculture in the tropics (there are already hundreds of books covering every possible technical aspect); rather, it is intended to bring together the tropical agriculture background in such a way that the reasons why the subsistence farming system is breaking down and development is so slow are highlighted. It is my view that unless one understands the fundamental aspects of subsistence farming as it exists now, and the complexities of introducing changes to the system, one cannot make meaningful plans for the future. Many authorities, governments, and international aid organizations confuse 'symptoms' with 'causes' – it is rarely worthwhile attempting to treat a 'symptom', though admittedly the determination of the 'cause' may be the more difficult and harder task.

In examining the subject of tropical agriculture it is postulated that subsistence farming is a fundamental system evolved many eons ago, and that (because it is a stable system) it permitted development in other fields, such as the development of languages, the written word, mastery of metals, scientific advances, the arts and material wealth of man. Additionally, this study reveals that an understanding of the problems related to the development of agriculture in the tropics requires wide experience, including having had close contact with the cultivators in the field. Agriculture is a multidisciplinary subject and not just the science of rotations, time of planting and plant populations.

Those concerned with the development of the rural masses in the tropical world must recognize that the subsistence cultivator is a hard-working and competent farmer, able to hold up his head with the best of the world's farmers. But we have to note that, in a situation where production is geared to home production, and in countries where populations are growing explosively, his farming and development options are limited.

Strangely enough, the best way to help subsistence farmers is to get people off the land and into the towns, but in saying this I recognize that the cost of an urban workplace is very high. This obvious point is often underestimated in national planning; the difference between the £100 rural workplace and the £30,000 urban workplace is not fully appreciated. Sadly for many developing countries, developments are nullified by the alarming yearly increases in population. There is just no way in which the small rural surpluses can meet the enormous development costs of the urban sector, and if the subsistence farmer's lands are being degraded because of population pressure then the future is indeed bleak.

Early in this book it has been said that the purpose of agriculture is to feed the people, that and nothing more, and that that is a worthy objective overriding Western economic targets. But it is also observed that rising populations are the major problem for the developing countries. Unless this problem is dealt with, then, for any community with finite land resources, functional landlessness and progressive starvation are inevitabilities, thus creating a class of people whose only hope is unpredictable charity. Oddly enough the symptom is apathy and not anger.

It is recommended that much greater thought should be given to the fundamental concepts and philosophies of development. The technology exists but the present day philosophies of development (in all senses), do not permit the developing countries to make full use of it. It may not be necessary, or even dietetically good, for man to have a luxury diet, but all mankind should be entitled to enough grain and vegetables each day to keep him and his family healthily and enjoyably alive and it should not be beyond the wit of modern leaders, making use of the available technologies, to achieve this objective.

The previous paragraph is perfectly valid, but in fact is typical of the bland statements of world politicians or international bodies, and as such makes little contribution to the practical task of meeting the urgent needs of the individual subsistence families in the harsher parts of the developing world. There is a need for more practical and positive recommendations, a need for key actions which can be supported and implemented by governments and other organizations, both in the developed and developing world. It will be said, of course, that there are many research institutions about the world all actively engaged in the solving of the problems of the subsistence cultivator, aimed at meeting the food needs of the populations, so action is already being taken by the responsible authorities. Sadly, these institutions are mainly concerned with the transfer of Western advanced agricultural technology to the developing world and their findings cannot be related to the circumstances of the peasant family – there is no developed economic infrastructure on which to 'hang' the 'advances'. It took the West many hundreds of years to develop its infrastructure of communications, markets, banking facilities, processing techniques, etc. before its agriculture advanced.

Obviously there are many ways in which famine can be avoided, development undertaken and progress achieved, but if there is to be a real advance then the fundamental problems must be faced. The cool towel on the forehead may soothe a man with fever, but it will not cure his malaria. My own priority recommendations would be:

1 A massive world propaganda campaign to make large families socially unacceptable in all countries, supported by comprehensive contraceptive aid programmes. Without a halt to the increase in world population the future is bleak for the subsistence farmers and their families.

2 Water and soil conservation must receive increased attention, and the insidious degradation of the tropical soils must be halted. The watersheds must be protected at all costs, or rehabilitated where possible. Western aid could make useful contributions in this field.

3 National policies should be directed at making cash crop production (food and primary commodities), an attractive proposition for small holders, by enlightened price and marketing policies. Rural communities, that is the subsistence farmers, must not be regarded simply as sources of cheap food for the urban populations. Conversely a rural population with a 'fair' share of the nation's money in its pocket will be a better base for urbanization.

4 All agricultural officers and agricultural research workers in the developing countries to be required to have had a minimum of three years' practical experience working in the field with the subsistence cultivators, ideally with only a bicycle or motorbike as a means of transport. During this period officers should be moved frequently between ecological areas and, if possible,

between countries. No officer should be accepted for ministry or planning bureau positions without this experience.

Less urgent issues requiring attention by the various bodies concerned with agriculture in the developing world are:

1 The Western countries must stop destabilizing the agriculture of developing countries by providing governments of these countries with cheap or free food (dumping), except in cases of natural disaster and as short term help. This aid is often accepted by the urban rulers for the urban populations as a means of avoiding having to face up to the need for internal changes in agricultural policies, for example the uneconomic price of bread in Egypt. If they cannot change these policies then, maybe, they could give a free bag of fertilizer with each bag of food aid.

2 In giving aid to developing countries greater emphasis should be placed on the provision of funds for the costly infrastructural elements of development, such as training, health, incentive goods. The inclusion of such items usually makes the internal rates of return look 'sick' and consequently they are often underestimated in project costings, but one has to acknowledge that it is difficult, for example, for an agricultural scheme occupying an area of four hundred thousand feddans to become viable if there is only one qualified local agricultural engineer for the whole scheme.

3 More aid should be given for small 'farming as a business' projects, which can grow from their own success. Most of the world's sugar estates started life as small plots. But failure must be an accepted risk to be taken by the donor.

4 A greater part of the aid should be without strings on the basis that aid well used will qualify for more.

5 Western governments must provide guaranteed long term markets for primary products. Fair minimum prices for primary commodities should be fixed, but related to quotas. By 'fair' is meant a price that gives the developing world and its subsistence farmers an adequate and attractive return for effort and not a price dictated by competition and the necessity to earn foreign exchange at any price.

Undoubtedly the best aid that the West can give to developing countries is to assist in urbanization and job creation in the urban areas. Unfortunately this is a sensitive issue as many of the developed countries have difficulties in organizing themselves to provide full employment for their own human resources.

It must also be understood by the developed nations that subsistence agriculture is a stable and quite sophisticated survival system (providing there is no population pressure). But it is on a 'plateau' or peak of development and has only limited further development potential (because of the farm power constraint). Development is not a continuous 'ladder' from subsistence farming to 'farming as a business', as they are two entirely different, and almost incompatible, systems. It is not possible to change the subsistence farming system to 'farming as a business', even with the injection of large amounts of development aid, without urbanization and the expansion of the markets.

References

1 ADB. Yearly. Reports by the Boards of Directors of the African Development Bank, African Development Fund covering each year. ADB, Abidjan.

2 ADB. 1973. Uses of Consultants by Asian Development Bank and Its Borrowers. ADB Information Office.

3 AGRICOLA. 1978. Handbook for the Ceylon Farmer. pp. 418. Ceylon Printers, Colombo.

4 AHMAD K.U. 1980. Bangladesh Agriculture and Field Crops. pp. 137. Hussain Art Press, Dacca.

5 AHMAD K.U. 1982. Gardener's Book of Production and Nutrition. pp. 448. Dacca Press, Sangstha.

6 ALIM A. 1974. An Introduction to Bangladesh Agriculture. pp. 432. Swadesh Printing Press.

7 ALIM A. 1982. Bangladesh Rice. pp. 321. Associated Printers, Dacca.

8 ARKIN G.F. and TAYLOR H.M. (Eds.) 1981. Modifying the Root Environment to Reduce Crop Stress. pp. 407. American Society of Agricultural Engineers Monograph.

9 BANGLADESH GOVERNMENT. Yearly. Statistical Pocketbook of Bangladesh. pp. 687. Statistical Division, Ministry of Finance.

10 BELL E.A. 1985. New Commercial Crops for Arid Areas. Journal of the Royal Society of Arts, Vol. CXXXIII, No. 5348, pp. 545–556.

11 BROWN M.L. 1979. Farm Budgets: From Income Analysis to Agricultural Project Analysis. pp. 136. World Bank Staff Occasional Papers, No. 29. John Hopkins University Press.

214   *Nowhere to Go but Down*

12   CENTRAL BANK OF CEYLON. 1979. Economic and Social
     Statistics of Sri Lanka. Vol. II, No.2, pp. 115. Statistics
     Department of the Central Bank of Ceylon.
13   CENTRAL BANK OF CEYLON. 1980. Review of the
     Economy 1980. pp. 324 plus 126 Tables. Prepared by the
     Department of Economic Research, Central Bank of
     Ceylon.
14   CHATTERJEE B.N. and MAITI S. 1979. Rice Production
     Technology Manual. pp. 139. Oxford and IBH Publishing
     Co., Calcutta.
15   CHAUDHURY R.H. 1980. (Ed.) Special Issue on Food
     Policy and Development Strategy in Bangladesh. pp. 185.
     The Bangladesh Development Studies Journal, Vol. VIII,
     Nos. 1 & 2, Winter–Summer 1980.
16   COLONIAL OFFICE. 1939. Colonial Service Recruitment
     Memorandum No. 4. His Majesty's Colonial Service:
     Information regarding the Colonial Agricultural Service,
     The Colonial Veterinary Service, the Colonial Forest
     Service, Other Appointments of a Biological Nature, and
     the Colonial Chemical Service. pp. 113. HMSO.
17   COLONIAL OFFICE. 1949. The Colonial Office List 1949.
     pp. 595. HMSO, London.
18   COLONIAL OFFICE. 1958. Report of a Conference of
     Directors and Senior Officers of Overseas Deparments of
     Agriculture and Agricultural Institutions Held at Wye
     College, Kent, September 1958. pp. 169. Miscellaneous
     No. 531.
19   CROWDER L.V. and CHHEDA H.R. 1982. Tropical Grass-
     land Husbandry. pp. 562. Longman.
20   DE DATTA S.K. 1981. Principles and Practices of Rice
     Production. pp. 618. Wiley-Interscience.
21   DE GEUS J. G. 1967. Fertilizer Guide for Tropical and
     Subtropical Farming. pp.727. Centre d'Étude de l'Azote,
     Zurich.
22   DEPARTMENT OF PUBLIC INFORMATION. 1984. Basic
     Facts about the United Nations. pp. 134. United Nations,
     New York 1984.
23   DOORENBOS J. and PRUITT W.O. 1977. Guidelines for
     Predicting Crop Water Requirements. pp. 144. FAO,
     Rome.

24 DOORENBOS J. and KASSAM A.H. 1979. Yield Response to Water. pp. 193. FAO, Rome.

25 DOW H., et al. 1955. East African Royal Commission – 1953 to 1955 – Report. pp. 480. HMSO.

26 DUNBAR A.R. 1969. The Annual Crops Of Uganda. pp. 189. East African Literature Bureau.

27 EARL D.E. 1975. Forest Energy and Economic Development. pp. 128. Oxford University Press.

28 EL KHATIB A.B. 1974. Seven Green Spikes 1965–1972. Water and Agricultural Development. pp.226. The Kingdom of Saudi Arabia, Ministry of Agriculture and Water.

29 EL SAYED S. 1977. Egypt: Strategies for Investment. pp. 223. American University in Cairo Printshop.

30 EL TOGBY H.A. 1976. Contemporary Egyptian Agriculture. pp 228. Published by the Ford Foundation.

31 FAO. 1970. Guideline for the Preparation of Feasibility Studies for Irrigation and Drainage Projects. pp. 25. FAO/IBRD Cooperative Programme, Rome.

32 FAO SOILS BULLETIN. 1979. Soil Survey Investigations for Irrigation. pp. 188. Prepared by the Land and Water Development Division, FAO, Rome.

33 FARBROTHER H.G. 1983. How to Make Irrigation Work : the View of an Agriculturist. Seminar paper delivered on 11 May 1983 to the Tropical Agricultural Association. See Newsletter, Vol. 3, No. 3, July 1983.

34 FARMER G. and WIGLEY T.M.L. 1985. Climatic Trends for Tropical Africa. A research report for the Overseas Tropical Development Administration. pp. 136. Climatic Research Unit, University of East Anglia.

35 FEDERAL MINISTRY OF AGRICULTURE AND NATURAL RESOURCES JOINT PLANNING COMMITTEE. 1974. Agricultural Development in Nigeria 1973–1985. pp. 558. The Caxton Press (West Africa).

36 GITTINGER J. 1972. Economic Analysis of Agricultural Projects. pp. 221. Economic Development Institute publication, IBRD. John Hopkins University Press.

37 GOVERNMENT OF UGANDA. 1966. Work for Progress. Uganda's Second Five Year Plan. pp. 185. Ministry of Economic Planning and Development.

38 GRIST D H. 1978. Rice. pp. 601. Longman.

39 HALE E. 1964. University Grants Committee: Report of the Committee on University Teaching Methods. pp. 173. HMSO.

40 IBRD/IDA/IFC. Yearly. Annual Reports of the World Bank.

41 IBRD. 1987. World Development Report. pp. 285. Published for the World Bank by the Oxford University Press.

42 ILACO B V. 1981. Agricultural Compendium for Rural Development in the Tropics and Subtropics. Commissioned by the Ministry of Agriculture and Fisheries, The Hague, The Netherlands. pp. 738. Elsevier.

43 INDONESIAN MINISTRY OF AGRICULTURE. 1980. Five Years of Agricultural Research and Development for Indonesia, 1976–1980. pp. 128. Published by the Agency for Agricultural Research and Development (AARD).

44 INTERNATIONAL INSTITUTE FOR LAND RECLAMATION AND IMPROVEMENT. April 1983. Wetland Utilization Research Project West Africa Phase I, The Inventory. Vol III: The Agronomic, Economic and Sociological Aspects.

45 JOHNSON B.L.C. 1982. Bangladesh. pp. 130. Heinemann Educational Books.

46 KRANZ J., SCHUMUTTERER H. and KOCK W. (Eds.) 1977. Diseases, Pests and Weeds in Tropical Crops. pp. 666. J. Wiley & Sons.

47 LEAKEY C.L.A. and WILLS J.B. (Eds.) 1977. Food Crops of the Lowland Tropics. pp. 345. Oxford University Press.

48 LILLESAND T.M. and KIEFER R.W. 1979. Remote Sensing and Image Interpretation. pp. 612. J. Wiley and Sons.

49 LITTLE I.M.D. and MIRRLEES J.A. 1974. Project Appraisal and Planning for Developing Countries. pp. 388. Heinemann Educational Books.

50 LYNN C. W. 1949. Agricultural Extension and Advisory Work with Special Reference to the Colonies. pp. 104. HMSO.

51 MACDONALD A.S. 1963. Some Aspects of Land Utilization in Uganda. East African Agricultural and Forestry Journal, Vol. XXIX, No. 2, October 1963, pp. 147–156.

52 MACDONALD A.S. 1972. Crop Acreage Trends in Uganda. pp. 144 plus Tables. Unpublished material.

53 MACMILLAN H.F. 1948. Tropical Planting and Gardening. pp. 560. Macmillan and Co.

54 MAHADEVAN P. and MARPLES H.J.S. 1961. An analysis of the Entebbe Herd of Nganda Cattle in Uganda. Journal of Animal Production, 3. pp. 29–39.

55 MAHADEVAN P. 1965. Dairy cattle breeding in East Africa. East African Agricultural and Forestry Journal, Vol. 30, pp. 320–327.

56 MAKHIJANI A. and POOLE A. 1975. Energy and Agriculture in the Third World. pp. 168. Ballinger Publishing Co., Mass.

57 MEADE J.E. 1968. The Economic and Social Structure of Mauritius. pp. 246. Frank Cass & Co.

58 MENDIS M.W.J.G. 1973. The Planning Implications of the Mahaweli Development Project in Sri Lanka. pp. 154. Published by Lakehouse Investments, Colombo.

59 MICHAEL A.M. 1978. Irrigation, Theory and Practice. pp. 801. Vikas Publishing House, Delhi.

60 MINISTRY OF OVERSEAS DEVELOPMENT. 1977. A Guide to the Economic Appraisal of Projects in Developing Countries. pp.160.

61 MORRISON F.B. 1961. Feeds and Feeding, Abridged. The essentials of the feeding, care and management of farm animals, including poultry. pp. 696. Morrison Publishing Co. Canada.

62 NICHOLAIDES J.J. et al. 1982. Improvements in Soil Management in Shifting in Latin America's Amazon Basin. pp. 36. Paper prepared for consultation with FAO on Improvements in Shifting Cultivation.

63 NIX J. 1985. Farm Management Pocketbook. pp. 177. School of Rural Economics, Wye College, UK.

64 OLDEMAN L.R and FRERE M. 1982. A Study of the Agroclimatology of the Humid Tropics of Southeast Asia. pp. 229. FAO/UNESCO/WMO interagency report published by FAO, Rome.

65 OVERSEAS DEVELOPMENT ADMINISTRATION. 1983. British Oveseas Aid: Annual Review. pp. 85. HMSO.

66 PAPACHRISTODOULOU S. 1976. Norm-output Data of the Main Crops of Cyprus. pp. 259. Agricultural Economics Report. Agricultural Research Institute, Ministry of Agriculture and Natural Resources, Nicosia.

67 PANABOKKE C.R. 1967. The Soils of Ceylon and Use of
    Fertilizers. pp. 151. Ceylon Association for the Advance-
    ment of Science.
68 PAXTON J (Ed.) Yearly. The Statesman's Yearbook. Statisti-
    cal and Historical Annual of the States of the World for
    each year. pp. 1696. Macmillan.
69 PURSEGLOVE J.W. 1975. Tropical Crops: Mono-
    cotyledons. pp. 607. Longman.
70 PURSEGLOVE J.W. 1977. Tropical Crops: Dicotyledons.
    pp. 719. Longman.
71 RAHMAN A., HAQUE M.S. and AHMAD M. 1984.
    Production Procurement and Agricultural Price Policy in
    Bangladesh. pp. 290. Published by the Centre for Inte-
    grated Rural Development for Asia and the Pacific, and the
    Institute of Business Administration, Dhaka.
72 RANGNEKAR, SHARU. 1974. In the Wonderland of Indian
    Managers. Vikas Publishing House, Sahibabad, U.P.
73 RASHID, HAROUN E.R. 1977. Geography of Bangladesh.
    pp. 579. University Press, Bangladesh.
74 ROUNCE N.V. and THORNTON D. 1936. Ukara Island and
    the Agricultural Practices of the Wakara. Tanganyika
    Notes: Records 1, pp. 25–32
75 RUTHENBERG H. 1980. Farming Systems in the Tropics.
    pp. 424. Oxford.
76 SANCHEZ P.A. 1976. Properties and Management of Soils in
    the Tropics. pp. 618. Wiley-Interscience.
77 SIERRA LEONE GOVERNMENT. 1957. The 1955 Report
    of the Department of Agriculture. pp. 45. Government
    Printer, Freetown.
78 SIERRA LEONE GOVERNMENT. 1957. The 1956 Report
    of the Department of Agriculture. pp. 31. Government
    Printer, Freetown.
79 SIERRA LEONE GOVERNMENT. 1974. National
    Development Plan 1974/75 – 1978/79. pp. 285. Central
    Planning Unit, Government Printer, Freetown.
80 SIMMONDS N.O. 1963. Feed Milling and Associated Sub-
    jects. pp. 377. Leonard Hill (Books) Ltd.
81 SIPRI. 1984. Yearbook. Stockholm International Peace
    Research Institute.

82　STEITIEH A.M. et al. 1978. A Manual for the Main Vegetable Crops grown in the East Jordan Valley. pp. 87. Faculty of Agriculture, University of Jordan.

83　SUKAMANDI RESEARCH INSTITUTE FOR FOOD CROPS, INDONESIA. 1979. Report on Research on Rice and Secondary Crops at Sukamandi, 1974–1979. pp. 65. Agency for Research and Development.

84　TOFFLER A. 1981. The Third Wave. pp. 544. Pan Books in association with Collins.

85　TOTHILL J.D. (Ed.) 1948. Agriculture in the Sudan. pp. 974. Oxford University Press.

86　TOTHILL J.D. (Ed.) 1940. Agriculture in Uganda. pp. 551. Oxford University Press.

87　UGANDA PROTECTORATE. 1911. Annual Report on the Department of Agriculture for the year ended 31st March, 1911.

88　UGANDA GOVERNMENT. 1967. Agricultural Production Programme. pp. 32. Published by the Department of Agriculture, Ministry of Agriculture, Forestry and Co-operatives.

89　UGANDA GOVERNMENT. 1965. Report on Uganda Census of Agriculture. Vol.I. Ministry of Agriculture, Forestry and Cooperatives, Entebbe.

90　UNIDO. 1977. Manual for the Preparation of Industrial Feasibility Studies. Prepared by the International Centre for Industrial Studies. Unido.

91　USDA. 1969. Diagnosis and Improvement of Saline and Alkali Soils. pp. 160. Agriculture Handbook No. 60. United States Department of Agriculture.

92　USDA. 1984. Agricultural Statistics 1984. pp. 558. United States Government Printing Office, Washington.

93　WMO/IRRI. 1980. Proceedings of a Symposium on the Agrometeorology of the Rice Crop. pp. 254. International Rice Research Institute, Philippines.

94　WORLD BANK. Uses of Consultants by the World Bank and its Borrowers. Information Offices.

95　WORLD SOILS RESOURCES REPORT. 1980. Agro-ecological Zones Project, Vol. 4. Results for Southeast Asia. pp. 39 and 11 maps. FAO, Rome.

96　YOUNG A. 1976. Tropical Soils and Soil Survey. pp. 468. Cambridge University Press.

Index